# Anti-Capitalist Britain

**History and politics titles from New Clarion Press**

Lawrence Black et al., *Consensus or Coercion? The State, the People and Social Cohesion in Post-war Britain*

John Carter and Dave Morland (eds), *Anti-Capitalist Britain*

Keith Flett and David Renton (eds), *New Approaches to Socialist History*

Duncan Hall, *'A Pleasant Change from Politics': Music and the British Labour Movement between the Wars*

Anne Kerr and Tom Shakespeare, *Genetic Politics: From Eugenics to Genome*

David Renton, *Classical Marxism: Socialist Theory and the Second International*

David Stack, *The First Darwinian Left: Socialism and Darwinism 1859–1914*

Leo Zeilig (ed.), *Class Struggle and Resistance in Africa*

*Forthcoming*

Mark O'Brien, *When Adam Delved and Eve Span: A History of the Peasants' Revolt of 1381*

# Anti-Capitalist Britain

*edited by*
*John Carter and Dave Morland*

**New Clarion Press**

© John Carter, Dave Morland, Anonymous, Molly Scott Cato, Colin Hines, Caroline Lucas, Alexandra Plows, Amir Saeed, Jonathan Purkis, Paul A. Taylor, Derek Wall, 2004

The right of the above named to be identified as the authors of this work has been asserted in accordance with the Copyright, Designs and Patents Act 1988.

First published 2004

New Clarion Press
5 Church Row, Gretton
Cheltenham GL54 5HG
England

*New Clarion Press is a workers' co-operative.*

A catalogue record for this book is available from the British Library.

ISBN paperback   1 873797 43 5
      hardback   1 873797 44 3

Typeset in Times New Roman by Jean Wilson Typesetting, Coventry
Printed in Great Britain by The Cromwell Press, Trowbridge

# Contents

# Contributors

**Anonymous** has been involved in various anti-capitalist, direct action, radical ecological and anarchist projects for the last ten years, including Reclaim the Streets actions, anti-summit demonstrations, anti-road protests, squatted social centres, critical mass cycle actions, anti-genetics actions, prisoner support, strike support and dole struggles.

**John Carter** works in the School of Social Sciences and Law at the University of Teesside. He uses some of the endless leisure time this provides to write about new social movements and recent anti-capitalist protests. His darkest secret is that he was once a member of the Labour Party. Following a long, slow anarcho-drift, he now *very much* isn't. He occasionally makes forays into the real world of anti-capitalist demos, May Days and actions, but has not yet learned how to juggle or stilt-walk.

**Molly Scott Cato** works as a green economist, seeking to develop a sustainable and just economy. Her doctoral research, focusing on work motivations and the future of employment policy in South Wales, was published as *The Pit and the Pendulum*. She currently works at the Welsh Institute for Research into Cooperatives in Cardiff, where she is part of a team carrying out an audit of cooperative activity in Wales. Molly is an active member of the Green Party, standing for election at all levels and currently speaking for the party on economic issues. She has researched and published papers on a wide variety of topics alongside her work on employment.

**Colin Hines** is the author of *Localization: A Global Manifesto* (Earthscan) and an Associate of the International Forum on Globalization, a San Francisco-based alliance of activists, academics and economists committed to challenging the adverse effects of globalization and free trade, and to developing alternatives such as localization. Before that he was the Co-ordinator of Greenpeace International's Economics Unit, having worked for the organization for 10 years. He has worked in the environmental movement for over 30 years on the issues of population, food, nuclear proliferation, new technology and unemployment.

**Caroline Lucas** is one of the British Green Party's first MEPs, and serves on the European Parliament's Trade and Environment Committee. She has written extensively on international trade and development, and is an

Associate of the International Forum on Globalization. Believing that politicians must be activists as well, she has a history of involvement in non-violent direct action and peace campaigning. She is currently a Principal Speaker for the Green Party.

**Dave Morland** works in the Sociology section at the University of Teesside. He was first introduced to Labour politics whilst an apprentice in the aero-engineering industry, but gradually became interested in anarchist ideas and activism. In the real world, Dave is an enthusiastic mountaineer and a long-suffering supporter of Sunderland AFC.

**Alexandra Plows** has been a direct activist since 1992, when as one of the 'Donga Tribe' at Twyford Down she helped to kick-start the anti-roads movement. Over the last decade she has taken direct action on environmental, human rights and anti-capitalist issues, including 'digger-diving', tree-sits and proactive blockading. Alex is a Research Associate at the Centre for the Economic and Social Aspects of Genomics (CESAGen) at Cardiff University, and she has published widely, with contributions in a number of recent texts on environmentalism, anti-capitalism and new social movements.

**Jonathan Purkis** teaches media and cultural studies at Liverpool John Moores University. He has been active in various radical, environmental, anticonsumerist and anarchist groups, and has written a PhD thesis and various articles on these movements. He is heavily involved in the journal *Anarchist Studies* and plays music with Huddersfield alt.folk band *Bar the Shouting*.

**Amir Saeed** is Senior Lecturer in the Department of Media and Cultural Studies at the University of Sunderland. His research interests lie in racism, human rights , media control and the so-called War on Terrorism. He is currently researching racism in the north-east of England.

**Paul A. Taylor** joined the Institute of Communications Studies at the University of Leeds in February 2003 as a Senior Lecturer in communication theory. His research and teaching interests centre on the politics of celebrity and digital culture, and he is a regular commentator for Radio 4 on media-related topics. His main forms of activism relate to red wine and an ongoing voodoo project against the global franchise formerly known as Manchester United.

**Derek Wall** is an independent academic and teaches political economy and green politics at Goldsmiths College and Birkbeck College. An associate editor of *Red Pepper*, his next book *Babylon and Beyond* will be published in 2005. He is a member of the Green Party and is an ecosocialist.

# Acknowledgements

Thanks are very much due to Chris Bessant and all at New Clarion Press. He has responded to our missed deadlines with good grace and worked hard to produce what we hope is an interesting and stimulating book. We would also like to thank all of our contributors, who have had much to put up with from us as editors. They (and we) have decided to forgo our respective share of the text's royalties. As a result, those moneys will be donated to various green and anarchist groups and to organizations supporting the Palestinian people.

Finally, John would like to thank Gill and Laura Hughes for their patience and support whilst he put together *Anti-Capitalist Britain*. Dave is deeply indebted to Liane Brierley, and their children, Fay and Alex, for tolerating his many failings and absences as both partner and parent during this and other publishing projects.

*Dave Morland and John Carter*
*Teesside, March 2004*

# Selective list of green, direct action and anti-capitalist groupings

Anarchist Bookfair: http://freespace.virgin.net/anarchist.bookfair

Campaign for the Accountability of American Bases: http://www.caab.org.uk

Corporate Watch: http://corporatewatch.org.uk

Earth First!: http://www.earthfirst.org.uk

Foundation for the Economics of Sustainability (FEASTA): http://www.feasta.org

Global Commons Institute: http://www.gci.org.uk

Globalise Resistance: http://www.resist.org.uk

Green Party: http://www.greenparty.org.uk

London Class War: http://www.londonclasswar.org

Indymedia (UK): http://www.indymedia.org.uk

May Day 2004 site: http://diy.spc.org/ourmayday

Medical Aid for Palestinians: http://www.map-uk.org

New Economics Foundation: http://www.neweconomics.org

No Sweat: http://www.nosweat.org.uk/index.php

Reclaim the Streets: http://www.reclaimthestreets.net

Socialist Workers' Party: http://www.swp.org.uk

Stop the War Coalition: http://www.stopwar.org.uk

Subvertisers: http://www.subvertise.org

Thomas Hurndall Fund for Palestinian Victims in the Occupied Lands: http://www.tomhurndall.co.uk

Urban 75: http://urban75.net

Veggies (vegan catering campaign): http://www.veggies.org.uk

Welsh Institute for Research into Cooperatives (WIRC), UWIC Business School, Colchester Avenue, Cardiff CF23 9XR

Wombles: http://www.wombles.org.uk

Yes-men (cyber hoaxers): http://www.theyesmen.org

# Introduction

## Dave Morland and John Carter

A chapter (and book) of this sort almost inevitably begins with Francis Fukuyama's predictions of the 'end of history'.[1] Following the fall of the Berlin Wall in 1989 and amid the break-up of the Soviet Union, he claimed (and celebrated) a watershed in world history.

In politics, the West had won the Cold War and capitalism had vanquished communism as a practical way of living – to the point at which it was no longer seen as a credible competing system. Similarly, in the battle of ideas and ideologies, the free market and liberal democracy had prevailed, becoming in the process models for the 'developing nations'. Fukuyama saw no serious alternative to capitalism on the horizon and regarded it as a system aligned to human nature. Future politics, therefore, were to be played out within that ideological framework – an ironing out of its kinks and inefficiencies.

Fukuyama's judgement in this respect was the latest in a long line of sociopolitical sermons preaching the end of ideological politics. Daniel Bell, for instance, made similar claims 30 years previously.[2] What made Fukuyama's pronouncement more dramatic was that it was preached in front of a backdrop of a bipolar international struggle that had blighted the lives of many for nearly half a century. This was, however, no mere temporary *détente*, but a seemingly permanent end to hostilities, and the realization of potentially huge markets with the fall of the Iron Curtain.

As the 1990s proceeded – probably capitalism's favourite decade of the twentieth century – this view of the free market rampant and unchallenged gathered supporting evidence. E-commerce and the rise of the Internet fuelled the stock market boom and dot.com entrepreneurs showed that it was possible to become a millionaire without actually making a traditional profit. In this perspective, branded neoliberal globalization was all conquering, commodifying more and more areas of social life.

In the UK (as elsewhere) this furthered processes of restructuring as Conservative regimes trashed the final remnants of the postwar consensus, disciplined the workforce and shrunk the legal space in which trade unions could operate. A fourth Tory victory in 1992 – the final leg of what was to become a generation in power – further undermined collective and communal loyalties, and promoted a narrow individualism rooted in consumerism, which was granted pseudo legitimacy within the framework of a property-owning democracy.

Perhaps the greatest victory of the right in this period was the widespread acceptance of its case that the only alternative to the free market was tarnished state socialism. And when the Tories rolled out TINA (there is no alternative), they effectively delivered a final judgement on the state of the political landscape. You could have either Reagan and Thatcher or the 'failed regimes' that had let down their people at almost every level – economically, politically and socially. These East European regimes, which were both brutal and inept, seemed a hardly enticing option. Alongside this the Labourist and Social Democratic parties of the West were successfully (and perhaps justifiably) tarred with the same brush. Their belief in top-down Keynesian economic management and bureaucratic public services seemed dated and the evidence was that 'nationalization plus the welfare state' had done little for the working classes. All of this promoted a view that the traditional left project had been abandoned by history. This was symbolized most poignantly in the Soviet Union by a small band of elderly Russians demonstrating in the snow outside the Kremlin, holding pictures of Stalin.

In the UK these trends led to the birth of New Labour – the epithet 'New' a formal recanting of the party's past. The key symbol here was the abandonment of its commitment to 'socialism' as expressed in Clause 4 of the party's constitution (in 1995). From this almost inevitably flowed the Third Way, a supposed amalgam of right and left. In this mix the right has contributed a belief in free markets, entrepreneurs and deregulation, whilst from the left Blair takes only an ill-defined 'fairness', rather than substantive equality. The product is a party that now celebrates the market (if still a trifle uneasily) and promotes a squalid managerialist politics. The postwar consensus had been replaced by a post-Thatcherite consensus.[3] New Labour had swallowed the bitter pill of neoliberal economic reality. Attempting to swim against the tide of global economic forces was perceived to be political suicide. Political survival was increasingly conditional upon the adoption of flexible labour markets and the maintenance of New Right monetarist policy.

Overlaid upon the 'victory of the right' paradigm, the 1990s also saw a growing belief in the inevitability of neoliberal globalization. In what was probably the dominant reading of this thesis came the contestable notion that power was draining away from the nation state. Capitalism was at once stronger and more diffuse, as evidenced in the power of the multinationals, e-transactions and the spread of Western lifestyle consumerism (rather than developments in the more defined battlegrounds of individual states). For radicals, as a result, it was becoming more and more difficult to lay a glove on to something that had melted into air.

Alongside this sense of capitalism both ever-present and decentred, paradoxically, came a growing awareness of strong concrete supranational agencies such as the World Trade Organization (WTO), International Monetary Fund (IMF) and World Bank. Year by year these bodies both policed and promoted the right's vision of globalization, closing down spaces in which alternatives might flourish.

The 1980s and 1990s, then, were a period of pessimism, at least for those who still bought into a traditional notion of left advance. How could the old ideas and weapons succeed in this new era – particularly the notion of building a movement within a nation state and around the organized working class? Sociologist after sociologist announced that this working class was no longer there, overtaken by economic change and the rise of the service sector, as other groups, such as the so-called 'underclass', came into their analytical sights. Moreover, the working class's strongest battalion, the miners, had suffered a devastating blow in the defeat of 1985 – a defeat that for many brought to an end a period of government-busting industrial militancy. Taken together these developments suggested that Marxist assumptions about the link between class position and political action were somewhere between overoptimistic and plain wrong.

In 2004, however, this picture has started to change. After the attack of 11 September 2001 and two wars on 'terrorism' an economic downturn has been accompanied by a seemingly long-term decline in the value of shares. Similarly, the dot.com boom, built as it was on speculation and hype, is over. Fukuyama's equation of the free market with liberal democracy also seems a tad overoptimistic. For a number of former Eastern bloc countries, the last decade has merely seen a transition from communist bureaucracy to a kind of economic gangsterism. Organized crime rather than human rights have found it easier to flourish in these circumstances. In a number of ways, then, history has not ended.

In this new context, the guardians of the new world order (WTO, G8, etc.) find that their international gatherings are now confronted by mass action. Rather than being celebrations of free trade and the market, these summits have seen the powerful and the rich retreat into luxury hotels, surrounded by lines of paramilitary police. Beyond these lines, however, to quote the slogan, it seems that Another World is Possible.

In the UK, as elsewhere, these highly visible set-piece protests coexist with a resurgence of campaigning and action more generally. At one level this can be regarded as an issue of *more*: *more* specific campaigns and *more* people participating in them, around issues such as transport, the environment, debt relief and the like. However, this book will argue that these discrete actions are not all that discrete and that a sense of coherence and convergence can be detected. Put simply, this amounts to the claim that there is now a definable anti-capitalist position and movement in the UK. With this, capital is once again under ideological attack. A heterogeneous mix of ecological, anarchist, socialist and liberal agendas has been gaining momentum, targeted at the worst excesses of neoliberal economic governance and cultural hegemony. Furthermore, whilst this movement is dynamic and changing, it also appears to be self-sustaining – a permanent carnival against capitalism.

However, the anti-capitalist movement is in no sense a reversion to the traditions of Marxist-Leninist anti-capitalism – a politics built upon the agency of the organized working classes, which viewed the state as the primary instrument of left advance, either after or instead of the revolution. Many people never shared those assumptions anyway and other anti-capitalisms always existed as at least sub-currents (particularly anarchism). But those other voices were often drowned amid the narratives of twentieth-century modernist, scientific socialism. With the twenty-first century comes a sense of new possibilities – perspectives rooted as much in moral critique as in analytical Marxism (and no less revolutionary for that). Also, and perhaps linked to these new visions, today's anti-capitalism can be seen as a more explicitly cultural (and even post-structuralist) assault on the free market, its values and its guardians.

Intellectually, all of this adds up to the justification for putting a book like this together. These phenomena are quite simply important and worth looking at. However, over the last couple of years the sight of people deploying against capitalism in new and vibrant ways also acted as a spur to us – as both activists and writers. This in turn led to a rolling programme of talking to people we knew and others we didn't to discuss their possible participation in the book. Like similar projects this involved us approaching people who had written interesting things (and were doing interesting things), following up suggestions and the like. It has been an organic project, therefore, in which we were not always sure what people were going to argue till we got their submissions. However, as is often the case, this approach has produced a series of contributions that are interesting in their own right whilst also hanging together as a collection. For that we would like to thank all of our contributors.

As a text, *Anti-Capitalist Britain* seeks to analyse the vitality of the new protest movement, both as a bundle of ideas in late modernity and also as a practical politics. Indeed, throughout there is an emphasis on the *relationship* between ideas and activism. For in today's anti-capitalism there is a real sense of groups and individuals consciously raiding the past for inspiration and, ultimately, producing something new from it. This sense of new ideas, new tactics and new visions runs through a number of the contributions here.

A word about our title and that word *Britain*. Is this a parochial jaunt, an attempt to analyse 'anarchism in one country' (to misappropriate a phrase from one Josef Stalin)? Well, no. Choosing the title *Anti-Capitalist Britain* was an attempt at mildly provocative irony – a seeming attempt to study things in a national framework that should only really be understood in a global context. In reality, though, what we are offering here is a case study of the particular that is grounded in the bigger picture. As such, we thought it would be worthwhile to look at the emergence and nature of the movement in one particular place – and how it has adapted to and developed the pre-existing left politics of the UK. We also thought it would be interesting to look at national-level developments given the welter of articles and books that have appeared recently analysing anti-capitalism as a general or international phenomenon. Moreover, our contributors are discussing domestic groups that are themselves linked into international networks, and activists whose work and outlook is explicitly internationalist (indeed, much more so than was the case with the old left). So, rather than seek to achieve the probably impossible task of providing an overview of the world movement, *Anti-Capitalist Britain* instead takes an inside-out approach. In this way, we use our domestic focus to show what is specific to the UK, whilst also commenting on developments elsewhere.

# The chapters

In our scene-setting opener we consider the origins and nature of the anti-capitalist movement, with particular reference to the UK. This first chapter examines the degree of continuity with previous movements, but also what is new. We especially identify an anarchist shift, towards a less authoritarian, prefigurative way of doing politics that has resonances in poststructuralism. This can be identified not only in what groups do but also in their organizational styles and ways of confronting the powerful. Following on from this we consider whether these loose networks, with their absence of centralized command structures, mean that the British anti-capitalist movement can properly be described *as a movement*. This almost inevitably leads on to the question of whether decentred, fluid organizations and actions display postmodern and poststructural characteristics.

In Chapter 2, Caroline Lucas and Colin Hines with their 'ten myths about globalization' challenge dominant readings of the subject – that globalization is inevitable and something that must be embraced by all nations to avoid falling behind. In place of neoliberal globalization, they propose an agenda of localization and sustainable trade. For these principles provide the conditions for community cohesion, cooperation and the reduction of poverty. Moreover, they reverse the dynamic towards environmental degradation and overexploitation that typifies the Bush/Blair/WTO model. Inherently, they also imply a post-capitalist future that could be created through the regulation and reorientation of present arrangements, rather than by insurrectionary means.

This issue of the location of green thinking within anti-capitalist politics is taken up explicitly in Chapter 3 by Molly Scott Cato. In particular, she ponders whether environmentalists still have something to learn from Marx. This chapter provides a breakdown of just what it is that Greens object to in the operation of free markets and out-of-control productivism, and how these are in turn destructive to the environment. By way of an alternative she sets out the principles that might underpin a new, green anti-capitalist politics – 'steady-state fairness', localization, cooperation and the reunification of production and consumption.

Writing from a subjective standpoint as a British-Muslim of Scottish-Pakistani origins, Amir Saeed demonstrates in Chapter 4 how Muslims in the UK are increasingly seen as 'others' or 'outsiders' by the press, government, the far right and the general public, and as people who make little attempt to integrate into mainstream British culture. Consequently, he argues that right-wing organizations have made political capital by associating Islam with terrorism – a position that is given some credence by recent government legislation and thinking. More importantly, by drawing on the writings of Huntington and Halliday, Saeed reveals how a new clash of civilizations is emerging. One result of this is the development of an anti-Muslimism, fuelled by events surrounding 9/11, which constitutes a new mode of racism. Saeed concludes his chapter by illustrating the views of ordinary British-Muslims on 9/11 and the War on Terrorism. His findings clearly indicate the increasing sense of isolation that Muslims feel in the UK today, and draw attention to some of the hostility they have endured since 9/11 was played out live around the world.

In Chapter 5, Derek Wall considers the life and work of the troubled Russian theorist Mikhail Bakhtin. He shows that Bakhtin's unique ideas – what might be called Rabelaisian social theory – have played a crucial role in the development of today's anti-capitalist movement. In particular, they underpin the street parties, road protests and other actions that have taken place under the Reclaim the Streets (RTS) banner. RTS and other direct actors have consciously deployed the traditions and practices of Carnival against power and the profit nexus. In this guise, some would argue that the anti-capitalist movement is at its most subversive – disrupting not only the hierarchies of capitalism but also those of Leninist leftism.

Alex Plows, in Chapter 6, draws on an ESRC study on environmental direct action networks in the UK to map out the historical development and current practices of anti-globalization movement mobilizations. In doing so, she explores how the growth of global environmental problems, the advent of the Internet and the recrudescence of neoliberalism during the 1980s feed into such mobilizations. By briefly examining direct action in the 1980s and the way in which certain direct action tactics and strategies cascaded down into the 1990s, Plows demonstrates how this played out in a micro context, triggering anti-capitalist and anti-globalization protests. By emphasizing that local circumstances often shape political action, her chapter incorporates activists' experiences of the 1980s peace camps, the miners' strike, the 1990s road protests and campaigns against genetically modified (GM) crops to illustrate how direct action in the 1990s increasingly led to an understanding of the bigger picture. Whilst arguing that opposition to globalization is not particularly new, it is suggested that the rise of the WTO played a central role in the rise of new biodegradable alliances of new social movements with the old left and conventional economic lobby groups that characterize this movement of movements.

In Chapter 7, Paul Taylor considers the way in which emerging technologies can be adopted and subverted so much that they become sites and means of protest themselves. His particular focus is on *hacktivism* and other forms of counter-cultural electronic performance. Embedded in a wider social scientific literature, Taylor's chapter traces the development of hacktivism from its purist routes in the 1980s. From this he identifies ways in which electronic activism has itself undergone change and, in some cases, been appropriated by the mainstream.

Jonathan Purkis draws a distinction in Chapter 8 between, on the one hand, safer forms of green consumerism and, on the other, an anticonsumerism that comprises an important aspect of the anti-capitalist movement. He shows that this deep green strand emerged out of the British Millenarian tradition and has its own Utopian vision. Moreover, it is this vision of another world that provides so much of what is radical in the wider movement. In this way it offers a critique not only of the consumer society but also of hierarchy *per se*. Purkis ultimately considers whether a 'discursive bridge' can be constructed between this vision and the dreams of the wider population, as a way of increasing the capacity of the anti-capitalist movement.

Writing from a personal perspective as a British-based protestor involved with Black Bloc during the Genoa action, in the final chapter Anonymous provides a meaningful insight into what actually happens during a big set-piece anti-capitalist protest. Reflecting on the extent to which communism and the radical left in general are deeply embedded in Italy's political culture and consciousness, Anonymous argues that a number of consequences follow. One of these is the generally warm welcome extended by Genoa city council to the huge numbers of protestors who descended upon the city. Such huge numbers, comprising different blocs of protestors, do present problems, however. In outlining some of those difficulties, Anonymous focuses on the role of Black Bloc during the protest. By charting its origins, ephemeral emergence and rapid dissipation after such events as Genoa, Anonymous demonstrates some of the issues surrounding the relationships between groups in such events, and illustrates how extemporaneous tactics emerge organically during protests like Genoa.

# 1

# Anti-Capitalism: Are We All Anarchists Now?

## *John Carter and Dave Morland*

In this chapter we consider the shape, dimensions and directions of the anti-capitalist movement (ACM) in the UK. We work through this initially at the level of description, seeking to trace origins and beginnings, as well as describing organizational styles and ways of doing protest. We argue that the ACM shows an anarchist shift in both its ideas and its (anti)politics. In the second half of the chapter we seek to draw more theoretical conclusions as to the nature of that anarchism as well as locating the contested social theoretical terrain on which the movement fights.

There is a sense in which this study of a particular movement can be regarded as a case study of anti-system politics in late modernity, for telling this story inevitably requires some consideration as to the nature of movements *per se*. As such we will at least implicitly be considering questions such as:

- How little organizational coherence can you get away with and *still be a movement*?
- How much can campaigners disagree about with regard to strategy, ideology and even ultimate goals and *still be a movement*?
- Has there been a cultural turn in UK anti-system politics?

We also need to note in passing a related question. That is, how much has the ACM been shaped and affected by the same trends that are shaping and reshaping the very capitalist system that it opposes? For the ACM also has become globalized and uses the tools of the information society – mobile phones and the Internet, most notably.

With all of this baggage in mind, we will resist any attempt to come to a simple or pat definition of the movement and will instead try to build up a picture of recent protests. In that we will draw conclusions derived from our position as observers and activists. We do this with a degree of humility, aware that others with better protest pedigrees and different perspectives may reach different verdicts. Furthermore, in our discussion of the rich variety of current actions and campaigns, we cannot even pretend to be comprehensive. We offer here only a snapshot and personal impressions.

## Timescales and origins

Getting into a debate as to *when* the ACM began may seem a little pedantic. However, the point at which we begin the story has a knock-on effect on questions of *what* and *who*. In other words, the process of dating the movement has an impact on whom and what we see as being part of it.

One (rather narrow) way of putting chronological parameters around the movement follows from the brief history set out in the introduction to this text. That points to the centrality of the 1990s, as the decade in which the market and neoliberal globalization reigned unchallenged. In those years we see the solidifying of the new world order with a more prominent role for the WTO and formal protocols such as the North American Free Trade Agreement in 1994. With a kind of stimulus–response model in mind, one could then note a starting point for the current phase of anti-capitalism as mass actions specifically aimed at the architecture of the new hegemony. This process of carbon dating the onset of the ACM (internationally) can be seen in a recent text inspired by the Socialist Workers' Party, with its 'Chronology of Anti-Capitalist Struggles'.[1] In this the authors set out a table of events, beginning with the famous Battle of Seattle (against the WTO) in December 1999. As an aside we might note that this conveniently forgets the more anarchist-inspired Carnival against Capitalism (usually referred to as the J18) which took place in June of that year. That saw both riots and street parties in London as the British leg of what was an international action.

There is a sense in which choosing Seattle as a point of departure *is* valid. Activists, commentators and journalists take it as a common reference point – the point at which the organizations that embody the new world order and its values become a permanent and very obvious target. In this sense, mass international actions around that period have two important effects with regard to perceptions of the movement:

- A name: the notion that there is something called an anti-capitalist *movement* – rather than discrete and unconnected groups of people who are in different ways pissed off with capitalism – becomes established.
- Perceiving the lines of force: these big demos also provided a focus and a sense of dramatic opposition. On one side were a heady mix of citizens, protesters and NGOs – and on the other bodies like the WTO and IMF who stood for and policed triumphal global capitalism.

There is, then, a sense in this line of argument that the ACM in Britain and elsewhere came into being at a particular moment. The market rampant with its associated environmental and social consequences was clearly one of the factors that opened up new possibilities (and reasons) for protest. Alongside and related to this was the phenomenon that Naomi Klein eloquently outlined in *No Logo* as the victory of the brand, the process of selling goods as pure image and lifestyle symbolism.[2] This was described by Guy Debord a generation earlier as 'capital accumulated to the point where it becomes image'.[3] However many billions the Nike swoosh and McDonald's arches may have made for their companies, they have also provided ever-present targets for protesters, Subvertisers and others, since they represent the dead-eyed consumerism of the present.

There is a further way in which a focus on the 1990s as a 'starting point' is plausible. It is in that decade that an empty space makes its presence felt – the space previously occupied by Leninism and hierarchical Marxism. With the disappearance of the Soviet bloc came a weakening of a particular and exclusive form of anti-capitalism. What went was the idea that for individuals to oppose capitalism required them (literally) to sign up to a centralized party with its dogma, 'line' and forms of bureaucratic politics. As *Do or Die* put it, 'now that the Soviet Union has ceased to exist, it has become a lot easier for those of us working in radical movements to conceive of a different society without having to refer to a failed model'.[4] As a result, today's ACM has a chance to reinvent itself for new times. The death of the old authoritarian Soviet anti-capitalism has cleared the way for more radical and vibrant ways of fighting money and all of its works.

Without wanting to withdraw anything from this notion – that a mass movement and new phase of struggle comes into being in the late 1990s – this is a narrative that tells only a partial story. The ACM has not only been shaped by current events and revulsion towards things as they are now. We also need to bring other players into our story and go back further to pick up on previous battles, movements and skirmishes. This isn't simply a process of noting antecedents or providing background. There is a real sense of continuity here, that revolts and ideas from the last 35 years are present in (and to some extent even *comprise*) today's ACM. Things may have been catalysed by the Battle of Seattle but they did not begin there.

In doing this we are really making a quite obvious and conventional point – one that highlights the importance of the late 1960s in the history of radical politics and protest. The 'moment of 1968', which is actually much less dramatic in the UK than elsewhere in Europe, does seem to usher in a new period in which the politics of protest takes a new form. That can be defined in terms of both scope and strategy. The 1960s and early 1970s witnessed a growth of campaigns related to social identities, such as gender and sexuality, in conjunction with heightened student radicalism and environmental awareness. These movements, however, were not cut from the old cloth and managed to develop new, less hierarchical forms of protest. Our contention is that these counter-cultures have contributed to the present counter-culture in important ways. Accordingly, they need to remain in focus amid contemporary discussions. Perhaps there is even a sense in which the different strands, analyses and lifestyles that have waxed and waned over the last three decades are only now achieving the status of *movement* – a coming together, however loosely.

Perhaps defensively we should add that this is to reduce a complex history to a couple of paragraphs and maybe needs to be qualified somewhat. We do recognize that there have always been significant crossovers between different movements – for example, feminism and the peace movement. Similarly, it smacks of determinism to suggest that today's movement is simply a product of what went before. We would, though, still maintain that the seeming victory of the market and liberal globalization has done much to produce the conditions of a *de facto* alliance amongst different strands of protest. We will return later to the question of whether this actually adds up to a *movement*.

This process of reclaiming and re-presenting the protest of the 1970s and 1980s has already been undertaken by George McKay.[5] He seeks to weave a number of 'post-68' movements into a single narrative of resistance, highlighting continuities and commonalities. McKay's book does this with chapters on:

- 1970s free festivals
- travellers (New Age and otherwise)
- punk, postpunk and anarchopunk
- the early (politicized) rave scene
- anti-road protests and camps
- the campaign against the 1994 Criminal Justice Act

To these we could add, at random, Greenham Common and other peace camps; environmental direct actions; Hunt Sabs; animal rights and the ALF; Class War, Stop the City and Henley Regatta 'visits'; street parties; hacking and any number of other movements from the last three decades. But what is the claim here – and how does this process of listing amount to a coherent history and sense that what went before is really part of what exists now? Are these not very different campaigns and is it not a post-hoc rationalization to say that all of these actors were 'really anti-capitalists'?

Well yes, these *are* diverse movements and any attempt to corral people with diverse motivations and ideas into a single story risks the sins of simplification. There is, however, enough commonality here to present these protests, movements and ways of living plausibly as contributions to what has now become a *de facto* joint enterprise. Those common features can be defined in four ways.

First, there is a tendency to work outside of formal political structures or even established pressure group activity – in fact, often, a conscious rejection of these structures and ways of working. Actions are not means of influencing Parliament and the powerful; they are active challenges and alternatives to that way of making decisions.

Secondly, linked to the point above, there has been in these movements an emphasis on *doing things* – direct action. Whether violent or non-violent (which the British scene has predominantly been) this is different from the traditional model of seeking to get our leaders to make changes *for us*. Direct action is about taking responsibility for change yourself – blockading a base, rescuing lab-tortured animals, preserving an ancient wood – not persuading bureaucrats and politicians to do it for you. In this sense, direct action not only challenges on an issue-by-issue basis, but also challenges accepted power structures and the set of assumptions that underpin parliamentary forms of governance. Consequently, not all direct actions are undertaken by anarchists, but direct action itself tends towards an anarchistic model of decision making. It may be that these features, in turn, have imbued protesters with a sense of vitality and empowerment, a feeling that with creativity and energy it is possible to live outside of the capital's sphere. Talking to veterans of the early Reclaim the Streets actions, anti-road camps and other early 1990s protests, there is a real feeling that this was the case, a sense in which a new generation was discovering the personal and political possibilities of do-it-yourself (DIY). Indeed, there may even be a sense that some of that vitality has been lost as a more permanent protest infrastructure has come into being over the last five years.

Thirdly, within many of the historic movements listed above (and equally among today's activists) there has always been a vision of *something else*, an awareness that there might be other ways of living beyond the circuit of capital. Often utopian, these alternatives have challenged the assumptions of consumerism, instrumental economic rationality and even modernity itself (a point to which we will return).

Fourthly, what activists from Greenham Common right through to the dsei protests of 2003[6] have managed to do is provoke the powerful and in doing so reveal the state's propensity for violence. Of late, in a period of deindustrialization and falling union membership, that provocation has less and less taken the traditional form of organized workers fighting industrial battles, though workers do still fight back against privatization and casualization. Instead, the British state has become more exercised about those who want to visit ancient stones, travel the land or party in the streets of the capital on May Day. In the Battle of the Beanfield[7] in 1985, the government's main weapons were truncheons. More recently, these have been augmented with the use of CCTV, the monitoring of e-mail traffic, the Regulation of Investigatory Powers Act and the deployment of public order and even terrorism legislation against protestors.

Perhaps most of all, the legacy of the last three decades, in all of its diversity, amounts to a sense of *presence*, an ongoing opposition to capitalism, the commodity form and the mega-machine. With this has also been passed on a set of ideas and experiences, ensuring that subsequent movements have something to draw on and develop in changing circumstances – tactics, analyses of power, musical taste, dress sense, etc. There is also a feeling of continuity at the personal level, in that whilst today's ACM is predominantly a young people's movement, it has also reinvigorated older activists and veterans of earlier battles.

## The contours of today's movement

If there is, then, a movement in the UK – more accurately, a movement of movements – it is worth listing some of the players. Here, our aim is to be illustrative rather than exhaustive – illustrative, that is, of the *type* of groups in action. In no particular order, these would include:

- *Reclaim the Streets* (RTS), which grew out of early 1990s road protests, particularly the M11 campaign (see Chapter 5). It has played a key role in organizing anti-car protests and street parties (indeed, in developing the very idea of street parties as a strategy). RTS has also been a key player in a number of May Day actions. The London RTS Collective no longer exists as a permanent organization, but recently reformed to organize the dsei protests.
- *Earth First!* – a network of deep-green environmental activists, responsible for developing direct action tactics. They include 'anti-civilizationists' and others opposing the negative effects of industrialization and mass society.
- The *Socialist Workers' Party* (SWP) – a Trotskyist grouping who believe that the revolution will have to be organized by a political party (more of them later).
- *Corporate Watch* – a network of activists and researchers producing reports on corporate power and its abuses.
- *No Sweat* – a movement against sweated labour, in solidarity with workers and campaigners in 'developing' nations.
- *The Wombles* – another network of activists with an emphasis on improving and coordinating demo tactics. They are notable for white overalls and other forms of padding/self-protection.

To this list we should add campaigns against specific multinationals such as ESSO, Nike and, of course, McDonald's. Closely linked to these is the work of Subvertisers,[8] who alter billboards and electronic adverts, using humour in a way that undermines brands and their messages.

In describing this anti-capitalist broad church, we would also want to include the various peace camps, campaigns against American bases,[9] debt reliefers, defenders of local woods and many others, operating as specific organizations or as less formal affinity groups. It is also important to stress the fluidity and temporality of these movements – there are no membership cards or subscriptions, and activists often move between different actions rather than staying with any kind of 'home organization'.

Another way to think about the ACM in Britain is by type of activity, which itself can be described spatially. In this way UK activists have participated in the big set-piece *international* demos against the WTO, G8 and other guardians of the new world order (in places like Seattle, Genoa, Nice and Evian). Below this, at the *national* level, a number of days of action are now well established as annual events or protests that draw in people from the whole country. Foremost of these is the reclaimed May Day – a day that used to exist as little more than an arid Trades Union Congress (TUC) rally. Now it has become a carnival of direct action where protesters take to the streets of London, directing protests against the arms industry, the square mile and other conspicuous targets of capitalism rampant.

Though essentially non-violent, these protests have nevertheless involved a clear element of confrontation with the police, over the right to occupy public space and protest.[10] In turn, the Metropolitan Police's tactics have evolved from their perceived defeat on May Day 2000, with a more aggressive stance involving the pre-emptive 'penning' of demonstrators, often for several hours. Moreover, with the backing of an increasingly authoritarian government, the police have been able to photograph, search and detain activists under the questionable provisions of recent public order and even terrorism legislation.

Such a mixture of fast-moving, unstructured protest with an equally 'robust' police response was played out in recent protests against the arms trade (dsei) in London. Other biggish national direct actions have taken place at American bases such as Menwith Hill and Fairford in recent months, where younger anti-capitalists have worked with often older peace activists, including those from the Campaign for Nuclear Disarmament (CND). We also cannot avoid mentioning the massive Stop the War Coalition march of February 2002, which drew in up to two million people from all backgrounds – the biggest political gathering the UK has ever seen.

In much of this there is a clear thread of internationalism, with activists travelling overseas, supporting campaigns in other countries and showing solidarity with the imprisoned. As well as this, many UK groupings and networks are in turn linked with parallel organizations elsewhere, such as Earth First!. This internationalism, underpinned as it is by the Internet, videostreaming and other new media, has created a situation where the parochialism of the old left has started to break down.

Just as important with regard to the work of the ACM is action at the local level – in fact, in terms of securing a long-term future and making actual change, it is more important. Examples of local work include the establishment of city-wide networks where activists and groupings advertise actions and campaigns, develop ideas and the like, again backed up by e-discussion lists and mailbases. More importantly, anti-capitalism takes place in physical communities, through participation in ongoing local campaigns affecting real places where people live. These often take the form of *resistance*, fighting against privatizations, destruction of woodlands and so on. However, anti-capitalists and anarchists have been at the forefront of establishing positive alternatives with the development of Social Centres. In many cases these began as squatted buildings, though some have a semi-official status in which activists have engaged with the local council to secure a form of official recognition. In turn, Social Centres such as London's Radical Dairy and the Sumac in Nottingham form a community resource where people can take courses and develop their own potential, as well as providing a base for activists. Often developing from derelict buildings, Social Centres offer an opportunity for anarchist DIY principles to be put into effect – in terms of self-management of the centre and also, literally, in relation to its renovation.

Inevitably, all of this diversity and localized action has produced the need for coordination and forms of *infrastructure*. That there are common enemies and a potential for common action has to be put into practice. At the national level, this task has been taken up by Indymedia,[11] an independent and non-commercial electronic newsite/wire (itself part of an international network of independent newscentres). Generated and run by activists, Indymedia consists of a rolling programme of analysis pieces, reports from demos, videostreams and announcements. It manages at once to embody a DIY principle whilst also being quite slick, patching together multimedia work in a range of formats. Indymedia also combines local reports on particular community campaigns (in conjunction with more recently established local Indymedia centres) with a consistent focus on overseas struggles.

Formatwise, *Schnews*[12] can be seen as a slightly more traditional activist 'newspaper', albeit in electronic form, coming out on a weekly basis with reports on previous and upcoming events. Beyond this, Urban75[13] is perhaps the other main national coordinated channel of communication for activists. A massive multimedia site including debates on a whole range of lifestyle issues, Urban75 has at its heart a series of discussion threads on direct actions, tactics and protest ethics. As a result, Special Branch routinely monitors traffic on these sites as well as infiltrating activist groupings – particularly in the run-up to May Day (in addition to the Met's more public strategy of photographing anyone attending planning meetings). Finally, in an electronic age, pretty much every grouping or campaign has its own website, with the usual set of 'links' and 'forthcoming events'.

In the non-cyberworld there are a variety of forums in which experiences are shared and tactics evolved. These include the annual Earth First! Summer Gathering and the Anarchist Bookfair. The latter of these has grown and grown, and now has workshops and discussions on all areas of libertarian theory and practice. This kind of event gives a sense of coherence to a movement that is, almost by its very nature, minimally cohesive and fragmented. This is particularly so for those living outside of London and other 'activist-rich' environments.

A word about the Socialist Workers' Party (SWP). Perhaps the main fault line (though not the only one) in the UK anti-capitalist scene is between the anarchists/direct actionists described so far and the Trotskyist SWP. There was an impression in the late 1990s that, as the ACM began to grow and mobilize, the SWP had become almost figures of fun. Still banging on about socialism and the planned society, still seeking to build the party and still strike chasing, the SWP seemed to be following the tactics of an earlier era. Alongside this was a vibrant and growing movement, made up of people who saw no need to sign up to a party line – or indeed saw no need for a party at all. Even worse, there was a sense that they were hanging on to the coat-tails of a new movement, with a view to stealing some of that energy.[14]

In the intervening period, SWP newspaper sellers have become a familiar sight at meetings and the party's access to high-quality printing facilities has ensured it has a visibility beyond its actual membership numbers. However, the core of the SWP's strategy has been to work through 'front organizations'. These include Globalise Resistance (with its SWP-paid organizer), the Stop the War Coalition and the Socialist Alliance. It is important here to define the term 'front organization': we are not suggesting that these organizations are numerically dominated by the SWP – though the party does have a significant presence on the coordinating bodies. Rather, SWP members and other hierarchical socialists spend a lot of time working in these bodies and through that play a major role in developing strategy – circulating pre-arranged draft resolutions, etc. They are also well placed to recruit activists into their own organization.

The aim of the SWP has been to maintain links with organized labour and, particularly, the new generation of anti-Blair trade unionists. It must be admitted that libertarian anti-capitalists have often neglected these essential links. However, what must be questioned is the direction the SWP wants the ACM to take. Time and again its emphasis has been on mobilizing large numbers of protesters, but ensuring that those protests remain orderly and legal, even to the point of having pre-arranged chants. To be avoided at all costs is direct action and spontaneity, in which demonstrators make their own (personal and collective) decisions as to what is appropriate. Instead the SWP has adopted the Grand Old Duke of York strategy of marching from A to B, listening to the usual suspects making speeches in Trafalgar Square and then going home. With this approach the SWP had a role (via the Stop the War Coalition) in getting two million people into Hyde Park on 15 February 2002 – admittedly a major achievement – but could do little to build upon this.

The underlying and persistent approach of the SWP is essentially one of *capacity building*, particularly building the membership of the SWP itself as a Leninist/Trotskyist party. With this the party's aim is to assume a leadership role within the working-class movement in times of militancy and, ultimately, revolution. This Bolshevik strategy, however, regards attempts to confront capitalism in the here and now by direct action as 'indiscipline'. The SWP also seeks to promote its 'line' – the party's analysis of the 'current phase of struggle' – through the pages of *Socialist Worker* itself and other publications. This line, updated for new times can be seen in a recent work by the party's leading theorist, Alex Callinicos.[15] Finally, it might be added that the SWP strategy has had a certain success of late. Most notably, it could be argued that May Day has been partially re-reclaimed: that is, wrestled back from the frisky direct action protests of 2000 and 2001. In conjunction with the South-East TUC, Globalise Resistance has managed to reinvigorate an A to B trade union march which has perhaps drawn some of the sting from the anarcho-protests taking place in central London on the same day.

By way of contrast, the rest of the movement, and certainly those involved in direct action, exhibit a kind of anarchist style of decision making and activism. This is not to claim that all non-Trotskyist anti-capitalists are self-proclaimed anarchists (though many are), but that non-hierarchical (or at least less-hierarchical forms) typify the movement. One way into this is with the notion of *leaderless protest.* This assumes that decisions on what to do evolve out of open, practical meetings which may then develop further in web discussions. Decisions on actions are, for want of a better phrase, *frameworks*. As such, there may be start times, themes, even objectives – but not any kind of attempt to marshal or *deploy* protesters. The emphasis is passed on to individuals and small affinity groups to determine their own approach and make their own ethical decisions as to the nature and limits of the protest. In particular, activists will exercise their own judgement as to the way they manage the (almost inevitable) confrontations that follow from aggressive policing strategies. From this it could be argued that these are collective protests, but without centralized (or, more specifically, hierarchical) control. Similarly, there is in such actions a heavy emphasis on personal judgement and responsibility. However, this does not mean that anti-capitalist protests are merely atomized and individualistic. There is in fact a feeling of common purpose and solidarity, something that is itself nurtured by a process of active disorganization.

In a point of qualification it should be noted that the lack of internal or formal hierarchy in groupings does not mean there is an absolute equality of influence. Inevitably, those who get involved, attend planning meetings and do the work will have more of an impact on outcomes. However, the key point is that influence does not derive from any formal position or office – posts such as 'chair', 'organizer' and 'secretary' are pretty much absent from anarcho-groupings. Importantly, this type of organization lacks any kind of implementation bureaucracy: that is, the notion that one group of people makes decisions and others put them into practice. In the ACM those who are part of the decision to do a particular thing are the ones who carry that out – activists. It should be noted that this is not always the case with the more traditional non-governmental organizations and charities. Anarchist politics, though, assumes a DIY method – there is no one else to do things for you.

Taking all this as a whole, the ACM (at least the non-Trotskyist ACM) displays a *prefigurative* politics. By this we mean that people seek to conduct their struggle and personal interactions in ways that mirror the kind of society they intend to build. A non-hierarchical future should be built by non-hierarchical methods or, to put it another way, means should mirror ends. This differs from the Leninist or Bolshevik notion that the future Communist society must be built by a disciplined and structured party in which strategy and analysis are 'owned' by defined leaders.

Demographically, the ACM has a distinctive age profile, in that activists are predominantly in their twenties and thirties (with, of course, older participants and, more recently, younger ones – schoolkids). In this the ACM is a mirror image of the mainstream parties, whose average age creeps up and up. As a result, the movement exemplifies and uses key aspects of youth culture in terms of music, dress and style – though, ironically, the big brands have developed so many lines of street clothes over the last decade that everyone now has protester chic.[16]

Another contrast worth drawing relates to the shift from *physical* to *symbolic* confrontation with the state. The former of these was paradigmatically represented by the miners' strike and Wapping disputes in the 1980s. These saw the deployment of class forces (marshalled by the unions and others) in large numbers against specific employers and the police. Whilst these were complex disputes and should not be reduced down to the physical attempt to blockade depots and pits, nevertheless those events were absolutely central to the actions and their success or failure. Our claim here is not that what might be called traditional class/industrial politics has gone away – though there has been an obvious diminution as union membership has dropped, the TUC has moved rightward and the right to strike has been curtailed by Parliament. Indeed, anti-capitalists of all hues have been keen to support and link with workers' struggles. Rather, we are suggesting that a new iconography and language of protest has developed, which in turn has gained its inspiration from pre-modern and pre-industrial sources. For example, May Day 2002 had a Carnival theme as an attempt was made to revive the anti-authoritarian revelry of the medieval fair with its lords and ladies of misrule. It is a rare demo now that does not have its fair share of stiltwalkers and jugglers (or, as more exasperated class war anarchists sometimes put it, *fucking jugglers*). In similar vein, balloons and samba music have been deployed against the state and tin foil against the armed police at Menwith Hill spy station.

Before this begins to sound too disparaging, we would argue that this kind of strategy can be effective in that it involves the *humiliation of power*, a process of showing a creative contempt for Leviathan. It breaks with Bolshevik assumptions that the power of the state must be combated with an equal dose of workers' power and an equal measure of muscle. Instead, *power itself* is combated and undermined. Yet, at the same time it would be wrong to suggest that anti-capitalist actions are purely fluffy, pink fairy pacifism. Protesters put themselves in harm's way and seek to break through the police cordons that are now routinely used to pen demonstrators. Activists also use their own physicality to interrupt the flow of nasty corporate activities – by climbing cranes, d-locking on to trains and such like (on protest tactics and strategies, see Chapter 9). In all of this there is also a healthy disrespect for keeping protests within the law.[17] Our claim, then, that a shift has taken place towards *symbolic protest*, needs to be understood in this context. It is not symbolic in the sense of passive or without effect – quite clearly these are vigorous and energetic actions. Rather, it is that symbols are deployed against capitalism, the arms industry, the police and the 'system'. These are symbols of fun, symbols that hint at new ways of living and symbols that undermine the assumptions that make the powerful powerful.

## Poststructuralist anarchism

All of this inevitably takes us into a theoretical debate, one that tries to identify relevant frameworks within which to understand the new politics and new movements. One starting point would be a rather bad-tempered argument that has been raging within anarchism over the last decade or more. At the core of this has been a case made by proponents of a traditional 'social anarchism' (notably Murray Bookchin), who in defending this school of libertarian politics have dismissed what they see as an emerging poststructural or 'lifestyle anarchism'. Other writers, perhaps more aligned with the strategies and ideas outlined so far in this chapter, have fought back and sought to work out a new terrain of politics and ideas.

The very idea of poststructuralist anarchism remains anathema to Bookchin. For him, poststructuralist anarchism is one version of lifestyle anarchism, which is nothing short of a narcissistic devotion to bourgeois hedonism. Owing much to Foucault, lifestyle anarchism:

> is little more than an introspective personalism that denigrates responsible social commitment; an encounter group variously renamed a 'collective' or an 'affinity group'; a state of mind that arrogantly derides structure, organization, and public involvement; and a playground for juvenile antics.[18]

Bookchin has produced a sizeable volume of anarchist texts, but his brand of social ecology has engendered considerable criticism within anarchist circles. One of his most vociferous critics, Bob Black, denies that there is any such thing as lifestyle anarchism. Rather, there are many different anarchists experimenting with many different ideas and theories. Bookchin has simply invented the term 'lifestyle anarchism' to 'collect all his political enemies for their more convenient disposal'.[19]

Despite the difficulties associated with Bookchin's analysis, the term 'lifestyle anarchism' does signal something useful. As we have illustrated above, it can be employed to categorize a number of varied but loosely united groups that have been central to recent modes of resistance. Certainly, it would be disingenuous to deny that anarchists have found themselves on a multitude of differing theoretical trajectories of late. Writers such as Perlman, Zerzan, Debord, Vaneigem, Black, Bey, Moore and May have produced significant and sometimes contentious contributions to the anarchist canon. These diverse inputs are rooted in a number of competing theoretical positions. One of those is *poststructuralism* – a position we will now examine with regard to its influence in and upon the ACM.

Associated most closely with the works of Foucault and Derrida, but deriving much of its cogency from Saussure's analysis of language and meaning as differential rather than referential, poststructuralism offers an alternative to a structuralist account of the human condition. Marx's argument about the economic base of society is a classic example of the way in which a social theorist attempts to explain the human condition by referring to an underlying structure that is susceptible to objective analysis, outside the discourse that constructs these structures. If structuralism was a reaction to the humanist position, in which the world should be conceptualized as the product of human beings, then poststructuralism is, in turn, a reaction to structuralism. Like anarchism, poststructuralism is difficult to define in a positive sense, whereas identifying what it rejects is comparatively easy. As Belsey has recently argued, poststructuralism 'is not a system, nor even, when you look at the details, a unified body of theory'.[20] But there are particular reasons for poststructuralism's repudiation of structuralist accounts, and these reasons afford insight into the nature of poststructuralism itself and the crossover between poststructuralism and anarchism.

For poststructuralists, structuralism failed in its critique of humanism for the reason that structuralists invested structures themselves with a surrogate agency.[21] Consequently, the writings of psychologists like Piaget and social theorists like Althusser endowed structures with a determining role in the production of subjects (or human beings). This is where the poststructuralists part company with structuralism. To understand this we need to journey back in history. One of the most famous philosophical accounts of knowledge is that provided by Descartes. In an attempt to discover what we can know for certain, Descartes employed his now famous method of doubt. The result was *cogito ergo sum*: I think, therefore I am. In other words, if Descartes could not be certain either that the external world was as it seemed or that he had a body, because his senses or an evil demon could deceive him, he concluded that he could have no doubt about the existence of his consciousness.[22] At the heart of this Cartesian position there occurs a separation of subject and object, with the subject (the consciousness) contemplating objects outside itself. Poststructuralists deny the separation of subject and object. They argue that the subject is an integral part of symbolic and cultural discourses and practices, and an object can only be known by a subject that resides within those discourses and practices. The antithesis between subject and structure is replaced by the 'contingent practices that produce both "subjects" and "structures"'.[23]

One of the most telling poststructuralist analyses may be found in Foucault's work on power. Here, power is conceptualized as resident within everyday cultural, political and social discourses. Moreover, power is perpetually reproduced within these discourses, and so poststructuralist thought endeavours 'to expose the politics that are at work in representations and to undo institutionalised hierarchies, and it works on against the hegemony of any single discursive system . . . in its advocacy of difference, pluriformity and multiplicity'.[24]

This poststructuralist analysis of power signals one way in which the transition from social anarchism to poststructuralist anarchism has occurred. Whilst May acknowledges that anarchists are ambivalent about whether the state is the major site in the exercise of power, he contends that at the heart of anarchism there lies an assumption about the suppressive nature of power.[25] It is in this sense that anarchists have targeted the state and the bourgeoisie as principal sites of resistance. Calls for the elimination of power wherever possible and the general decentralization of power to local communes or communities are reflective of anarchism's endeavours to cage the negative effects of power. Indeed, the tradition persists in some anarchist quarters. Strands within the group Class War, for example, remain committed to class struggle with acts of resistance directed against the bourgeoisie and the state. Sceptics might argue that such an approach is now hopelessly outdated and completely misses the target. The point of the poststructuralist critique, though, is that it is now futile to talk of a target. There is no longer, if there ever was, one target to aim for.

Social anarchism's vilification of the state as the locus of power and oppression is what characterizes it as a strategic and therefore redundant ideology.[26]

Within the poststructuralist writings of Deleuze and Guattari, power is visualized as inhabiting the rhizome of political, social, economic and cultural networks. Its distribution along the flows of these networks may result in occasional concentrations of power at interconnections between different networks, but there is no epicentre of power for poststructuralism. One example of a concentration of power is the WTO, but there are many others. For this reason, power must be resisted across these networks. Consequently, there is no one primary site of resistance, but multiple locations and modes of resistance. This poststructuralist outlook is pivotal in the shift away from what May regards as a strategic ideology to a tactical philosophy, such as poststructuralist anarchism.[27]

Thinking about power in terms of networks or rhizomes reflects poststructuralism's emphasis on totalities. And it is this view that informs a further development in poststructuralist anarchism. For nineteenth-century social anarchists like Bakunin, the principal enemy is capital and the bourgeoisie as its representatives. For poststructuralist anarchism, such a narrow focus would be inappropriate. The poststructuralist stress on totalities suggests a broader vision of system-wide oppression. Poststructuralist anarchists encounter oppression and power across a wider totality. Thus Moore suggests that 'the focus of anarchism is not the abolition of the State, but the abolition of the totality, of life structured by governance and coercion, of power itself in all its multiple forms'.[28] To be sure, poststructuralist arguments on power are central to its consideration of the state and the practices within which it is situated. Accordingly, May claims that thinkers like Lyotard, Deleuze and Foucault have developed

> a new type of anarchism. This new anarchism retains the ideas of intersecting and irreducible local struggles, of a wariness about representation, of the political as investing the entire field of social relationships, and of the social as a network rather than a closed holism, a concentric field, or a hierarchy.[29]

Within poststructuralist anarchism, the notion of resistance reflects the nature of power as system-wide oppression. There is clear overlap here with the Situationist heritage that confronted and simultaneously subverted the spectacle of capitalism, and in so doing signalled a shift away from economistic attacks on capital as the structural epicentre of power. A poststructuralist understanding of resistance suggests that alternative modes of opposition are utilized to subvert this systemic oppression. In this sense, resistance transcends the political and also assumes social and cultural forms. It is these modes of resistance and subversion that are central to the ACM.

# The anti-capitalism movement and poststructuralist anarchism

It is our contention that the hallmarks of the present ACM are markedly anarchist, and specifically a poststructuralist anarchism at that. There are a number of conceptual bridges that link the movement with poststructuralist anarchism and we explore some of these below. However, it would be disingenuous of us to claim that the ACM is a uniform movement that shares one common perspective. As we illustrated above, there are fault lines running through the movement. One of the main divisions here segregates Trotskyite socialists from contemporary anarchists. Consequently, it is better to talk about a movement of movements. Nonetheless, others have also noted that anarchism is pivotal to the ACM.[30] It is partly for this reason that the ACM is a dynamic, organic and acephalous movement.

In that sense, when we refer to the ACM as a new social movement we are talking about something quite different from the old social movements of the twentieth century, many of which were essentially labour movements. During the last century, capitalism was increasingly opposed by people operating within modernist categories: either from a definite social position – usually working class and within a class-based organization (party or union); or from within, by deploying a grand ideological narrative such as socialism. This frequently led to pre-determined conclusions. Marxism, being the pre-eminent ideological narrative of the left, occupied the role of a quasi-religion. In other words, the terrain of ideological and political struggle was clearly mapped out well in advance of any practical action by the labour movement itself.

In global terms, both in terms of the struggle between the two superpowers and in an ideological sense, there raged a battle of world philosophies. This struggle presented something of a barrier to alternative and emerging social movements in the 1970s and 1980s, such as the women's movement and the environmental movement, if only to the extent that socialists were inclined to dismiss such concerns as something that would be resolved during the transition to a post-capitalist society. Socialism was a child of the French Revolution and the Enlightenment. Accordingly, it exhibited a Promethean faith in progress, science and technology, as well as its own revolutionary potential. Anti-capitalism, then, insofar as it amounted to various socialist political organizations and the labour movement, possessed an organizational and ideological clarity (and even exclusivity) during this period.

Today that is no longer the case. To begin with, the focus of the ACM has changed significantly. The political realm has largely, if not absolutely, been forsaken for modes of resistance that are cultural and symbolic in nature.[31] This shift in the nature of resistance signals one of the conceptual bridges that links the ACM with poststructuralist anarchism. As Ruggiero has observed, what separates new social movements from the labour movements of old is that the former 'refuse to engage in building up a superior representative entity, such as a party or an all-embracing organization'.[32] Both poststructuralist anarchism and the ACM embody an anti-representational politics. Or, to be more accurate, they are both anti-political.

Additionally, the ACM is emblematic of another crucial difference that separates it from the old labour movements. Anyone familiar with labour movement politics during the 1970s and 1980s in the UK should recognize the hierarchies and organizational structures that were at the heart of this movement. Images of trade unions leaders marching into Downing Street for beer and sandwiches with the Labour government as they discussed the movement's latest grievances, or memories of Scargill's leadership of the miners' strike in the 1980s are significantly different from the contemporary dynamics of the ACM. As Anonymous illustrates in Chapter 9, groups involved in the present ACM, such as Black Bloc, are without leadership, structures or permanent organization. This is not to deny that there were no instances of spontaneity, direct action or autonomy within old labour movement actions. Wildcat strikes and flying pickets were often spontaneous modes of direct action that were autonomous from the broader organizational structures of the labour movement. As Alexandra Plows argues in Chapter 6, certain tactics and strategies present in the ACM today have cascaded down from previous protest groups. But the important point here is that the loose and flexible organizational structures of the ACM are one of its defining hallmarks. Similarly, its leaderless, spontaneous direct action, which facilitates 'on the ground' autonomous strategies of resistance, which in themselves emerge organically inside the protest event and often dissolve immediately after the event, are indicative of a very different mode of resistance from that of the 1970s and 1980s.

Memories of trade union leaders appearing on television barking out demands either to their bosses or to the government are illustrative of another critical difference. One outcome of this anti-representational and heterogeneous movement of movements is that its activists refuse to negotiate over the movement's goals or objectives. Groups like Earth First!, for instance, are not in the business of entering into negotiations with recognized authority or power structures inside central government. As Welsh has maintained, protests are 'staged on the movement's own terms'.[33] Even if these broad theoretical brushstrokes disguise some of the contrasts within the ACM, it is clear that the movement, in the UK at least, grew out of anarchist and radical environmentalist groups that simply won't play the game of nominating leaders to broker agreements with governments, which subsequently betray simultaneously the radical principles of the movement and the dedication of its activists.

It is here that we find another conceptual bridge between the ACM and poststructuralist anarchism. In contrast to the structuralist and representational mode of politics harboured by the SWP, which many protestors believe is guilty of vampirism and coat-tailing tactics insofar as it has locked on to the ACM to make political capital for the party, the anarchist elements of the movement operate strategies of resistance that resonate with poststructuralism. The rejection of representational politics and the emergence of cultural and symbolic resistance exemplifies not only a different feel to political protest as a process, but also a discrete appreciation of what needs to be resisted. That resistance is no longer centred on building a revolutionary party to lead the working classes to power, but assumes many different guises, addresses multiple sites of power and oppression, and is reflective of a poststructuralist understanding of power as rhizomatic – of oppression occurring across totalities and systems. There are multiple targets because there are multiple sites where power and oppression manifest themselves. Correspondingly, resistance needs to address these multiple sites in multiple ways. In that sense, images of protestors engaged in fluffy tactics, Social Centres recycling cooking oil into green diesel, and cooperatives pooling labour and skills under LETs initiatives are all an integral part of an anarchist culture that is not only striving to deprive established mechanisms of power and any semblance of moral jurisdiction, but also engaged in a prefigurative construction of autonomous zones and autonomous capacity building.[34] It is precisely this, May contends, that renders anarchism as a poststructuralist and therefore tactical philosophy.[35]

The process of building alternative practices represents another bridgehead between the ACM and poststructuralist anarchism. Before exploring this, however, a few words are warranted about the context within which the ACM operates. As a protest movement, the ACM increasingly finds itself working in and partially defined by a set of global economic and political practices. To be sure, the circumstances of neoliberal globalization are beginning to frame the ACM, providing a context and target for protests. More importantly, these practices have led to a growing awareness among protestors that what they oppose and resist is no simple and singular manifestation of economic power. Instead they frequently perceive a system that reaches into culture, consumption and lifestyles across the globe. As Plows indicates in Chapter 6, the more protestors participate and develop ties with other organizations and networks, the more they develop an awareness of different linkages, such as the connection between consumerism in the developed world and exploitation in the developing nations, and between the growth of corporate branding and the elimination of local diversity.

> Before the onslaught of globalisation 'the system' was sometimes hard to recognise in its diverse manifestations and policies . . . But the

reduction of diversity in the corporate landscape and the concentration of power within international institutions such as the IMF, the WTO and the financial markets has clarified things and offered a focal point for protest and opposition.[36]

Articulation of the bigger picture, of the systems and networks of oppression and power that encompass the globe, has certainly been one of the dividends that the protest movement has taken from its experience of resisting organizations such as the WTO and G8.

The other major contextual factor has been the alleged victory of the liberal-democratic, free-market capitalist model of government. With the collapse of the Berlin Wall and the cessation of the Cold War, commentators like Francis Fukuyama were swift to pronounce the final victory of capitalism over communism toward the end of a century that had witnessed the triumphal progression of economic liberalism across the globe.[37] Such claims leave much to be desired, not only in terms of the theoretical and philosophical grounding of their historical assertions, but also quite simply in their accuracy. It would be more accurate to say that these events led inexorably to public discussion on the crisis in Marxist thinking. To be sure, declarations of liberalism vanquishing a now moribund and forever irrelevant communism led to much introspection on the part of Marxist scholars, and more generally to the decline of 'systematic' left thinking. Paradoxically, however, the decline of left thinking may have presented an opportunity for the emergence of new radical analyses. These analyses embody an instinctive conception of capitalism as a holistic but multidimensional entity. Consequently, the ACM seeks to combat capitalism in diverse and inventive ways – in the workplace, shopping mall, cyberspace, streets, etc. This has resulted in a subtle but important shift. When capitalism was seen to exist primarily in the workplace and in the extraction of surplus value, only those predominantly involved in that workplace struggle could be regarded (or regard themselves) as anti-capitalists. However, as analyses of capitalism have shifted on to other terrain – consumerism, lifestyle and the generation of desire – then protesters in those fields have been redefined. Twenty years ago someone opposing Shell was an environmentalist – now they are/ would regard themselves/associate with other anti-capitalists.

Taking advantage of this decline in left thinking, anarchists and the ACM are now occupying the theoretical space vacated by socialism. This brings us back to the other conceptual bridge between the ACM and poststructuralist anarchism. In constructing alternative practices, anarchists and the ACM are engaged in a mode of opposition that has a long history within anarchism. Kropotkin's article 'Act For Yourselves', which was originally published in the nineteenth century, has echoes in the DIY culture of today's movement, and is reflective of the ways in which anarchists have striven to establish autonomous zones in the forms of free schools and communes, for example, that are practices of resistance against dominant paradigms.[38] Undoubtedly, such practices provide an environment in which those particular practitioners derive a sense of meaning both about their own forms of direct action or practice and about that which they oppose.

Poststructuralist writers like Deleuze and Guattari refer to such activities as 'becoming minoritarian'.[39] By developing alternative practices through social forums and other networks and organizations, contemporary anarchists are challenging dominant parent practices and simultaneously escaping oppression. In a sense this is what sociologists refer to when they talk about counter-cultures. But what is especially important from a theoretical perspective is that here we have examples of practices that are concurrently modes of criticism. Building alternatives to dominant paradigms is essentially a prefigurative experiment in new ways of living. This mode of criticism and resistance, MacKenzie has recently termed 'ontological constructivism'.[40] This is the way poststructuralism perceives the critical act as the construction of alternative ways of life. As Deleuze and Guattari see it, the concept of majority 'assumes a state of power and domination, not the other way around. It assumes the standard means, not the other way around.' Accordingly, it is imperative to distinguish between 'the majoritarian as a constant and homogenous system; minorities as subsystems; and the minoritarian as a potential, creative and created, becoming'. In becoming minor, 'a nondenumerable and proliferating minority . . . threatens to destroy the very concept of majority'.[41]

# Conclusion

A sensible question to ask at this juncture is, where does that leave us? Or to be more definitive, how can we best describe the nature of the ACM? To begin with, we are in no doubt that the ACM is a social movement of some importance. How important and how influential it proves to be are questions that cannot be addressed or answered in this chapter or at this time. We are equally clear that we have witnessed the development of a movement that sometimes has the feel of an organized coincidence. By this we mean that there is a sense in which the ACM refers to: a collection of people attending the same demonstrations; a group of protestors who feel no need to join exclusive organizations; a set of cross-references and the facilitation of mutual support through numerous websites; and a series of bonds, occasionally weak and ephemeral but sometimes stronger and more enduring, between local and national networks. Certainly, most anti-capitalist groups are themselves minimally cohesive coalitions – and the movement as a whole is a minimally cohesive movement of movements. Generally, these coalitions possess an orientation that is simultaneously anarchistic and what some may describe as postmodern.[42]

The ACM unquestionably envelops an overlapping series of economic, cultural and political protests – but within a broad cultural turn. In a related sense, the movement also exhibits the ability of groups with diverse and even opposing ideas to work together. More specifically, these groups display *a lack of concern* about the issues of message coherence, ideological compatibility and tactics. From both a practical perspective and a theoretical standpoint, the ACM has begun to challenge a series of contemporary orthodoxies. Its ability to muster hundreds of thousands of demonstrators to protest against the WTO, for example, and its underscoring of a multitude of lived alternative practices, both in the UK and elsewhere, signifies a movement, both heterogeneous and prefigurative in nature, that has captured the imagination of those willing to resist the homogeneous cultural oppression and environmental and economic exploitation of the planet and its population.

# 2

# Time to Replace Globalization: A Green Localist Manifesto for World Trade

## *Caroline Lucas MEP and Colin Hines*

The purpose of this chapter is to challenge the growing myths about the alleged benefits of ever-increasing trade liberalization, and in particular to tackle head-on the greatest myth of all – that economic globalization is inevitable. We also make clear that an alternative to this damaging process exists, that a radically different set of trade rules can bring about the necessary transition, and that the EU must play a key role in delivering it.

Globalization is not driven by irrefutable economic laws, nor is it governed by ineluctable market forces. And, by the same token, it has not happened by an accident of nature or divine intervention. Despite the public relations efforts of some to convince us otherwise, the WTO system is just one design for the world's economy. It is not inevitable like the moon's pull on the tide, or the force of gravity. The establishment of the WTO and the global trade rules it oversees was an enormous task. If we do not like the outcome, we can choose alternatives to it. To underline our point, we set out a framework constitution for a different global institution with different rules and a different end goal.

In contrast to the ten myths of world trade, we posit one overriding reality: that a planet of finite resources and increasingly unmet social needs cannot sustain an economic system based on ever-increasing international competition and ever-greater free trade, the product of a single global development model driven by, and serving, corporate interests. As the German economic philosopher Wolfgang Sachs argues in his book, *The Development Dictionary*, 'the only thing worse than the failure of this massive global development experiment would be its success'.[1]

The reality is that this process poses an enormous threat to the environment and is on a collision course with attempts to control climate change.[2] Trade accounts for a growing share of an increasingly fossil fuel-hungry global economy, and the transport it depends on is one of the fastest-rising sources of greenhouse gas emissions. Moreover, even at its optimum performance level, its long-term benefits go only to a minority of people who sit at the hub of the process, while the rest are left fighting over fewer jobs and less land, living in increasingly violent societies on a ravaged planet.

The adverse effects of globalization have long been apparent to those on the ground in poor countries. These range from Indian peasant farmers made bankrupt by cheap imports, resulting from the dismantling of protective tariff barriers, through to rising death rates in Russia following the collapse of social infrastructure and the rise of gangster capitalism. Richer countries are now also beginning to feel their effects more widely, with the recent fall in the values of stock markets and the resulting decline in consumer confidence bringing rising unemployment and insecurity, as jobs disappear, share values are destabilized and pensions shrink.

It is therefore both necessary and timely to set out an alternative proposal for a radically different way to organize the world's economy in order to achieve genuine sustainability. The one presented here is a process of 'localization'. This is a model that is beginning to be increasingly advocated both North and South. In essence it means that the focus of a country's economic policy is to protect and strengthen its local and regional communities by producing as many goods and services as feasible and appropriate from within its own borders. This obviously does not mean putting an end to all international trade. It simply means trying to meet more of our basic needs from closer to home, with long-distance trade reverting to its original purpose – the quest for what cannot be obtained domestically. Later in the chapter, we set out in detail some of the changes to world trade rules which would be needed to achieve this alternative vision, and outline the key role which the EU must play to bring this about.

# Getting the terms straight – globalization

Before challenging the myths of the alleged benefits of economic globalization, it is crucial to clarify what is meant by the term.

Linguistic clarity is vital, since the advocates and beneficiaries of globalization misuse the indisputable benefits that can accrue from constructive international flows of information and technology to justify the destructive processes of economic globalization. In her former role as International Development Secretary, Clare Short typified this approach when her department's official statements asserted that 'globalization means the growing interdependence and interconnectedness of the modern world'.[3] This woolly, cosy definition allowed Short to wax lyrical about the spread of democracy and human rights without understanding that these have very little to do with economic globalization as most activists understand it.

By *globalization* we mean the ever-increasing integration of national economies into the global economy through trade and investment rules and privatization, aided by technological advances and driven by institutions like the WTO. The relentless effort by multinational corporations to eliminate 'barriers' to trade has led to a loss of democratic control by nation states and their communities over their own economic affairs. The process is driven by the theory of comparative advantage, and the goal of ever-increasing international competitiveness.[4] It is occurring increasingly at the expense of social, environmental and labour improvements, and leading to rising inequality for most of the world. This is very different from the process of 'internationalism' – the positive global flow of technology, ideas and information, together with growing international understanding and cooperation.

By 'localization' we mean a set of interrelated and self-reinforcing policies that actively discriminate in favour of the local. In practice, what constitutes 'the local' will obviously vary from country to country. Some countries are big enough to think in terms of increased self-reliance within their own borders, while smaller countries would look first to a grouping of their neighbours. This approach provides a political and economic framework for people, community groups and businesses to re-diversify their own economies. It has the potential to increase community cohesion, reduce poverty and inequality, improve livelihoods, promote social provision and environmental protection and provide the all-important sense of security.

Localization is the very antithesis of globalization, which emphasizes a beggar-your-neighbour reduction of controls on trade and contorts all economies to make international competitiveness their major goal. Localization involves a better-your-neighbour supportive internationalism where the flow of ideas, technologies, information, culture, money and goods has, as its end goal, the protection and rebuilding of national and local economies worldwide. Its emphasis is not on competition for the cheapest, but on cooperation for the best.

# Ten myths about globalization

## Myth 1: 'Globalization is the only effective route to development'

Conventional wisdom has it that globalization has accelerated the world's economic growth, and that the only argument is over how that growth has been distributed. A closer look at the facts, however, reveals a very different picture.

From 1960 to 1980, virtually every nation in the developing world was developing along the lines of the 'Import Substitution Model', by which locally owned industry was built through government investment and high tariffs. During this era of increasing national government control and ownership, per capita income grew by 73 per cent in Latin America and by 34 per cent in Africa. By comparison, since 1980, growth in Latin America has come to a virtual halt, increasing by less than 6 per cent over 20 years, while African incomes have declined by 23 per cent.[5] Also during this period, more than a decade of life expectancy was added to nearly every nation on the planet. From 1980 to today, the era of increasing globalization, life has become brutish and shorter. Since 1985, life expectancy has been falling in 15 African nations. Even the IMF has admitted that 'in the recent decades, nearly one-fifth of the world population have regressed' – arguably 'one of the greatest economic failures of the twentieth century'.[6]

Recently, a group of US researchers has drawn up a globalization scorecard which compares the period from 1980 to 2000 – the era of Reaganite neoliberal globalization when the drive for capital deregulation, privatization, and the lifting of barriers to international investment was at its height – with the period from 1960 to 1980 when most developing countries had a more restrictive and inward-looking economy.[7]

They discovered that the poorest countries went from a per capita growth rate of 1.9 per cent annually in the period 1960–80 to a decline of 0.5 per cent a year between 1980 and 2000. The middle group of countries did worse, dropping from annual growth of 3.6 per cent to growth of just under 1 per cent after 1980. The world's richest countries also showed a slowdown.

Using the United Nations Development Programme's Human Development Index, which widens assessments of welfare from purely income measurements to include, among others indicators, infant mortality, literacy and gender empowerment, the researchers found that between 1980 and 2000 there was a 'very clear decline in progress'.

For life expectancy, the picture was similar. Only the richest countries showed a higher rate of improvement in the past 20 years. Among middle-income and poor countries, progress in reducing child mortality and raising school enrolments was faster before 1980.

But what of the East Asian 'Tigers', which seem to have reaped enormous benefits from the world economy? In fact, their development strategies were very different from those being prescribed to poor countries today. Countries like South Korea and Taiwan had to abide by few of the current rules during their formative growth period in the 1960s and 1970s, and faced far less pressure to open their borders to capital flows. These countries combined their outward orientation with unorthodox policies: high levels of tariff and non-tariff barriers, public ownership of large sectors of banking and industry, export subsidies, domestic-content requirements, patent and copyright infringements, and restrictions on capital flows, including foreign direct investment. Today it would be impossible to replicate these strategies without breaking the rules of the WTO or IMF.

## Myth 2: 'Greater integration into the world economy is good for the poor'

The WTO, alongside other international finance agencies, incessantly repeats that greater integration into the world economy is the only way for the world's poorest countries to develop. In recent years, faith in integration has spread to political leaders and policy-makers around the world.

Such integration, however, is more than just lowering barriers to trade and investment. Countries must now comply with a long list of admission requirements, from new patent rules to more rigorous banking standards, and undertake complex institutional reforms that took today's industrialized countries generations to achieve.

This is bad news for the world's poor. By focusing on international integration, governments in poor countries divert human resources, administrative capabilities and political capital away from more urgent development priorities such as education, public health and industrial capacity. Blind adherence to the integrationist faith leaves less space for the development of domestic economic strategies based on domestic investors and domestic institutions.

Moreover, analysis by the United Nations Conference on Trade and Development (UNCTAD) found that income gaps between North and South have continued to widen and that globalization has contributed to this trend. In 1965, the average per capita income of the G7 countries was 20 times that of the world's poorest seven countries. By 1995, it was 39 times as much. In almost all developing countries that have undertaken rapid trade liberalization, wage inequality has increased, most often in the context of declining industrial employment of unskilled workers and large absolute falls in their real wages, of the order of 20–30 per cent in Latin American countries.[8]

More than 80 countries now have per capita incomes lower than they were a decade or more ago, and as the United Nations Development Programme (UNDP) points out, it is often the countries that are becoming even more marginal which are highly 'integrated' into the global economy.[9] In spite of the fact that exports from Sub-Saharan Africa, for example, have reached nearly 30 per cent of GDP (compared to just 19 per cent for the leading industrialized countries of the OECD), the number of people living in poverty there has continued to grow.

Indeed, studies reveal no systematic relationship between a country's average level of tariff and non-tariff barriers and its subsequent economic growth rate. If anything, the evidence for the 1990s indicates a positive relationship between import tariffs and economic growth. The only clear pattern is that countries have dismantled their trade restrictions as they have grown richer. Today's rich countries, with few exceptions, embarked on economic growth strategies behind protective barriers but now display low trade barriers. As US economist Dani Rodrik concludes, the globalizers have it exactly backwards: integration may be the result, but it is certainly not the cause, of economic and social development.[10]

## Myth 3: 'Developing countries have most to gain from a new world trade round'

According to Mike Moore, Director-General of the WTO, the future of world prosperity depends on an agreement to launch an ambitious new trade round at the next WTO ministerial meeting. A number of developing countries have good reason to question this assumption. Sub-Saharan Africa, for example, has lost an estimated $569 million per year from the last Uruguay Round.[11]

Moreover, the costs of implementation are significant. World Bank economist Michael Finger has estimated that a typical developing country must spend $150 million to implement requirements under just three WTO agreements (those on customs valuation, sanitary and phyto-sanitary measures, and trade-related intellectual property rights). As Finger notes, this sum equals a year's development budget for many least-developed countries.[12]

Indeed, a significant number of developing countries are not in favour of launching a new trade round. Many are insisting that outstanding issues negotiated during the last round of trade talks, the Uruguay round, be resolved before a new round begins. These include revising the agreement on intellectual property rights to take account of public health needs, delaying implementation of investment measures, operationalizing the commitment to 'special and differential treatment' for poorer countries, and honouring the market access commitments made by the industrialized countries at Marrakesh and still not implemented. On the eve of the G7/8 Summit in July 2001, 30 African countries, including the regional giants South Africa and Nigeria, signed a declaration in Addis Ababa rejecting new powers for the WTO, while in late August the South Asian Association for Regional Cooperation, which includes India and Pakistan, called on WTO members to oppose a broad new round of trade talks. The EU, on the other hand, is adamant that it is essential to include new issues such as investment, competition and government procurement in a comprehensive and ambitious new round.

Although not a formal part of the new round, the WTO's Agreement on Agriculture is also a highly contentious issue for developing countries. India has been a particularly outspoken critic, since its huge agricultural sector is being devastated by WTO rules forcing India to lower its protective tariffs. Prakash Singh Badal, the Chief Minister of the most prosperous state in the so-called breadbasket of India, Punjab, warned last December that 'the implementation of the WTO Agreement in its present form would lead to bloodshed in the country . . . signing of the WTO amounts to signing the death warrant for the farm sector'.[13]

Much play is made of the fact that the majority of WTO members are developing countries and that therefore they have the upper hand in the institution. This is to ignore cynically the realities of international politics, whereby the more powerful countries – particularly the EU and USA – dominate the proceedings. Although nominally one country, one vote, in fact voting does not generally take place in the WTO at all – instead, power is brought to bear in the corridors and back rooms.

The reality of this power imbalance was seen in the content of September's first draft of the Ministerial Declaration for the WTO Conference. It failed to reflect the concerns that many developing countries have been expressing for a long time over implementation issues, and all the elements that the developing countries have been objecting to are there in the draft text.[14]

## Myth 4: 'Comparative advantage is the most efficient way to ensure a prosperous world'

The advocates of free trade claim that all nations benefit by trade because of the principle of 'comparative advantage'. According to this 'do what you do best, and trade for the rest' approach, nations do best from international trade when their industries specialize. By mass producing those goods where they can make maximum use of the factors of production which are in abundance locally (whether land, climate, natural resources or labour), countries are able to gain a price advantage over their competitors. Thus, according to the theory, a nation should narrow its focus of activity, abandoning certain industries while developing those in which it has the greatest 'comparative advantage'.

If a country has a significant amount of low-cost labour, for instance, it should export labour-intensive products; if it has a rich endowment of natural resources, it should export resource-intensive products. International trade is then said to grow, as nation states export what they can produce most cheaply and import what others produce most cheaply. As a result, efficiency and productivity would increase in line with economies of scale, and prosperity would be enhanced.

This ivory tower theory ignores the reality of the differences in power between traders and producers as well as those between nations. The nature of comparative advantage for a country may alter completely if it has the power and resources to gain such advantage. Thus through long-term planning, education and investment, Japan has made its wealth on manufactured goods, despite being poor in natural resources and energy. But for poor countries, as their economies now stand, free trade means continuing in their relatively powerless role as low-cost producers of primary goods for western consumption.

These theories therefore bear no comparison to today's reality. The free flow of goods *and* capital means that investment is now governed by *absolute* profitability and not by comparative advantage between countries. Today, the increased size and the global spread of transnational corporations (TNCs) has been paralleled by a massive increase in the amount of capital flowing round the world. In 1996 alone, for example, total world cross-border investment flows amounted to some $310 billion. Developments in computing and information technology, plus a deregulation of controls on capital by nation states, now mean that around $1.3 trillion is transferred every day around the world.[15] As one economist concludes:

> When capital is mobile it will seek its absolute advantage by migrating to countries where the environmental and social costs of enterprises are lowest and profits are highest. Both in theory and practice, the effect of global capital mobility is to nullify the Ricardian doctrine of comparative advantage. Yet it is on that flimsy foundation that the edifice of unregulated global free trade still stands.[16]

As if to prove the point, the WTO refers to the theory of comparative advantage as 'arguably the single most powerful insight in economics'.[17]

## Myth 5: 'Anti-globalization protesters are all white, middle-class rich kids, whereas the Third World wants more free trade'

The Seattle and post-Seattle protests in the USA and Europe have been termed a 'new movement'. But these much publicized protests, derided by supporters of globalization as the 'antics' of the 'white, privileged and middle class' are actually just the tip of a far more global iceberg. In the South, a much deeper and more wide-ranging grassroots movement has been developing for years, largely ignored by the media. Indeed, the northern protesters are echoing the same concerns as their southern counterparts.

Protests and demonstrations organized by the southern poor have been aimed at policies that hurt their livelihoods and, in some cases, undermine the democratic foundations of their countries. This 'hidden' movement has a global reach and represents a deep unease over economic policies that keep the poor in poverty.

Among the largest demonstrations have been those in India, where in the early 1990s half a million people demonstrated against the adverse effects of the policies of the WTO's predecessor, the General Agreement on Tariffs and Trade (GATT). Indian farmers' coalitions are currently fighting the large-scale export agriculture promoted by WTO rules, by countering the illegal rollback of land reform policies to enable TNCs and domestic industries to buy agricultural land for growing luxury crops for export; and by opposing new export policies encouraging the slaughter of 'sacred' animals in slaughter houses for meat exports. Thousands of villages in Gopalpur in Orissa have also blocked the establishment of a new steel plant by Tata and Nippon. The plant is only for export production, and will use iron ore from newly opened mines and energy from new dams, which together will cause millions to be uprooted and displaced.

Other countries where big demonstrations have occurred include Argentina, Bolivia, Brazil, Colombia, Costa Rica, Ecuador, Honduras, Kenya, Malawi, Nigeria, Paraguay, South Africa and Zambia.[18]

Moreover, hundreds of NGOs and groupings from global civil society both North and South signed on to 'WTO – Shrink or Sink!' – a sign-on letter demanding radical reform of the WTO. The signatories agreed that

> The time has come to acknowledge the crises of the international trading system and its main administering institution, the WTO. We need to replace this old, unfair, and oppressive trade system with a new, socially just and sustainable trading framework for the 21st century . . . We need to protect cultural, biological, economic, and social diversity; *introduce progressive policies to prioritize local economies and trade*; secure internationally recognized economic, cultural, social and labour rights; and reclaim the sovereignty of peoples and national and sub-national democratic decision-making processes.[19]

Of the nearly 80 countries that were represented in the signatories' list, 44 were developing countries and seven were from central and eastern Europe.

## Myth 6: 'More globalization means more jobs'

According to the International Labour Organization, at the beginning of 1999 there were some 150 million people unemployed worldwide and up to one billion under-employed – a third of the world's labour force. In the words of then ILO Director-General Michael Hansenne, 'the global employment situation is grim, and getting grimmer'.[20]

The situation is worst of all for developing countries and those in eastern Europe. However, even across the industrial world, pressure to reduce real wages and downsize labour forces has been a hallmark of policy since the late 1970s. This has been largely the result of competition between rich countries as they have opened up their markets to foreign capital, mergers and acquisitions, as well as to imports and the relocation of companies to other countries. Pressure on jobs in rich countries has also been increased by competition from low-waged, but increasingly high-skilled exporters from the Asian economies and China, and by the actual or threatened relocation of industries to lower-waged, less regulated economies. Often the threat of relocation alone is enough to introduce a sense of discipline to the workforce, limiting their expectations of better wages and conditions.

At the same time, both manufacturing and an increasing part of the service sector are being driven down globalization's competitive path of ever more automation and the 'downsizing' of its workforce. Increased job losses far too frequently result in redeployment to lower-paid, part-time, more insecure work, or simply to unemployment.

Recent examples include the Dutch-owned Corus Steel, which bought British steel works and then closed them, and BMW's purchase of Rover, and its subsequent downsizing of the company before the management buyout. Even more symptomatic of the waning power of elected leaders over transnational corporations was the fact that when the US-owned company Motorola shut its factory in Scotland, with the loss of 3,000 jobs, Prime Minister Tony Blair could not even reach the chairman on the telephone to discuss the issue.[21] Perhaps most symbolic of the loss from relocation of jobs once thought secure for the northern working class in Britain was the transfer of cloth cap production from Leeds to China in an effort to remain competitive. Moreover, in both rich and poor countries, the push to attract and keep private investment in national economies has led to strict curbs on the funding of public provision for basic needs, so that taxes can be reduced while inducements to foreign investors are increased.

Globalization also offers no security for workers in developing countries as they are constantly forced to compete with other workers from even poorer countries. This situation will be made worse when, as expected, China joins the WTO at the ministerial meeting. The country's rural majority will be further disadvantaged by cheap food imports, especially from the USA, and will join the 100 million who are already looking for urban work. This recipe for ever lower Chinese wages at a time of export emphasis will further devastate its Third World competitors – China has already captured Northern textile markets from poor competitors such as Bangladesh. With technology transfer and automation, China will potentially also be able to beat OECD competition and increasingly dominate the markets in Europe and the rest of the North in a huge range of goods. Shougang Steel, for example, has already become so expert in computerized production techniques that it won a contract to install the control systems for a US steel maker.[22]

## Myth 7: 'If globalization is replaced, we will return to the disastrous protectionism of the 1930s and the communist era'

According to economic orthodoxy, the goal of 1930s protectionism was for each protected industry or country to hide behind higher tariff barriers in order to provide a respite from competition. In theory, this would enable it to increase its economic viability and then compete for foreign markets at the expense of others. The result was said to be that the more countries raised such barriers, the less trade there was between them and, as a result, the 1929 slump turned into a depression.

However, Professor Eckes, a former adviser to President Reagan who has studied the relevant archives and diplomatic correspondence, recently revealed that the tariffs which were raised – which were themselves not very high – caused little retaliation between countries. It was the depth of the global depression, not the irritation of tariff increases, that forced governments to restrict trade and currency flows, and to concentrate on domestic economic recovery. The myth that protectionism was a major cause of the depression is therefore wrong.[23] Rather, the depression was so deep because the laissez-faire ideology of the time failed to allow enough governments to pump adequate public expenditure into their economies to overcome the decline in consumer expenditure. It was only the Second World War that eventually provided sufficient demand to pull the world out of depression.

A further challenge is to rescue the language of protectionism. Peasants are lampooned as 'protectionists' for resisting trade liberalization and for trying to preserve an 'inefficient' way of life. Workers and businesses are described as 'standing in the way of progress' if they express worries about their livelihoods being undercut by imports. Consumer and environmental organizations are criticized as 'green protectionists' when they attempt to prevent free trade from rolling back hard-won environmental or product safety regulations or the introduction of more stringent measures. But if we look at the meaning of protection, interesting questions follow. Protection of what? For whom? For what ends? To whose benefit?

It is the answer to these questions which makes localization very different from 1930s protectionism. Rather than raising barriers in order to compete in foreign markets at the expense of others, localization raises barriers in order to protect and rediversify the national provision of goods and services. The old protectionism served the short-term interests of the powerful elites and national companies; localization seeks to protect *public* interests such as health, the environment, safety standards and poverty eradication against the interests of the free-trading elite. The old protectionism sought to preserve gross inequalities within and between states; localization seeks the reverse, arguing that today's challenges cross all geographical and social boundaries.

Localization also differs from the closed, protectionist economies attempted by communist regimes because internal competition, the international flow of ideas and technology, and the introduction of resource taxes will ensure that the stagnation and environmental degradation so often found in these closed-off regimes will not be repeated. Finally, it is crucial to note that localization is not against all international trade; rather it seeks to reduce unnecessary trade in goods and services that can be conveniently produced domestically.

## Myth 8: 'To recover from the attacks on the Twin Trade Towers we need more globalization, not less: to be anti-globalization now is to offer unwitting support to terrorism'

The anti-globalization movement of which we are part is committed to non-violence, and we have repeatedly distanced ourselves from the tiny minority who wish to use violence. To suggest otherwise is misleading and dishonest.

Far from giving succour to terrorists, we are committed to addressing some of the factors which currently generate a fertile breeding ground for terrorism – poverty, inequality and situations where people see no hope of improvements, feel no sense of security and have no chance for a better future. Globalization exacerbates these factors – replacing globalization, then, is a crucial part of an overall strategy to combat terrorism.

However, after the appalling atrocity in New York, it is the pro-globalizers who are regrouping behind their usual misinformation about the benefits of free trade. They are using the understandable political bipartisanship in the aftermath of 11 September 2001 in order to bounce Congress into making it easier for President Bush to agree to a new WTO 'round'. Far from leading to greater international security, this would further reduce nations' control over their economies, and increase inequality.

In the aftermath of 11 September, Tony Blair proposed that the monument for those who died should be that the international community shapes a world where all people have justice, prosperity and freedom to develop individual potential. He too recognized that this was the way to deal with some of the causes of terrorism. For him, however, the issue is not how to stop globalization:

> The issue is how we use the power of community to combine it with justice. If globalization works only for the benefit of the few, then it will fail and will deserve to fail. But if we follow the principles that have served us so well at home – that power, wealth and opportunity must be in the hands of the many, not the few . . . then it will be a force for good and an international movement that we should take pride in leading. Because the alternative to globalization is isolation.[24]

Yet with this statement, Blair reveals a fundamental naivety in failing to understand the historical fact that the WTO rules were initially developed by and for large corporations. The reality of these rules of economic globalization is that they pit nation against nation, rich against poor, in a commercial war to conquer other people's markets, under the battle cry of 'international competitiveness'. Experience shows that this leaves little room for Blair's hopes for justice, prosperity and freedom.

Moreover, his straw man of pitting isolation as the only alternative to globalization is belied by the fact that communities all over the world are increasingly recognizing that globalization is an obstacle to the ends that they want, not a vehicle to achieve them. Instead, they are demanding a new focus on cooperation to achieve the protection and rebuilding of economies, North and South.

## Myth 9: 'The WTO is democratic, accountable and driven by elected governments'

Many decisions affecting people's daily lives are being shifted away from local and national governments and are instead being made by a group of unelected trade bureaucrats sitting behind closed doors in Geneva. They are now empowered to dictate whether the EU has the right to ban the use of dangerous biotech materials in the food it imports, or whether people in California can prevent the destruction of their last virgin forests, or whether European countries have the right to ban cruelly trapped fur.

At stake is the very basis of democracy and accountable decision making. Indeed, globalization is characterized by the establishment of supranational limitations on the legal and practical ability of any nation to subjugate commercial activity to other policy goals. It has aptly been described as a 'slow-motion coup d'état' over democratic governance worldwide.[25]

Thus, under the WTO's rules, the race to the bottom is not only in social and environmental standards, but also in democracy itself. So-called free trade deals virtually guarantee that democratic efforts to ensure corporations pay their fair share of taxes, or provide their employees with a decent standard of living, or meet environmental targets are met with the response that such measures could undermine their international competitiveness; followed closely by a threat to relocate to countries with less stringent standards.

It is not hard to see why. Corporate interests share a common, perverse outlook which makes the globe first, and foremost, a common market and source of capital. Governments, laws and democracy are factors that restrict their exploitation. From this perspective, the goal is to eliminate market barriers on a global scale. From any other perspective, such barriers are seen as valued safeguards on unfettered economic activity – that is, every nation's laws that support their economies, their citizens' health and safety, the sustainable use of their land and resources, and so on.[26] Indeed, the globalization process, and the trade rules that guide it, have been driven over the past three decades by the world's leading business and governmental elites. They have been instrumental in achieving free trade agreements such as the General Agreement on Tariffs and Trade's Uruguay round (spearheaded by the International Chamber of Commerce) and, in the EU, the single market and currency (via the European Roundtable of Industrialists).[27]

Their power has been increased by the additional armoury of the WTO's international trade rules, to ensure the global economy is further shaped to their advantage. The following example is a case in point. The extraordinarily controversial issue of intellectual property rights was put on the Uruguay round agenda by a committee of 13 major companies, including General Motors and Monsanto, which lobbied governments to include their proposals in the trade talks. In the negotiations that followed, 96 out of the 111 members of the US delegation working on intellectual property rights were from the private sector. Little surprise, then, that the final agreement serves corporate interests, and undermines poor people's access to knowledge and technology.[28]

The extent of their success is seen by the credible fact that 47 of the top 100 economies of the world are TNCs, 70 per cent of global trade is controlled by just 500 corporations and a mere 1 per cent of TNCs are responsible for half the total foreign direct investment in the world.[29]

## Myth 10: 'Globalization is inevitable'

The political consensus around the 'globalization is inevitable' myth initially appears daunting. According to Renato Ruggiero, former Director-General of the WTO, trying to stop globalization is 'tantamount to trying to stop the rotation of the earth'.[30] For Bill Clinton, globalization is 'not a policy choice, it's a fact'. Tony Blair has called it 'irreversible and irresistible'.[31]

Such descriptions of globalization are clearly deliberately designed to pre-empt any serious analysis of the phenomenon, to forestall any critical examination of its underlying interests and driving forces, and ultimately to prevent radical alternatives being proposed. Yet such crude economic determinism is neither politically acceptable nor intellectually tenable.[32]

Translated into less abstract terms, what such concepts refer to, of course, is the worldwide expansion of the corporate production and investment strategies of giant transnational corporations, together with the investment strategies and speculative financial transactions of powerful banking, insurance, stockbroking and other financial organizations. Yet the global expansion of such economic and technological agencies has required – and has been actively promoted by – political processes, particularly the actions of governments to create national and international conditions conducive to their perceived needs.

The opening up of almost all countries and all economic sectors to the global operations of such industrial and financial agencies has demanded the removal of impediments, particularly 'unacceptable' regulatory terms and conditions, identified as 'barriers' to business or 'distortions' in the functioning of market forces. This requires, and is producing, the increasing deregulation and liberalization of trade and investment operations, financial and labour markets, service sectors and other national and international economic functions.[33]

The shameful fact is that governments have so little control over economic globalization precisely because they have systematically *chosen* to give away power to unaccountable bodies like the WTO. By giving up the right to condition investment in a country on certain societal standards, or the entry of products into domestic markets on compliance with national rules, for example, political leaders have deliberately eliminated whatever leverage they had on corporate behaviour.

The choice before us, then, is not between the rules of the current international economy on one hand, and the chaos of no rules on the other. Rather, we can devise a different set of rules, with different strategies and goals.

Globalization is not like gravity or the pull of the tides, nor is it a God-given state of grace that must therefore be with us forever. It is a set of policies shaped by corporate pressure groups and carried out by politicians. It is perfectly possible to replace it with a different end goal for the world economy. This could come about if a different set of pressure groups and others persuade the public and eventually politicians to move in a completely different direction: to shift away from the ruthless international competition of globalization to a post-globalization alternative – the protection and rebuilding of national and local economies everywhere. Indeed, it is the purpose of this chapter to help begin such a process.

## What's the alternative to globalization?

Economic globalization is under unprecedented attack as millions of people, from the Mexican jungle to the streets of London, become ever more aware of the destruction and devastation it brings with it. It is therefore time for a comprehensive and radical alternative, based on a new direction for the global economic system. It must reduce inequality, improve the provision for basic needs and fully protect the environment. Its end goal must be to support and increase the democratic control and involvement of citizens in the rebuilding of sustainable national and local economies worldwide.

Localization is just such an alternative – a set of interrelated and self-reinforcing policies that actively discriminate in favour of the more local. It provides a political and economic framework for people, community groups and businesses to re-diversify their own economies. It has the potential to increase community cohesion, reduce poverty and inequality, improve livelihoods, promote social provision and environmental protection, and provide the all-important sense of security.

Over a period of time, there would be a gradual transition away from dependence on international export markets (with every country trying to compete with each other, leading to a downward spiral of social and environmental standards) towards the local and national provision of as many goods and services as feasible and appropriate. Long-distance trade is then reduced to supplying what cannot come from within one country or geographical grouping of countries. This has the environmental advantage of no longer requiring the transport of so many goods over unnecessary distances. It would allow an increase in local control of the economy, and offer the potential for its benefits to be shared out more fairly.

Localization is the very antithesis of globalization, which emphasizes a reduction of controls on trade and contorts all economies to make international competitiveness their major goal. Localization involves a supportive internationalism where the flow of ideas, technologies, information, culture, money and goods has, as its end goal, the protection and rebuilding of sustainable regional, national and local economies worldwide. Its emphasis is not on competition for the cheapest, but on cooperation for the best.

Among the policies that have been proposed as part of this long-term policy package are:

- localizing money, so that the majority of it stays within its place of origin, using controls on capital flows, a Tobin tax, and control of tax evasion, including offshore banking centres
- a 'site here to sell here' policy for manufacturing and services domestically or regionally, so that market access is dependent on physical presence, making the threat of relocation less effective
- the reintroduction of protective safeguards for domestic economies (e.g. tariffs and quotas)
- local competition policy to eliminate monopolies from the more protected economies
- increased democratic involvement both politically and economically to ensure the effectiveness and equity of the shift towards more diverse local economies
- ecological taxes on energy, other resource use and pollution to help pay for the economic transition towards localization
- the reorientation of the end goals of aid and trade rules so that they contribute to the rebuilding of more sustainable local and national economies[34]

The policy mix will obviously vary in practice to some degree from country to country. Some countries are big enough to think in terms of increased self-reliance within their boundaries; smaller countries would look to a grouping with their neighbours.

# Rewriting the rules for sustainable trade

### GATT – the old rules

The General Agreement on Tariffs and Trade (GATT) was established in 1947 as a mechanism to negotiate the continuous lowering of tariffs between its members. Since its formation, there have been eight 'rounds' of trade negotiations, focusing first on tariffs, and later including non-tariff barriers, with the most recent round leading to the creation of the much more powerful World Trade Organization in 1995. The WTO requires that the laws of every member must conform to those of the WTO. It has the power to judge a country's compliance with its rules, and – critically – to enforce the rules with sanctions.

### GAST – the new rules

We propose replacing GATT with the General Agreement on Sustainable Trade (GAST). The end goal of GAST is *not* to ensure the unimpeded and ever-increasing international trade in goods and services, but to promote a more sustainable and equitable economic system by strengthening democratic control of trade, stimulating industries and services that benefit local communities, and rediversifing local and national economies.

# Comparison of WTO rules with those of the General Agreement on Sustainable Trade

### Article 1

#### Most-favoured nation treatment

The most-favoured nation (MFN) rule requires WTO member countries to treat products from one WTO member as favourably as they do products from any other member. In other words, discriminating between foreign producers is prohibited. This rule raises serious doubts about the validity of international trade-related environmental conventions (e.g. the Montreal Protocol, CITES and the Basel Convention) which actually require that *less* favourable treatment be accorded to countries which are not fulfilling their obligations under these environmental conventions. As a recent WTO case involving the banana trade between several Caribbean islands and the EU illustrates, the MFN rule also prohibits the use of special trading relationships to support development cooperation programmes with poorer nations.

This would be changed under the GAST rules to:

> Provided it is not at the expense of domestic goods and services, states shall give preferential treatment to goods and services from other states which respect human rights, treat workers fairly, and protect animal welfare and the environment.

## Article III

### National treatment

The national treatment (NT) rules require that imported and locally produced goods be treated equally. Thus, under WTO rules, it is unlawful for governments to favour, or otherwise promote, domestic products above imported goods.

This would be changed under the GAST rules to:

> Trade controls that increase local employment with decent wages, enhance protection of the environment, and otherwise improve the quality of life are encouraged. States are urged to give favourable treatment to domestic products and services which best further these goals.

### Process and production methods

The rule on process and production methods (PPMs) makes it unlawful for governments to discriminate against individual countries' goods because of concerns about the damaging or unethical processes that may have been used to produce or harvest them. This makes it impossible, for example, to protect domestic producers with high environmental or animal welfare standards (e.g. producers of free-range eggs) from unfair competition from foreign producers that do not meet such standards (e.g. producers of eggs from battery cages).

This would be changed under the GAST rules to:

> Members are permitted and encouraged to make distinctions between products on the basis of the way they have been produced in order to further the aims of sustainable development.

## Article XI

### Elimination of quantitative restrictions

Under this article, WTO members cannot limit or impose quantitative controls on exports or imports through quotas or bans. This is very problematic from an environmental and social perspective. Consider the implications of such a rule when applied to measures such as an export ban on unprocessed resources like timber; or an embargo against the export of agricultural commodities from a country suffering food shortages; or a prohibition against trade in endangered species; or a ban on the export of hazardous wastes to less developed countries.

This would be changed under the GAST rules to:

> Quantitative restrictions should be permissible. For those products which are imported, preferential access should be given to goods and services going to and coming from other states which, in the process of production, provision and trading, respect human rights, treat workers fairly, and protect animal welfare and the environment.

## Article XX

### General exceptions to WTO rules

In theory, this article allows the adoption or enforcement of measures to protect public morals, to protect human, animal and plant life or health, or to conserve finite natural resources, provided they are not arbitrary or unjustifiably restrictive. In practice, it has been interpreted extremely narrowly, and has failed to offer the protection it promises. With only one exception, the WTO has struck down as an illegal trade barrier every single domestic environmental, health or safety law that it has reviewed, including the US implementation of a global endangered species treaty concerning sea turtles.

This would be extended under the GAST rules to:

> Article XX exemptions should allow trade interventions for a wide range of purposes that further sustainable development, e.g. sanctions against human rights violations; tariffs for the maintenance of environmental, food, health and animal welfare standards; enforcement of treaties on environment and labour rights.

### The Agreement on Technical Barriers to Trade

In the jargon of international trade law, all environmental standards and regulations are, prima facie, considered technical barriers to trade. The actual provisions of the TBT agreement are detailed and complex, but reduced to bare bones, it establishes:

- an international regime for harmonizing environmental standards that effectively creates a ceiling – but no floor – for environmental regulation
- a detailed procedural code for establishing new laws and regulations that would be difficult for even the wealthiest nations to meet

At present, when nations fail to observe the WTO's rules, they are vulnerable to international trade complaints and sanctions and the TBT rules have emerged as important new weapons for challenging government regulatory initiatives.

This would be changed under the GAST rules to:

> All international environmental and social standards and regulations are considered as effectively creating a floor for governing the conditions for trade between parties. Any country with higher levels should experience positive discrimination in terms of trade. Poorer countries for which such standards are at present too expensive should receive financial support to help them improve their standards, and once setting a future date for such improvements, should experience positive discrimination in trade terms.

## The Agreement on Sanitary and Phytosanitary Standards

The provisions of this oddly named agreement are very similar to those found in the TBT agreement, but deal with laws and regulations that concern food and food safety, including pesticide regulation and biotechnology. As with TBT rules, the SPS agreement has proved a useful device for undoing government regulatory initiatives that are unpopular with large corporations. In theory, the text of the SPS agreement appears to permit the use of the precautionary principle. In practice, however, in the interpretation of disputes by the WTO, this principle has not been recognized as a justifiable basis upon which to establish regulatory controls. A recent example of this was the WTO's ruling against the EU ban on the importation of beef produced with growth hormones.

The SPS agreement also seeks to remove decisions about health, food and safety from national governments by delegating them to international standard-setting bodies such as the Codex Alimentarius – an elite club of scientists based in Geneva. Because of its location and composition, Codex is an institution that is singularly inaccessible to all but a handful of international corporations and business associations that are capable of maintaining delegations in Geneva. Codex standards often fall substantially short of those established by jurisdictions closer and more responsive to the interests and views of consumers and health advocates.

This would be changed under the GAST rules to:

> All laws and regulations that concern food and food safety, including pesticide regulation and biotechnology, are considered as effectively creating a floor for governing the conditions for trade between parties. Any country with higher levels should experience positive discrimination in terms of trade. Poorer countries for which such standards are at present too expensive should receive financial support to help them

improve their standards, and once setting a future date for such improvements, should experience positive discrimination in trade terms.

The 'precautionary principle' is a justifiable basis upon which to establish regulatory controls affecting trade when the risks warrant action, even in the face of scientific uncertainty about the extent and nature of potential impacts.

## The Agreement on Trade-Related Intellectual Property Rights

By attaching the prefix 'trade-related', this agreement transforms an entire domain of domestic policy and law into one that is subject to WTO regulation. The essential thrust of the TRIPS agreement is to compel all WTO member nations to adopt and implement patent-protection regimes.

This virtually provides US and European multinationals with global patent rights which can now be enforced by retaliatory trade sanctions. The rights of indigenous communities to genetic and biological resources that are held in common are ignored. The result is to facilitate the appropriation of the genetic commons by corporate interests, which can then demand user rents from the communities that should be the proper 'owners' of the genetic resource.

This would be changed under the GAST rules to:

> Global patenting rights should not override the rights of indigenous communities to genetic and biological resources that are held in common. For products, fees should be able to be levied to cover the cost of development, plus a reasonable level of profit, but such patenting rights must have a limited timeframe and fully reimburse the parties whose knowledge contributed to the patented entity. Patents on life are prohibited.

## The Agreement on Trade-Related Investment Measures

TRIMs set rules for investment in the production of global goods and services. While this investor-rights agenda is constructed according to the same principles as national treatment and most-favoured nation treatment, which are common to all WTO agreements, it goes much further in two critical ways. The first is to allow individual investors virtually unqualified access to international enforcement mechanisms that may be invoked by them directly against nation states. It would be difficult to overstate the implications of this radical departure from the norms of international treaty law which, with the exception of international human rights, has never created rights even for the benefit of individuals, let alone multinational corporations.

In other words, under the North American Free Trade Agreement (NAFTA), for the purposes of enforcement, foreign investors are accorded the same status as nation states. The other critical departure of this proposed investment regime from the norms of international trade law is to be found under the heading 'performance requirements', which actually constrain the implementation of domestic investment regulation, even when applied only to domestic investors.

This would be changed under the GAST rules to:

> No individual investor may invoke international enforcement mechanisms against investment regulations of nation states. The implementation of domestic investment regulations shall not be constrained by trade rules, provided that the former improve social and environmental regulations domestically.

## The Agreement on Agriculture

The vision expressed by this WTO agreement is of an integrated global agricultural economy in which all countries produce specialized agricultural commodities, and increasingly supply their food needs by shopping in the global marketplace. Protective barriers to foster indigenous farming, for example, are not allowed; neither are subsidies to support poorer farmers.

This would be changed under the GAST rules to:

> Protective barriers should be introduced to enable countries to reach maximum self-sufficiency in food, where feasible, with long-distance trade limited to food not available in the country or region.

# The role of the European Union

## A Green European lead at the WTO

Many of the world's leaders who will gather at the forthcoming WTO ministerial meeting are planning to use the occasion to launch yet another expansion to the scope and powers of the WTO. This 'round' of new trade negotiations would include not only industrial tariffs and agriculture, but also the so-called 'new issues' – among them, investment, competition policy and government procurement.

The European Commission is taking an aggressive lead in pushing for this new round. However, the European Parliament has the power of veto over the EU's position on the outcome of any new round of negotiations, and its position, therefore, is key. The Greens/EFA Group in the European Parliament, the fourth largest group, is opposed to this new round.[35] Instead, we are calling for a thorough and independent review of the social and environmental impacts of the last 'Uruguay round' of negotiations. Our aim is to develop an alternative economic system based on stronger local and regional economies, a far more equitable distribution of resources and a genuine commitment to sustainable development.

In my role as a member of the European Parliament's Trade Committee and an EU delegate to the ministerial meeting, I shall of course be advocating this 'review and reform' agenda, and making the case that the current trade system degrades the environment and exacerbates inequality. More than that, however, I shall also be demanding a far more fundamental change to the direction of the European Union – away from promoting globalization towards supporting a transition to localization.

## A cooperative Europe is the key

It will be impossible for such a radical change to be introduced by one country alone. Individual countries will need to cooperate in this project on a regional basis, but without falling into the trap of 'globalization' on a smaller scale, i.e. in 'free trade' blocs. Regional blocs, such as the EU and North America, should have a key role to play. Indeed, these two blocs are the only ones politically and economically powerful enough to be a counterweight to overcome the forces which are the major beneficiaries from globalization – transnational companies and international capital. Unfortunately, the prospect for the USA is of four years of a Bush programme of deliberately rolling back key social and environmental protection in order to promote ever-greater free trade. The EU must therefore take on the mantle as the major engine for change.

Given the problems facing the present global economy, once such a debate begins in Europe, it is likely to be echoed in other regional blocs, all of which have political and local activists seeking radical improvements in the way their countries' economies are organized.

What is required to achieve this is a far bolder, more ambitious and radically different vision of a Europe of genuine stability and cooperation, based on the rebuilding of sustainable local and national economies across the whole European continent, and throughout the world.

The EU should therefore move away from its present emphasis on ruthless internal and external competition leading to unsustainable growth. Its new goal of rebuilding and rediversifying local and national economies must be the key to its economic interaction with the central and eastern European countries and the rest of the world. In short, the Treaty of Rome should be replaced with an Internationalist Treaty of Home.

The inherent conflict between the WTO's international trade rules on one side, and the needs of the environment and development on the other, is one of the most important foreign policy flash points of the day. Unless the priorities of world trade are fundamentally altered, then the opposition and protests that it will provoke will form one of the most significant fault lines in the politics of the early decades of this century. The WTO ministerial meeting must be the turning point; localization, the new direction.

# 3

# The Watermelon Myth Exploded: Greens and Anti-Capitalism

## *Molly Scott Cato*

> All people, all living things, are part of the earth life, and so are sacred.
> No one of us stands higher or lower than any other. Only justice can
> assure balance: only ecological balance can sustain freedom. Only in
> freedom can that fifth sacred thing we call spirit flourish in its full
> diversity.
>
> Starhawk, *Declaration of the Four Sacred Things*[1]

## Economic radicals but not Marxists

Many Greens have travelled a circuitous route to arrive at the conclusion
most of us share today: our economic system lies at the heart of our environmental problems. My personal route took me via an undergraduate
course in economic and social theories with more than a nodding acquain-
tance with Marx, hence the distinctly Marxian origin of many of the
concepts I will use in this chapter. Many in the Green Party would feel
uncomfortable in identifying themselves as anti-capitalists, or even accepting that the Green Party is a party of the left. For many the old slogan
from Die Grünen, 'Not left, not right, but ahead', despite its rather smug
ring, sums up best the party's position on the left–right continuum.

I have never shared this nervousness about putting Marx and his fol-
lowers in to bat on my side, and some of his analytical concepts – my two
personal favourites are *alienation* and *commodity fetishism* – seem of
almost infinite intellectual value. However, identity is an important strand
of radical politics and, if the label of Marxist or anti-capitalist is off-
putting to some, I am happy enough to avoid it. It really is the ideas that
matter and, when we all agree that there is something radically wrong
with our economic system, centring on the way it is permitting the

corporate destruction of the planet and her people, it is of secondary importance whether we label that anti-capitalist or not.

For the first part of this chapter I will focus instead on what Greens identify as the problems with capitalism, and then I will spend the rest of the chapter describing ways we have found to change these. Like other political parties, the Green Party has its policies constantly under debate, so the views expressed here represent a personal view.[2] I must give credit for the ideas presented to the deep and intense thinking that has taken place in the green movement over the past 30 years; the conclusions, however, are my personal responsibility. In no way does this chapter represent an official Green Party view.

The chapter revolves around the four central problems with capitalism from the perspective of green economics:

- its reliance on perpetual growth
- the unfair extraction of the value of labour
- the creation of profit in the gap between production and consumption
- the alienation created by the systems of both production and distribution

Aside from the first, which is a particular concern for environmentally focused critics, all these points are shared by other critics of capitalism, but they may have a particular green slant.

The point has no doubt been made in other chapters but bears repeating here that the main contrast between the capitalism we are threatened by in the twenty-first century and that of the previous two is the growth in corporate size, power and reach. Good students of Marx and Engels' collected works are aware that the latter picked up many ideas while managing his father's Manchester-based cotton mills, making him an employee of a *de facto* multinational. But the scope of international business in the second half of the nineteenth century bore no relation to the extent of global connections today. There is no space to explore these differences here.

It should be pointed out at the outset that a green philosophy of change is incremental and bottom up. This would distinguish the locus of change we propose from classical socialist models. Two more ex-hippy slogans may help to make the point. The first is 'Small is beautiful', which is the rubric that has stuck in the public consciousness in connection with green thinking. This is a neat slogan for a complex philosophy that extends from questioning the scale of economic organizations and societies to respecting diversity in species, cultures and political systems. Secondly, we have 'What goes around, comes around', suggesting that major and violent political changes are likely to put in train a sequence of events that will harm those instituting the changes. Subject to the time constraints that Greens are more aware of than most, political and social change must be allowed to develop at its own pace. Spiritual development and advance at the level of consciousness are considered to be as important as state or centrally imposed policy making.

# The four central problems of capitalism

## The shark

Capitalism is often characterized as a shark. The shark is a great survivor of the animal world and its ruthlessness is recognized. However, it is the shark's need constantly to move forward that is the central explanation for this identification. Because sharks have only primitive gills, without constant forward motion they suffocate and die. In a similar way, capitalism is reliant on economic growth for its very survival.

The need to put an end to economic growth is the first principle of green economics. It stems from the origin of the environmental movement with the publication of *The Limits to Growth* in 1974.[3] It seems self-evident that, within the closed system of planet earth, we will in the end either use up all available resources or be confronted with our own waste, but this point still evades conventional economics. Early proponents of the need to move towards a non-growth or 'steady-state' economy used the contrasted images of the cowboy and the spaceman to explore our attitude to our environment.[4] The cowboy, who finds his apotheosis in American capitalism, is always pushing outwards, expanding his available resources, finding ever new frontiers to exploit. The spaceman, by contrast, is forced to recognize the limits of what he has brought on his small ship:

> Earth has become a single spaceship, without unlimited reservoirs of anything, either for extraction or for pollution, and in which, therefore, man must find his place in a cyclical ecological system which is capable of continuous reproduction of materials even though it cannot escape having inputs of energy.

It is an interesting ironic development of this contrast that, with the Mars escape project now itself using up a large quantity of earth's resources, the cowboy will meet the astronaut at the final frontier: space.

Neoclassical economists have never accepted the reality of planetary limits. Efficiency and technology are posited as solutions, enabling ever-growing populations and ever-increasing levels of consumption.[5] The proponents of the limits thesis were ridiculed because their early predictions about resource depletion were far too pessimistic. In fact, it is the other side of the equation, our waste overload, that has come to limit economic activity. The debate has been effective at the international political level, leading to the Brundtland definition of sustainability which, for all its shortcomings, forces two basic principles of green economics on to the international agenda: the recognition we that need to balance our needs with those of future generations (the intergenerational principle), which itself implicitly relies on the fact that planetary resources are limited (the limits principle). Since the publication of *Our Common Future*, the Brundtland Commission's report, capitalist apologists have mutated this principle into that of 'sustainable development', which pretty much means business as usual. However, the recognition of limits is there and can be used to our advantage.

There is a politically powerful coda to the limits-to-growth thesis, which helps to explain why it has been so controversial. The argument about where the limits fall, and precisely how much we can afford to use of the earth's resources, will keep many academics busy for a long while, but what is inevitable is the conclusion that follows from the acceptance of the idea of a limit. If there is only a fixed amount to go round, this makes the question of how that amount is shared of immediate political salience. Hence the various specious justifications for global inequity – with their ever more desperate slogans: remember trickle-down, and all boats rising on the tide? – are invalidated. If children die in poverty in Malawi, that really is my problem, just as the poverty wages of factory workers on Tyneside are the direct consequence of my relative affluence. The economics of the bicycle pump, where the planet can be endlessly inflated until all have enough, is found to be morally bankrupt.[6]

## The entrepreneur as Fat Controller

I hazard a guess that I am not alone amongst contributors to, and readers of, this book, in being rather confused about what is meant by an entrepreneur. The dictionary informs me that it relates to an 'undertaking', but my rusty French suggests a derivation closer to 'take between', suggesting exactly my conception of capitalist enterprise: the removal of profits between the producer and the consumer. Along with this etymological basis of my disdain goes an equally powerful mental picture. Perhaps it is because the concept of capitalism was invented in the nineteenth century, or because my own research focused on the coal masters of South Wales, but I find myself trapped with the mental image of a character from *Thomas the Tank Engine*, the Fat Controller.

Being ever vulnerable to accusations of wanting to return to the horse and cart, I have to overcome these innate prejudices and recognize that, while we may not all hold business people in the high esteem that neoclassical economists and politicians do,[7] in any developed society the goods and services that we wish to buy and use will need to be produced for us by businesses. How those businesses are organized and how they interact with their customers is a question that green economics is working its way towards, as described later.

For now it is sufficient to describe the inadequacy of the entrepreneurship model of capitalism, which is currently so popular with policy-makers that it has been introduced into the school curriculum at the expense of music and art. Some economics textbooks suggest that 'enterprise' is such a vital quality to an economy that it should be listed as another means of production, alongside land, labour and capital. It seems clear to me that, in spite of the mushrooming of intellectual property claims so that they now include such things as natural species and the phrase 'shock and awe', what is valuable about enterprise cannot be the property of an individual. Those who develop a new product should acknowledge that they not only stand on the shoulders of giants, but are actually hitching a free shoulder ride. What an entrepreneur is much more likely to do is to spot a market opportunity where something can be sold for a profit, identify something that can be bought cheap and sold expensive, or create an unnecessary need and then exploit it. None of these seems a laudable aim from a social or environmental perspective.

The entrepreneur is likely to be a single male individual, unentangled by social or family ties; he is likely to be greedy; he is likely to be selfish. He uses his ability to exploit others' needs and vulnerabilities to advance his status at their expense, and to ensure an unequal distribution of power and wealth in his favour. Entrepreneurs have no need to subscribe to values such as compassion and empathy that hold a human society together. If children die because AIDS drugs are too expensive in their countries, this is a price that must be paid to protect intellectual property rights. If the clothes we wear are made by children or slaves, this can be justified because of the need to compete in the jungle of international competition. These are the social and economic costs of enterprise capitalism and it is our right as world citizens to reject them as unacceptably high.[8]

## The absolute disadvantage of international trade

The international system of trade has become a hot political topic over the past few years. The debate is framed in terms of an opposition between free trade and fair trade; both sides seem to have mastered the discourse high-ground. The position of the free-trade supporters is morally and ideologically bankrupt. In successive rounds of the General Agreement on Tariffs and Trade (GATT), culminating in that in Uruguay in 1993, they bullied poorer countries into reducing tariff barriers, while all the time the richer nations protected their own farmers to the tune of millions of dollars a year. Fair trade is clearly preferable, yet this position is itself somewhat misguided and naïve from a green perspective. Trade is a competitive game that nations engage in on the assumption that they can win. But the rules of the game, the terms of trade, will always be controlled by the powerful nations, primarily the USA and the EU. Poorer nations must engage in trade to obtain foreign currency for goods they cannot make at home. But this should only ever happen once their own domestic needs are provided for. The current situation – where green beans that were grown in the countries of southern Africa, whose people are starving, are being sold in UK supermarkets – is the logical endpoint of the international trading system, whether free or fair.

Food security should be a priority for all countries; only food surpluses should be exported, and only when these goods cannot be produced by the importing countries. As Caroline Lucas, Green Party MEP, put it when launching the New Economics Foundation's Local Communities and Sustainability Bill, 'What are the implications of these principles of free trade? Essentially that communities and nations abandon self-reliance and embrace dependence. That we abandon our capacity to produce many items and concentrate only on a few. That we import what we need and export what we produce.' She went on to explain the consequences of trade for poorer nations with the following example:

> Two years ago, the US brought a successful case against India at the WTO which forced India to remove key quantitative restrictions or import barriers on food imports. This externally imposed import liberalisation has resulted in dramatically falling farm prices, and has decimated rural incomes. The price of coconuts has fallen 80%, coffee prices have collapsed by over 60%, pepper prices have fallen 45%. The most dramatic effect is on edible oil, where India's domestic production has been effectively wiped out as highly subsidized soya from the US and palm oil from Malaysia flood the market due to low import duties. Imports now account for 70% of the domestic consumption. Significantly, the response from both Indian academics and activists has been to call for the re-introduction of import controls, thus challenging the very linchpin of the globalisation process, which depends upon ever reducing tariff barriers.[9]

An UNCTAD report in 1997 showed that out of a sample of ten Latin American countries, in nine of them the differential in earnings between skilled and unskilled workers had increased as a result of opening up markets to international trade, and that in most of the countries the real purchasing power of the least-skilled workers had actually declined, in several cases by more than 20 per cent. In 1999 a paper from the World Bank reported on data for a sample of 38 countries between 1965 and 1992, showing that opening markets up to trade had reduced the incomes of the poorest 40 per cent of the population, while increasing those of the richer groups. Developing countries have spent these 30 years on the economic rollercoaster of international trade because of the dogma from international bodies suggesting that this will end poverty. The richest people in these societies have used this international game to increase their own wealth, while the poor in the same societies have grown poorer.[10]

So much for the economic case for trade: the environmental consequences are just as serious. Work by the pressure group Sustain has drawn
attention to the absurdities of what Caroline Lucas and Colin Hines called
'the Great Food Swap'. Here are some of the shocking statistics produced
by such research:

- One shopping basket of organic products could have travelled
  241,000 km and released as much carbon dioxide ($CO_2$) as an average
  four-bedroom house does while cooking meals over 8 months.
- In 1998 the UK imported over 60,000 tonnes of poultry meat from the
  Netherlands, to which it exported 33,000 tonnes of the exact same
  product.
- For every calorie of carrots flown into the UK from South Africa, 66
  calories of fuel are used.[11]

All of this unnecessary trade has a devastating impact on the environment in terms of $CO_2$ production and related issues of pollution and
congestion. A report from the New Economics Foundation contains dis-
turbing data about this relationship, including the fact that during the
boom of the Asian Tigers Indonesia, Malaysia, Thailand and the Republic
of Korea in 1980–96, their emission of $CO_2$ increased by between 100 and
278 per cent.[12] Figure 3.1 shows the relationship between total global
trade and this climate change pollution.

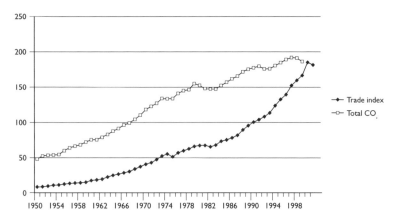

*Note*: The trade figures are calculated as an index based on 1990 = 100 and including agricultural and mining products and manufactures. The $CO_2$ emissions are
for solid, liquid and gas fossil fuels, divided by 33 to achieve appropriate scaling.
*Sources*: $CO_2$ data are from Oakridge Research Laboratory, California; trade data
are from the WTO.

*Figure 3.1*  The increase in global trade is matched by an increase in $CO_2$
emissions

The arguments for increasing trade should be rejected, whether they are couched in terms of more jobs in the West or higher standards of living in the South. These arguments have been rehearsed for nearly 60 years now, while the poor countries have grown poorer, the corporations richer, and the planet warmer. Globalization increases the distance between production and consumption, allowing more opportunities for larger profits to be siphoned off along the way. That is the reality behind the arguments in favour of trade.

## Life in the jungle

Work under capitalism is an unpleasant business. Marx reserved a special place for work in his analysis: he considered it to be the central expression of what he referred to as our 'species-being'. It is because what we do as a species is to work that the mutation of work into its capitalist form is so socially and psychologically damaging. It is this process which Marx refers to as 'alienation', meaning that the items which people produce with their work are appropriated by the minority of people who own the means of production: that is, the employers. In today's terms, this means global corporations. As Marx puts it in his *Early Writings*:

> This fact simply means that the object that labour produces, its product, stands opposed to it as something alien, as a power independent of the producer. The product of labour is labour embodied and made material in an object, it is the objectification of labour . . . In the sphere of political economy this realization of labour appears as a loss of reality for the worker.[13]

In other words, the process of work and the creation of products that are bought and sold by others destroy the individual's sense of self and radically undermine her or his identity. In the globalized economy, these identities are further undermined by the loss of connection between producer and consumer, as the geographical distance between them extends.

In modern discourse, the unpleasant effects of an inhumane work environment are defined as stress. Here are some statistics relating to workplace stress:

- The CBI puts the total cost to the economy of mental health and stress problems at £5 billion a year.
- A 1996 report from the Institute of Management said that 'an estimated 270,000 people take time off work every day because of work-related stress; this represents a cumulative cost in terms of sick pay, lost production and NHS [National Health Service] charges of around £7 billion annually.
- A Health and Safety Executive supplement to the 1990 Labour Force

Survey estimated that 183,000 workers took time off work suffering from work-related stress, depression or anxiety in the preceding year.[14]

The statistics convey nothing of the suffering that work-related stress can cause – the loss of confidence that is sometimes incurable, the sleeplessness, the health symptoms ranging from ulcers and migraines to loss of joy in life and suicide. Capitalism is an economic system that relies on the work of the many; the side-effects of that work are of no concern.[15]

A recent Datamonitor survey found that 12 million Europeans, most of them in well-paid but highly stressful jobs and with young children, are 'downshifting': that is, reducing their hours of work and taking a cut in salary. Another 2 million have given up on formal employment altogether, and they are mostly better-educated people in their thirties and forties.[16] These sorts of statistics fill me with delight, not only because some people are escaping wage-slavery, but also because they are the talented people, the very people capitalism relies on to come up with the new adaptation that allows it to survive. If you do not feature in these statistics yet, make sure you do soon.

# Four green solutions

Since its early development in the seventeenth century, the economic form of organization that came to be known as capitalism has crept into more and more areas of our life. In the UK, our ability to provide for our own needs has been reduced by laws relating to the ownership and use of land, by trade laws, by laws relating to taxation and employment. In developing societies, self-provisioning subsistence systems are being broken down by relocation schemes and the removal of people from their land. The capitalist system is now supported by an international network of legislation, especially the competition and free trade laws of the World Trade Organization, and an equally powerful system of ideological and cultural support.

The Green Party does not underestimate the power of this structure. We have developed policies for a sustainable and equitable economic system to replace capitalism, but we are also working to replace it in as many areas of our lives as possible. Within the dominant paradigm of capitalism, this is not an easy business. It is hard to think outside the box, whether in terms of doing something for nothing or challenging the value of work. But it gets easier with practice. In addition to attacking the economic system that threatens the planet and its people, Greens try to marginalize its role in their individual lives.

The following sections give some ideas for changes to the economy that we can all work towards in our workplaces, communities and homes. Every time you buy from a local cooperative rather than a supermarket, you have struck a blow against capitalism. Likewise when you give up your job for an international company and spend the time growing your own food or caring for your own children. When you visit a Green Party home, you almost always find evidence of self-provisioning: home-made clothes, chutneys, bottled tomatoes, self-made furniture. Capitalism grows by drawing more and more areas of our lives into the marketplace. The more we can claim back, the more we weaken that system.

## Steady state plus fair shares

The first and most successful response by green economics to the problem of the capitalist shark is the call for a 'steady-state economy'. Herman Daly, a former employee of the World Bank, made this case in 1973.[17] Along with other economists such as Hazel Henderson and Maria Mies, Daly argued that a capitalist economic system takes too narrow a view of what constitutes the economy, focusing exclusively on *intermediate means*, including the neoclassical means of production of land, labour and capital, but ignoring the *ultimate means*, the planet herself. Hazel Henderson developed her cake analogy for how such a system operates, whereas Maria Mies compares such an economy to an iceberg, with only a small amount of it visible above the waterline and the majority invisible below it.[18]

Recognizing the limits on available resources makes the issue of distribution much more pressing. An interesting new twist is offered by the urgency of the need to deal with the problem of climate change by reducing carbon dioxide emissions. A policy response to this problem also neatly ties up the issue of global poverty by proposing $CO_2$ limits shared on a global per capita basis. The model, developed by the Global Commons Institute and known as Contraction and Convergence, proposes limiting $CO_2$ to a level that matches the planet's carrying capacity and then simply dividing by the number of citizens on the planet. At 2000 levels this equation works rather neatly, since there were around 6 billion people on the earth and the carbon dioxide output limit is 6 billion tonnes. Hence every citizen on planet earth could have a share of around 1 tonne per year. Since current actual emissions are much higher, global output needs to be reduced by between 60 and 80 per cent within a few decades, by reducing production, switching to energy-efficient technologies, and moving towards renewable forms of energy production. The UK needs to cut emissions by 85 to 90 per cent to carry out its share of this programme.

So the solution to climate change is achievable, but better than this the Contraction and Convergence model offers a way towards redressing the world poverty problem at the same time. The poorer countries are poorer precisely because they do not have so much economic activity, which is linked to their energy use. So an exchange can be arranged between their unused carbon dioxide quota and the excess of consumption goods in the developed world. A simple illustration can be given by comparing the USA and India. With a population of some 285 million people (5 per cent of the world's population), the USA produces around 25 per cent of the world's total output of $CO_2$. By contrast India, with just over a billion people, has around 17 per cent of the world's population but produces only 289 million tonnes of $CO_2$, about 5 per cent of the world's total.

---

**Ten ways to challenge capitalism that wouldn't frighten your grandmother**

1. Arrange to buy your vegetables through the nearest organic box scheme.
2. Switch all your bank accounts to the Nationwide or another mutual building society.
3. Shop at the Cooperative – better still, join your local coop.
4. If you work in the private sector, cut your hours of work by at least half.
5. Cook more at home, for yourself and your friends.
6. Don't vote, unless the party you vote for has stated anti-capitalist economic policies.
7. Whenever you are talking to somebody involved in business, ask them if their business is a cooperative, and have something to back yourself up if they ask why you asked this question.
8. Get an allotment.
9. Cut down on your coffee intake, and make sure that what you do buy has been fairly traded.
10. Before you buy anything ask yourself how much you know about who made it and how, and move towards products where you have more information and closer ties.

---

## Localization

The localization agenda addresses several of the problems with capitalism identified above. The impulse towards increasing the quantity of goods produced locally and reducing the expansion of international trade came as a result of concern about the huge levels of carbon dioxide needlessly produced as biscuit-carrying juggernauts pass each other on Europe's congested road network, or as we find vegetables on our supermarket shelves grown in countries whose people are starving. However, it is clear that relocalizing the economy offers opportunities to address the problems of growth and exploitation, too. If the entrepreneur profits by extracting the arbitrage profit between the production economy and the consumption economy (that is, the difference in prices between two markets), the further apart those markets are in terms of geography and level of development, the larger is the profit to be made.

Interestingly, Marx had something to say about this issue of localization:

> *The Times* of November 1857 contains an utterly delightful cry of outrage on the part of a West-Indian plantation owner. This advocate analyses with great moral indignation – as a plea for the re-introduction of Negro slavery – how the Quashees (the free blacks of Jamaica) content themselves with producing only what is strictly necessary for their own consumption, and, alongside this 'use value', regard loafing (indulgence and idleness) as the real luxury good; how they do not care a damn for the sugar and the fixed capital invested in the plantations, but rather observe the planters' impending bankruptcy with an ironic grin of malicious pleasure . . . They have ceased to be slaves, but not in order to become wage labourers, but, instead, self-sustaining peasants working for their own consumption. As far as they are concerned, capital does not exist as capital, because autonomous wealth as such can exist only either on the basis of direct forced labour, slavery, or indirect forced labour, wage labour.[19]

Thanks to Derek Wall for this quotation. He notes that, in his opinion, Marx was not proposing localization as an economic model, 'but it makes the point well and it fits in with the idea of *ital*, i.e. the Rastafarian principle of producing what you need locally which is a key part of their religion. Ital means vital and natural, and if you remove the first three letters of "capitalism" you may find you have a different economic system.'

The name most often associated with the localization concept is Colin Hines. In 1999 he and his co-author Tim Lang summarized its goal as:

> to seek to challenge the defeatism inherent in accepting the inevitability of free-market policies. Its essence is to allow nations, local governments and communities to reclaim control over their local economies; to make them as diverse as possible; and to rebuild stability into community life . . . It would ensure a transition from the present situation to one where whatever goods and services can be provided locally are provided locally, where the reduction of 'product miles' (distance from producer to consumer) is an environmental virtue not an economic restriction.[20]

Green economists are developing ideas for such a locally based system for the exchange of goods based on the principle of *trade subsidiarity*. The Green Party in the UK supports a strong interpretation of political subsidiarity, with political power exercised by default at the lowest level and only passed upwards with the consent of local people. By analogy we may suggest that goods should always be made by preference in the local community, with people only looking further afield when local supplies are unavailable. Import and export duties can be imposed to encourage this sort of trading pattern. Such a system would encourage the movement towards a food economy based on seasonal produce, with exotic items such as bananas and coffee becoming much more expensive and hence luxury items.[21]

Just as the call for a limit to growth is criticized on the grounds that it would cut the poor world off from the benefits of economic development, so this proposal for strong local economies can be portrayed, by supporters of fair and unfair trade alike, as cutting citizens of developing countries adrift. The paramount need to cut $CO_2$ emissions requires us to reduce drastically the level of international trade. But green economists also believe that the international trade system will always be rigged in favour of the stronger nations, so that persuading poorer countries to get involved in the game will always operate to our advantage rather than theirs.

Strong local economies will also have considerable benefits for those who live in them in the UK. In Wales, huge amounts of public money have been spent on a strategy of supporting foreign companies rather than building up the local economy. Between 1988 and 1998 almost £800 million was spent in Regional Selective Assistance,[22] or corporate social security as it is known to its critics. The most prominent disaster of the inward investment policy was LG, a South Korean electronics company that received £248 million of public money in return for a promise to create 6,000 jobs; in reality the maximum number created was only ever 2,000 and earlier this year, within five years of the factory being opened, LG announced that all but 350 jobs would be cut. Rather than failing to guarantee long-term security, this public money could have supported many sustainable local businesses.

Instead of looking abroad for foreign saviours, greens propose focusing on our own indigenous resources. An example is the hemp and flax project at Bangor University, a research project to resuscitate the UK's native textile crops. In London, Bioregional has resuscitated the lavender fields of south London that were a source of local employment in the seventeenth and eighteenth centuries.[23] More widely, greens propose the development of economies along bioregional lines, with each region's boundaries being drawn so as to encompass most basic resources: sufficient productive agricultural land, water, energy and so on. The aim would be to achieve maximum self-sufficiency within these bioregions.

Practical achievements along these lines have progressed furthest in the case of the food economy. Food is a natural candidate for localization, since it travels poorly. In addition, food scares have undermined trust in the global food economy, making people willing to pay more for local supplies whose provenance they know.

In Wales a local campaign group, Powys Food Links, has been working together with the Regeneration Institute of Cardiff University to expand the amount of local food procured by local authorities for institutional meals in schools, hospitals and care homes. This offers what researchers refer to as the 'multiple dividend':

> Locally sourced food offers a number of benefits – what we call the *multiple dividend* – including healthier diets, local markets for local producers, lower food miles, as well as a better understanding between producers and consumers, the two ends of the food chain that have become divorced from each other and need to be re-connected.[24]

The campaign achieved a major success with the decision by Llanidloes Cottage Hospital to buy food supplies from local producers, which had numerous benefits in terms of the health of patients and the local economy. Through the Powys Public Food Procurement Partnership, established in October 2002, local government and health authorities are able to work with producers and local people to develop the multiple dividend approach to local food purchasing.

Developing strong local economies is not without problems. The dead hand of the corporations in developing trade rules at the European and global levels is clear and limits the scope for local authorities to purchase locally. This is why political change is necessary. But we can make a huge impact on trade by reducing the amount of imported goods we buy and making a conscious decision to support our own local economies.

## Cooperation

Perhaps the most personally damaging aspect of capitalism is psychological and physiological damage, as detailed above. This goes beyond diagnosed mental and physical ill-health; it represents the waste of millions of human lives whose creative potential is destroyed by mindless, exploitative work. Liberation from wage slavery is an essential step on the road to a green economy and it is one we can take within the existing economy by creating cooperative workplaces.

My home country of Wales has two sources of pride in this field: the inventor of the cooperative employment form was Robert Owen, from Newtown in Powys; and the world's only cooperatively owned coal-mine – Tower Colliery – is near Hirwaun in the Cynon Valley. Cooperatives directly address one of the central problems of capitalism by putting ownership and control back in the hands of the people who do the work. This eliminates the possibility of exploitation and profiteering, since profits will either be shared between workers or invested in the business. The absence of shareholders creates the additional advantages of increasing the local multiplier – since the money generated by the business is not siphoned off outside the local area – and tying the capital of the business into the local economy, in a process known as capital anchoring.[25] Cooperatives also tend to generate positive spillovers in the local economy, increasing social capital and lowering rates of crime. Employees who feel a part of the business they work for are less alienated and happier people. The potential for success of these businesses is high, since energy that has been spent in conflict between bosses and workers can be unified in the effort to keep the business alive in the long term and to create well-paid, secure jobs.

The creativity of green activists in developing new economic forms is boundless. Local Exchange Trading Schemes (LETS) are a way of exchanging goods in communities with insufficient money supply. The Institute for Community Currencies grew out of the extension of LETS into a real currency – beacons – in Brecon. Based at University College of Wales, Newport, they are seeking to develop a system of community currencies in the depressed economies of the Valleys. The currencies will provide extra liquidity to invest in projects that have insufficient collateral or profitability to gain funding from commercial banks. The Institute aims to establish 16 pilot Community Time Banks spread across the six local authority areas of the Valleys, laying the foundation for a Valleys currency. This is a practical response to the leakages of money from the local economies of South Wales that have led to persistent low levels of economic activity.

Developments in Argentina since the collapse of its banking system in 2000 are reassuring about the prospects for local economies following a possible financial collapse, and also provide inspiration for those of us building sustainable alternatives while that system continues to totter along. In Argentina it was the middle classes who lost most: the rich already had their assets in Swiss bank accounts, while the poor had never had much money to start with. People responded to the loss of liquidity, as cash was withdrawn from the economy, by setting up barter clubs and by creating their own currencies. Local authorities created money called *patacones* and also *kapones*, which were promises to pay their staff at some point in the future. Both these were used as money, as were agricultural crops including soya and grain. By November of 2002, General Motors was so desperate for sales that it was accepting payment in grain. As more information emerges from Argentina, it is clear that we can draw two important conclusions: there is life after capitalism; and people are ingenious and creative in developing methods of exchange.[26]

For more ideas about how a post-capitalist economy might look, you could try visiting Glastonbury Festival. While there last year I found it really useful as a model to help envision how economic exchange might work. Much of what was being exchanged actually had no economic value: it was ideas, love and communication. There is also a vast range of capitalist enterprises selling unnecessary and wasteful products. But the entire festival made me think of what medieval markets might have been like, and how these might be reborn in the twenty-first century. Each market in medieval England had its speciality: the Nottingham Goose Fair is the best known. Glastonbury has two specialities: music and environmentalism. It is a showcase for new bands and for new ideas about the planet. Much of what I am writing here has developed out of discussions at the Green Field speakers' forum. And around these central activities has grown up a whole range of performers and suppliers of goods and services to the festival-goers. Each group has its own venue and its own field; there is identity and sense of purpose. Makers of hemp clothes share ideas for improving the fibre quality; folk musicians share tunes and lyrics. The feeling is what we might be looking for in a post-capitalist economy.

## Reuniting producers and consumers

Capitalists generate profits by taking an unfair share out of the middle: that is, between producers and consumers. Reuniting those who produce goods with those who consume them removes this source of profits and is thus the most fundamental threat to capitalism. Again it is the food economy that has made the most progress in this direction, through organic box schemes and community-supported agriculture (CSA). The first system involves the ordering and delivery of boxes of seasonal organic vegetables from a local supplier via a wholefood shop or direct to homes. In the second, CSA, a more complex relationship is built up, with the eventual consumers of farm produce paying for their year's supply at the beginning of the growing season, thus offering a high level of commitment to the farmer and providing her or him with the capital to produce the year's crop. Another link between local producers and consumers is offered by the network of farmers' markets that are springing up all over the country, from the first in Bath in 1997 to more than 270 by the turn of the century.[27]

The next step in building a green economy will be to develop similar ideas for other products. Progress is being made in this direction through localization initiatives, but these do not really go far enough. The missing link is strengthening organizations of producers and to achieve this we may have to look back to the system that was destroyed to allow capitalism to thrive: a system of guilds.

Three methods that 'entrepreneurs' of today specifically favour as a method of gaining maximum profits were specifically banned by the guilds, namely:

- forestalling – buying up merchandise before it reached the market: that is, acting as middleman and extracting value without producing anything
- engrossing – stockpiling to force prices up
- regrating – buying and reselling where prices might be higher

Rather than generating profit, the objective of the guild was to ensure the quality of the product. Given the environmental prerogative, we might extend this to build a concern for sustainability into modern guilds' agenda. Other significant economic powers of the guilds included:

- setting quality standards for production – those not meeting them could be expelled
- setting the price paid for materials and labour and for final products
- when necessary, fixing production quotas for members to ensure sufficient to meet needs and prevent competition between members
- guaranteeing loans for members who needed to buy equipment or premises
- operating a system of risk sharing and pooling of assets – for example, in the case of expensive export ventures

Guilds' influence went far beyond production and distribution. They gave producers a sense of identity and a status in the local community. Each guild would be responsible for various civic functions, such as defending the city walls or policing the town. Guilds filled many of the roles that we identify as missing in our modern communities: training, social restraint, group identity. Space is limited in this chapter and these ideas are only in nascent form. However, the producers' guild is an idea that has much to offer in response to many of the problems of modern social and economic life.[28]

Of course, the best way of cutting down the distance between producer and consumer is to unite them in the same person – a solution known as self-provisioning. There is nothing particularly radical here; after all, it was only a few generations ago that every family had a few chickens and a pig in the backyard. The family allotment would have provided a free supply of healthy, organic vegetables. The Green Party proudly boasts of being the only party with a policy on allotments, and has recently helped lobby the government to carry out a review of this neglected local service. The idea is also being taken up in more glamorous quarters. Castro's latest revolutionary idea is 'organoponic gardening', which is described as 'a system of concentrated, organic urban vegetable cultivation' based on urban market gardens. This has been a natural response to trade sanctions against the country and is being taken up by Hugo Chavez's government in Venezuela.[29]

# Conclusion

Traditional visions for replacing capitalism have used words like 'overthrow' or 'topple', imagining the violent and sudden removal of an overpowering system. This focus on the top of the system has never been the green way. My vision for the end of capitalism in the UK is more like watching nature take over from a defunct old building. Almost invisibly at first, and then with greater strength, the roots and creepers and leaves break through, until the building crumbles and nature takes hold. For the millions who maintain it, capitalism offers cheap rewards in return for much effort and grief. For all of us who want an economy that reflects our human nature and recognizes the earth as our mother, I have a simple message: just do it.

# 4

# 9/11 and the Consequences for British-Muslims

*Amir Saeed*

## A personal reflection

Before detailing and presenting an analysis of the material, it must be made clear that I am a British citizen of Pakistani origin. If asked, I would describe myself as of Scottish-Pakistani background. Indeed, the notion of hybridity was my initial research area in academia. From national iden-tity[1] to sport[2] to music,[3] my research was initially focused on how minority groups adapted to accepted and formulated cultures (of incorpo-ration and resistance) within a different context. The events of 9/11 and subsequently have made me question my own notion of hybridity. In-creasingly I feel and see Muslims having to emphasize their Britishness. As Ansari notes, 'Muslims in Britain have had to think about themselves in reaction to being rejected and constructed as the "other". Their identifi-cation with Britishness is frequently questioned.'[4] In a similar vein, Balibar writes, 'the racial-cultural identity of "true nationals" remains in-visible, but can be inferred (and is ensured) *a contrario* by the alleged, quasi-hallucinatory visibility of the "false nationals": the Jews, "wogs," immigrants, "Pakis," natives and blacks'.[5] In short, the events surround-ing 9/11 and especially the 'War on Terrorism' have made me pay closer and closer attention to my religious roots. My secular outlook, in recent months, has been replaced by a more religious and (I say so hesitantly) more Islamic perspective.

It is with this personal background that I have approached this current research. Given that academia is supposed to be rational, objective and scientific, my conclusions may be open to criticism. However, the writing of As'ad Abukhalil (describing his most recent book on *Bin Laden, Ter-rorism and Islam*) may provide some thought to critics of a subjective approach:

> The style and tone of this book is emotional, and may strike the academic reader as odd. But hiding behind the cloak of objectivity is often used more to conceal than to reveal. We are not supposed to feel or to express anger, especially against the US government, which academia often treats with more than a tinge of patriotism . . . living in the US makes me say: for the purpose of the Anti-Arab, I am a proud Arab. I cannot and could not write about the events described with detachment and distance.[6]

Thus it was from a very sympathetic approach that I started on this current research.

# National and international concerns

During the 1990s, interest in the whole Muslim community in the UK increased significantly. Beginning with national issues such as the Rushdie affair and international matters such as the 1991 Gulf War, a series of events brought Muslims into the media spotlight and adversely affected the Muslim population in the UK. New components within racist terminology appeared, and were used in a manner that could be argued was deliberately provocative to bait and ridicule Muslims and other ethnic minorities. Many social commentators have noted that media language has been fashioned in such a way as to cause many to talk about a 'criminal culture'.[7]

Since 9/11 British-Muslims' loyalty to the UK has been further questioned with polls indicating that British-Muslims should make a special effort to emphasize their Britishness.[8] The perceived support amongst British-Muslims of Bin Laden, Palestinian suicide bombers and Kashmiri separatists has been further fuelled by recent events in the north of England. The disturbances there have in some quarters been presented as a particular problem with the Muslim community and not with the British-Asian community as a whole. Kundnani suggests:

> The popular press first blamed 'outside agitators', then blamed the community leaders who had failed in their allotted role: to control 'their people'. Then it was the inherent separatism of Islamic culture that was to blame – these people did not want to integrate: they were 'self-segregating'.[9]

Recent comments by a variety of mainstream politicians appear to substantiate these populist beliefs. Labour politicians like David Blunkett and Peter Hain have both made recent comments that have suggested that British-Muslims must make more effort to integrate into society. Blunkett has suggested 'oaths of allegiance', 'not marrying spouses from the Indian subcontinent', and the introduction of 'English Language Tests'.[10]

Pakistani and Bangladeshi communities in particular have been represented as separatist, insular and unwilling to integrate with wider society. Furthermore, the old stereotypical image of 'Asian passivity' has been replaced by a more militant aggressive identity which is meant to be further at odds with 'British secular society'.[11] The concept of culture clash has been reintroduced to imply that British-Muslims are at odds with mainstream society.

Furthermore, it could be suggested that the issue of asylum seekers/ refugees has been conflated with the issue of (Islamic fundamentalist) terrorism to create a new form of racism.[12] Faisal Bodi argues that

> The inordinate fear planted in our minds first asked us to make an imaginary connection between 9/11 and Saddam Hussein, now demands that we invent more mental dots to connect terrorists with asylum seekers. Seeing a political opportunity, the right has fused the less popular xenophobia with the more popular Islamophobia.[13]

Previously, Bodi had noted that the far right has increasingly used Islamophobia as its main weapon across Europe.[14] He suggests that New Labour, rather than challenging these views, is pandering to the right to win votes. In a similar fashion, Fekete notes:

> What has finally set the seal on xeno-racism, legitimising even further its populist appeals and inflammatory expression in the press, is the passing of the Terrorism Act 2000. This, the first permanent antiterrorism law in twenty-five years, directly targets exile organisations. Even as Macpherson in his report into the death of Stephen Lawrence warned of the danger of stereotyping black communities as criminal, the government gave legitimacy to a new set of stereotypes: asylum seekers are phonies and fraudsters; refugees are terrorists and the enemy within.[15]

For example, the tabloid newspaper, *The Sun* notes that due to weak asylum laws 'Britain is now a Trojan horse for terrorism'.[16] Fekete points out,

> In the UK, Home Secretary David Blunkett announced new reception arrangements and the introduction of identity cards for asylum seekers who will be tracked from arrival to removal because, in the past, terrorists have used the asylum system to gain entry to the UK.[17]

Writers from both ends of the political spectrum have debated the reasons for and consequences of 9/11 and subsequent events. However, the views of Muslim minorities in the West have been silenced in favour of fundamentalist or extremist opinions, which it could be suggested support the claim that Islam is inherently confrontational.[18]

# West versus Islam – the clash of civilizations

It appears that all across the West, the clash of civilizations debate has taken root. The basic premise of Huntington's thesis is that a new cold war is taking place based not upon economics or politics but on culture.[19] Sardar and Davies illustrate how Huntington's thesis has been appropriated:

> a Dec 3 2001 issue of the *National Review*, with a drawing of George Bush as a medieval crusader on the cover contained an article headlined 'Martyred: Muslim murder and mayhem against Christians', in which the author cites with approval the conclusion in Samuel Huntington's book, *The Clash of Civilisations and the Remaking of World Order*: 'The underlying problem for the West is not Islamic fundamentalism. It is Islam, a different civilisation whose people are convinced of the superiority of their culture and are obsessed with the inferiority of their power.'[20]

This example may well help explain why many Muslims look upon the War on Terrorism as a War on Islam.

However, as Halliday clearly points out, even prior to Huntington's thesis Islam was presented as a threatening 'other'.[21] Said's *Orientalism* provides the classic framework in understanding relationships between the 'West' (and the 'Rest') and Muslims in particular.

> In newsreels or newsphotos, the Arab is always shown in large numbers. No individuality, no personal characteristics, or experiences. Most of the pictures represent mass rage and misery, or irrational (hence hopelessly eccentric) gestures. Lurking behind all of these images is the menace of the jihad. Consequence: a fear that the Muslims (or Arabs) will take over the world.[22]

Halliday points out that this notion of an 'Islamic' threat has recently taken a more 'inward' direction centring on Muslims living in the West.[23] Halliday also illustrates how anti-Muslim sentiment has fostered and found voice in countries across the West (and also in Israel and India).[24] Fekete states, 'Humiliated, stigmatised and held responsible for the crimes of a small group of individuals, Muslims believe that powerful influences in European society now feel free to vent their fury against their cultural and religious traditions.'[25] Despite assurances from the UK Prime Minister, Tony Blair, and 'President' George Bush that the War on Terrorism was not a war on Islam, the events of 9/11 have given rise to a number of negative comments about Islam by leading players.

Fekete and Halliday both provide useful summaries and commentary on a number of anti-Muslim, anti-immigration and anti-Islam statements written and supported by leading members of the political community in the West.[26] Halliday, however, notes that a distinction must be made between Islamophobia and anti-Muslimism:

> The tone of this rhetoric is often alarmist, and encompasses racist, xenophobic and stereotyping elements. The term 'anti-Muslimism' is used here to signify such a diffuse ideology, one rarely expressed in purely religious terms but usually mixed in with other rhetorics and ideologies . . . It involves not so much hostility to Islam as a religion . . . But hostility to Muslims, to communities of peoples whose sole or main religion is Islam and whose Islamic character, real or invented, forms one of the objects of prejudice. In this sense anti-Muslimism often overlaps with forms of ethnic prejudice, covering peoples within which there may well be a significant non-Muslim element, such as Albanians, Palestinians or even Caucasians.[27]

In short, it appears that what Halliday is arguing is that 'anti-Muslimism' is almost a new form of racism that discriminates not only on physical traits but also on religious characteristics.

For Halliday the term 'Islamophobia' is inaccurate because it is too uniform. Halliday points out that usage of this term implies that there is only one Islam and that all Muslims are homogeneous.[28] Put briefly, Halliday is proposing that Islamophobia as a term suggests fear of Islam as a religion, not fear of the people who follow Islam.[29] 'The attack now is not against Islam as a faith but Muslims as a people, the latter grouping together all, especially immigrants, who might be covered by the term.' However, Halliday does acknowledge that such academic debates might not prove fruitful for victims of such prejudice.[30] Furthermore, Fekete and Abukhalil point out that post 9/11 some of the critics of Muslims have actually questioned the Islamic concepts of jihad and the hadiths of the Prophet Muhammad.[31]

Whilst at times the War on Terrorism has been argued as just that and not a war on Islam, it appears that many British-Muslims are not convinced. Seven out of ten British-Muslims believe the war on terror is a war on Islam, according to an ICM poll.[32]

# British and Muslim

It could be suggested that from these recommendations the onus is on the minority community to integrate within mainstream culture. Failure to do so then implies 'problems' with that particular minority community. The implication here is that due to their Islamic identity, Muslims cannot by nature be loyal to the British state. However, it has been argued that mainstream politicians are pandering to the right and fuelling populist beliefs for their own political agenda. If, however, they were to look at recent research undertaken in the area of national identity and ethnic minority communities, many of their concerns would appear to be unsubstantiated.

Academic work by Professor Tariq Modood notes that the 'Pakistanis and Bangladeshis, often regarded as culturally conservative and separatist, are more likely to think of themselves as being culturally mixed than some groups'.[33] That research was the largest ethnic minority study conducted in the UK, and Professor Modood and his colleagues certainly found that British-Pakistanis and British-Bangladeshis did see themselves as belonging to two cultures and did not perceive a major problem with this dual identity. Further empirical work in Scotland again clearly shows that Asians and Muslims living in Scotland regard themselves as having a bicultural hybrid identity. When given the choice, Pakistanis in Glasgow clearly had an identity which reflected both their ancestral roots and also their Scottish surroundings.[34]

Indeed, the most recent survey on Muslim opinion shows that the majority consider themselves British-Muslims.[35] Post-9/11 polls conducted by the British-Asian newspaper *Eastern Eye* show overwhelmingly that British-Muslims perceived themselves as loyal citizens despite opposing US/UK bombing of Afghanistan.[36] This right to disobey is, however, one of the cornerstones of democracy and one should consider that white Britons who may oppose government policy are not usually questioned about their loyalty. Fekete notes:

> Muslim communities across Europe have spoken with anger about the way in which the media have demonised them as terrorists if they exercised their democratic rights to oppose, in any way, the nature of the war in Afghanistan . . . Muslims who do so are immediately suspected of fundamentalist inclinations or asked for their anti-fundamentalist credentials.[37]

# The present study: British-Muslims post-9/11

## Sample and methodology

Drawing on focus group studies, this section details the views of ordinary Muslims and how they view 9/11 and the subsequent War on Terrorism. British-Muslims from a variety of ethnic backgrounds voice their opinions on these events and also on how they feel they are perceived by wider society.

Four focus groups were conducted, involving a total of 27 participants (17 male and 10 female). Two of the focus groups were conducted in Glasgow at the office of a youth organization. Two were conducted at the University of Sunderland. All of the participants were volunteers and British citizens. All of the participants interviewed stated that they were religious, although this did vary to a degree. A Likert scale noted that religion was *important* or *very important* to all of the participants. The sample was achieved by contacting individuals through youth organizations, and these individuals then contacted friends, etc. In short, a system of purposive sampling was employed.[38] As well as providing demographic details such as age, the participants were also asked to affirm their ethnic origin and to describe themselves in national terms.

The sample were told from the outset that the focus groups were about 9/11, the War on Terrorism and its effect on British-Muslims. Indeed, a number of the participants offered to come back and participate in any further research on this topic.The participants requested that the focus groups themselves consisted of both males and females. An additional questionnaire was completed by the sample on attitudes to race, religion and ethnic relations in the UK.

The interviews were semi-structured, thus allowing the respondents to explain issues of importance to them while at the same time maintaining an informal flow to keep in line with the aims of the research. A semi-structured interview was favoured because it was felt this would allow the respondents more scope to express themselves, although there are some disadvantages with semi-structured interviews and focus groups.[39] The interview was structured into three main parts:

- initial reaction to 9/11 (including thinking about initial causes)
- the subsequent War on Terrorism
- the effect of 9/11 and the War on Terrorism on British-Muslims

At times the participants also talked about related issues, such as Islam and its diversity, the role of women and what constitutes a Muslim.

Academically, the respondents' views were linked to previous research work and theoretical concepts. Moreover, it was hoped that the views of ordinary Muslims might be given a chance to be heard. Each extract from the respondents is preceded by demographic information in the following order: gender; age; ethnic origin; and self-description.

## 9/11 initial reaction

Various commentators have pointed that after the terrorist attacks of 9/11 not just the USA but the whole world was changed.[40] Parenti notes, however, that the American reaction was one of amazement and wonder about why the USA was attacked.[41] All of the respondents noted horror at the attack, but also bewilderment at initial American reaction.

Female, aged 23, Palestinian, British-Muslim:

> It was like watching a film. It just was not real . . . My mother came in and both of us were transfixed. This is what happened in films not in real life I said . . . At that point my uncle said yes but that was what

Palestinians were saying about the massacres at Shabilla in 1982 [*sic*]. That was a nightmare.

It was then I started thinking that Americans and Palestinians were both victims for the first time.

Male, aged 24, Pakistani, Scottish-Muslim:

It was surreal. It just did not seem real. I was in a cash 'n' carry at the time and we all rushed to the television. No one was celebrating. Everyone seemed shocked. A couple of people said something like 'we are going to be in for it now'.

For a number of the respondents their shock was linked to seeing their faith being exploited.

Female, aged 23, Pakistani, Scottish-Muslim:

Innocent people died and my faith does not allow me to celebrate that. I kept thinking this is a movie and I was waiting for the commercials to start. Even now when you see pictures of it you think 'Did that happen?'

Female, aged 23, Pakistani, Scottish-Muslim:

Islam means peace. It does not mean war like this. The people who did this hijacked our grievance and religion. They have now linked Islam to destruction for many people. This is not right. What happened on 9/11 was unbelievable but it was not Islam. I have to stress this. Those people did not deserve to die . . . You cannot imagine the horror those victims went through. You would not wish that on your worst enemy. No, it just was not right.

Following the events of 9/11, various leading figures did question the loyalty of British-Muslims. Furthermore, the media highlighted the extremists in Islam who applauded or cheered the events of 9/11.[42] This, it seemed, was proof of the 'fact' that British-Muslims were separatist and hostile to the UK. However, as surveys in the British-Asian newspaper *Eastern Eye* and the *Guardian* have shown, British-Muslims do consider themselves part-British.[43]

All of the Muslims also felt that their voice and concern was being overlooked in favour of more radical views to justify hostility to Muslims. They argued that, even though they opposed the views of Bin Laden, they still felt that the consequences behind 9/11 were not adequately examined. The following two extracts come from the same focus group.

Male, aged 34, Algerian, British-Muslim:

> September 11th was a crime and horrible, but has anyone in America asked why? No one cares that Sharon is killing Palestinians, no one cared too much about the Chechnya or Kashmir. When Muslims are getting killed, the West looks away. This is not fair. Even now Blair and Bush give guns to kill Muslim children and then say they are not anti-Muslim. That is a joke. I am not saying 9/11 was right, I mean look who's paying for it now – Muslims – but when Muslims are killed, who says stop?

Male, aged 26, Nigerian, British-Muslim:

> (*Nodding in agreement*) Yes, it seems to the West we only matter when we retaliate. But how many times do you expect us to turn the cheek? All over the world Muslims are getting attacked and the British and Americans know about it. But we are the enemy when we stand up. I spoke to non-Muslim friends and tried to explain how I felt. Straight away I was accused of sympathising with Bin Laden. No, it seems if we raise our voices, somebody shouts 'Taliban'! (*Group laughs.*)

Female, aged 22, Pakistani, Scottish-Muslim:

> I work in a big office and after 9/11 people seemed to think I had to defend all Muslims. When the bombing started some of the people were against it but most seemed to take offence, saying that America had to retaliate. They also seemed to imply that I supported Bin Laden . . . I did get pissed off; most of the people had never even heard of the Taliban before 9/11.

Anasari points out that post-9/11, Muslims felt increasingly isolated and alone. Several newspapers brought out special reports, which examined this feeling of marginalization.[44] However, even prior to 9/11 the Runnymede Trust pointed to a process of social exclusion of British-Muslims in society[45] – an occurrence that seems to be running parallel to developments in the rest of Europe.[46]

## The War on Terrorism

In this section the participants debated the ongoing War on Terrorism. Only two people did not see it as a war on Islam.

Female, aged 26, Indian, British-Muslim:

> After 9/11 states that sponsor terrorism have to be stopped. Islam itself has nothing to do with terrorism, therefore it can't be a war against

Islam. Both Bush and Blair have spoken with Muslim leaders to express this.

Female, aged 19, Pakistani, British-Muslim:

Yes, you know and I know that Islam has nothing to do with terrorism, but then why are nearly all the countries like Iraq, Iran and Yemen predominantly Muslim countries?

Female, aged 26, Indian, British-Muslim:

(*Replies*) But Iraq is a secular state not a Muslim state.

Female, aged 19, Pakistani, British-Muslim:

Yes but Bush is trying to make links between Iraq and al-Qaeda. Also if you ask anyone in the street they would say Islamic terrorism not Christian terrorism. For most people, Muslims are thought of as terrorists. I know and you know Islam has nothing to with terrorism but the average person in the street does not care.

## The effect of 9/11 and the War on Terrorism on British-Muslims

Male, aged 22, Moroccan, British-Muslim:

This is total bullshit! The Israelis kill us, nothing is said. The US gives them guns, no one cares. Yet we are the terrorists. No, this is a new war against Islam.

Female, aged 28, Pakistani, British-Muslim:

If the War on Terrorism is not against Islam, why is it everyday we see Muslims linked to terror in the media? No one cares about the Americans funding the IRA or that Sharon is a terrorist. It seems they want to go after the Muslims first. India, Russia, Indonesia, Israel, it's just an excuse to attack Muslims. But when we fight back, we are wrong. However, when Britain, the USA and Israel fight back, it's justified. (*Group nods and acknowledges*)

Male, aged 26, Nigerian, British-Muslim:

What is worse is that British people, I mean white people, believe this crap and in some place like Oldham, Burnley, everyone thinks

Muslims are terrorists. I mean what the BNP is pushing is that Muslims and asylum seekers are all going to attack Britain, so people are getting really scared.

# Conclusion and discussion

The previous extracts bring a number of interesting themes into play. The respondents seem to be invoking the 'ummah': the global Islamic community which supersedes nationality. Explained briefly, there are two tiers to Muslim identity, one related to faith and one related to country, but faith overrides any other component of identity. Jacobson notes that

> In this way, the boundaries defining Muslim identity may also be strengthened; the young Muslims are likely to feel that although within British society they are members of a relatively small and weak minority, their religious beliefs and practice traverse the globe and history and are thus components of what is a vast and (potentially at least) powerful force.[47]

Participants may be drawing strength from an Islamic identity that can provide solidarity with other Muslims, as well as an avenue of escape from being constantly identified in negative terms; the logic of this process implies a positive (re)conceptualization of Islamic identity transcending local, negative attributions. Certainly recent evidence in the UK suggests that British-Muslims, from a variety of different ethnic groups, are willing to assert an Islamic identity in the face of real and perceived prejudice.[48]

Thus in some respects the concept of the 'ummah' and conceptualizations of political blackness draw upon similar feelings of exclusion and empowerment. However, the 'ummah' is in many ways a romantic concept of Islam. As Halliday points out, Islamic communities are heterogeneous and also prone to internal violent conflict.[49] Linked to this, the term 'Muslim' may also need to be discussed – for example, is a Muslim one who adheres to or follows the principles of Islam, or one for whom Islam is the master signifier?[50] This also led to a debate amongst participants in the study between what is Islam and stereotypes of Muslims. The respondents seem to suggest that the wider society does not understand Islam and formulates opinions based on media discourse. However, as various others have pointed out, the media tend to emphasize an extreme view of Islam.[51] This in many respects reflects how the media erroneously represent minority groups in general.[52]

The interesting final section of the discussion notes how terrorism has been defined to mean the actions of particular groups and not of states. Chomsky notes how dominant and popular definitions of terrorism discount the possibility that western capitalist states engage in such acts.[53] Pilger argues:

> The documentation of American terrorism is voluminous, and because such truths cannot be rationally rebutted, those who mention them, drawing the obvious connections between them, are often abused as 'anti-American', regardless of whether or not they themselves are American. During the 1930s, the term 'anti-German' was deployed against critics the Third Reich wished to silence.[54]

It is evident that 9/11, alongside the issues of asylum seekers and the resurgence of far right politics, has left many British-Muslims feeling isolated and devalued. Rather than challenging these perceptions, it seems that more and more politicians are willing to place greater responsibility on British-Muslims to integrate.[55] Fewer onuses seem to be placed on giving equal and fair access. The media must also share some responsibility in trying to present a fairer impression of Islam; however, as Poole and the Runnymede Trust's research points out, this cannot be assumed.[56] Given the biased reporting of ethnic minority groups in the past, it seems unlikely that the media will play an active role in championing the causes of British-Muslims. Ansari notes, 'British-Muslims have responded to the challenges of living in Britain in a variety of ways . . . Often feeling devalued, humiliated and stigmatised by mainstream society, they explore strategies to resist the onslaught of what they perceive as hegemonic ideology and political culture.'[57]

This bleak assessment of the current climate is in many ways reflected by the participants in this study, who voiced their frustrations with great passion, anger and eloquence. For some, a process of 'assertive distinctiveness'[58] may occur where views may become even more polarized into 'them' and 'us'.

# 5

# Bakhtin and the Carnival against Capitalism

## Derek Wall

The 1940s. Two hundred miles out of Moscow, the philosopher Mikhail Bakhtin may be a little way from the front line but he isn't having a good war. Since childhood he has suffered from osteomyelitis, a disease that causes inflammation of the bones, particularly the long bones of the arm and leg. Secondary symptoms include a foul-smelling discharge from the sinus and non-healing ulcers. At the age of 12 he mastered Kant's *Kritik der reinen Vernunft* – what else is there to do when you are a bed-ridden pre-teen in the era before television, let alone PlayStation 2? Typhoid made matters worse: June 1929 saw him suffer paraphrenitis of the kidneys and in 1938 his right leg was amputated. He taught from a couch, walked with sticks and in old age in a Moscow old people's home took pills by the handful. During the 1940s his one great comfort was tobacco. Because cigarettes papers were in short supply, he smoked much of the manuscript of one his important but soon consumed books to generate his roll-ups.[1]

The 'Carnival against Capitalism', the City of London, 18 June 1999. Ten thousand protesters are on the streets, many of them masked, the masks contain on their reverse side the message:

> Those in authority fear the mask for power partly resides in identifying, stamping and cataloguing: in knowing who you are. But a Carnival needs masks, thousands of masks; and our masks are not to conceal our identity but to reveal it . . . The masquerade has always been an essential part of Carnival. Dressing up and disguise, the blurring of identities and boundaries, transformation, transgression; all are brought together in the wearing of masks. Masking up releases our commonality and enables us to act together, to shout as one to those who rule and divide us 'we are all fools, deviants, outcasts, clowns and criminals'. Today we shall give this resistance a face; for by putting on our masks we reveal our unity; and by raising our voices in the street together, we speak our

anger at the facelessness of power. On the signal follow your colour. Let the Carnival begin.[2]

Capitalism can only survive by constant growth. Marx famously noted that 'accumulate, accumulate . . . is Moses and the prophets' for capitalist companies and the system as a whole.[3] Those of us who believe that such growth restricts human potential, fuels injustice and is ecologically unsustainable face a series of painful dilemmas. For a start, capitalism seems so ingrained and structural, at a time when structuralism is out of fashion, that resistance appears unacceptable. Economic growth is the devil's gravity, if an act accelerates economic exchange we strive for it, everything has to be 'economic'. Yet economics, in a capitalist form, seems to serve contradictory purposes for living things. I am told that every mobile phone comes with an old-style public phone box worth of waste, yet unless we keep throwing them away and buying new generations the industry risks going into recession. Faced with global deflation, we all need to embark on an orgy of borrowing, shopping and overproducing – acts that will cement our alienation and harm other living things.

Few in the anti-capitalism movement acknowledge that we live within a social world that demands another way of life. To put the brakes on destruction will demand the most thoroughgoing of revolutions. The dilemmas inherent in this task are also often ignored by academics, who sometimes see anti-capitalist struggles as sites within which to try out ornate theory, and by political groups, which frankly view protest as an opportunity to sell papers, recruit members and accumulate their own activist capital.[4] Many 'anti-capitalists' simply want a kinder, fairer system rather than a different world.[5] Others are obsessed with finance capital, arguing that the simple creation of social credit can breed an ecologically sound economic system based on debt-free money.[6] Social creditors and others often have a conspiratorial view of what is wrong. Indeed, it is deeply worrying how often within the movement one comes across the idiocies of David Icke, who sees Jewish-Masonic cabals and lizards running the Matrix.[7]

'Getting there',[8] to a society that rejects accumulation, and 'being there' – that is, seeding new non-exploitative mediations with each other and the rest of nature – will be problematic. I believe that the Russian theorist Bakhtin can help us in both these tasks. In fact, his ideas have been used to inspire innovative anti-capitalist action. Here I am going briefly to outline his biographical details, then show how he directly motivated Reclaim the Streets (RTS) to undertake 'Carnival against Capitalism', before looking at the value of his key themes for anti-capitalist struggle. Thankfully this isn't original, but I would like to bring together in one place the critical insights published by others, so as to outline Bakhtin's utility to green anti-capitalists and provide for more dialogue. Graeme

Chesters and John Jordan, who have been active in the direct action movement, cite Bakhtin as a source of inspiration.[9] Bell and Michael Gardiner note his contribution to debates on ecology.[10] Michael Steinberg, along with Gardiner, Colin Barker and others, argues that he provides important insights into the political nature of language.[11] Having examined these perspectives, I will argue that Bakhtin shows that one does not have to throw out Marx and revolutionary commitment when constructing a politics that is open and based on dialogue. Indeed, long-standing traditions of ecosocialism that can be strengthened with an infusion of Bakhtin excess illustrate that polyphonic Marxism can get on the streets and struggle for ecotopia too!

# Bakhtin

Bakhtin, born in 1895, spent most of his life writing about philosophy and literature. He worked as a schoolteacher, but illness cut this career short. Like many Soviet intellectuals he fell foul of Stalin and he was lucky to be exiled to a remote town rather than a camp, where his infirmities would probably have led to death. There is fierce debate about whether a series of important works were written by him or associates in the so-called Bakhtin circle. He left some work incomplete, much was lost and the history of the publication and translation of the remainder is pretty torturous. The Stalinist landscape until 1957 meant that some of his ideas may have been self-censored and other themes generated as a hidden satire on the regime.[12]

Since his death in 1975, Bakhtin has been hailed by some as the most important thinker of the twentieth century.[13] His key ideas, which include heteroglossia, dialoguism, polyphony, the chronotope and carnival, are fascinating, diverse and impossible to summarize adequately. Heteroglossia, to provide a crude outline, is the concept that multiple languages exist in any society. Dialoguism, in turn, is not merely about dialogue but argues that meaning, indeed life itself, is possible only via interaction. Polyphony is the theme not only that diverse languages exist but that even individuals are multiple voiced. The chronotope, inspired by Einstein, refers to particular and discrete time-space sections.[14]

Amongst Bakhtin's titles, *Rabelais and His Work* is the most important for understanding his influence on the anti-capitalist movement.[15] It celebrates the medieval tradition of carnival, reflected in the novels of François Rabelais where the social world was pushed upside down and rebellion became the festival of the oppressed. Generally in the West he has been a resource for postmodernists, but for Reclaim the Streets via *Rabelais and His World* he was exploited for revolutionary practice.

RTS was created to fight the car. Evolving out of the 'No M11' campaign and Earth First! (EF!), RTS invented the street party where thousands of activists occupy and enjoy road space. Such street parties have diffused around the world and RTS has increasingly and explicitly promoted revolutionary anti-capitalism. RTS cannot be understood without Bakhtin and his account of the carnival.

# Let the carnival begin!

RTS started as part of Earth First!'s 'ban the car' campaign, which was put together by EF! founder Jason Torrance.[16] Torrance argued that the car was fuelling the greenhouse effect and wrecking the environment in diverse ways.

> The car's effect on our environment doesn't stop at direct exhaust pipe pollution but also extends to extraction of minerals for production, oil use including transportation dangers, and disposal of old cars . . . each year 23 million tyres are discarded in the UK alone and 28 million gallons of motor oil go missing, presumably finding their way into our freshwater systems.[17]

The first Gulf War was blamed on oil addiction to drive the great car economy before Torrance turned to the social ill-effects of the automobile.

> In today's society the car has become the norm, a symbol of wealth and prosperity. In reality it is the most destructive item an individual can possess. The worldwide slaughter of humans and other species amounts to hundreds of thousands each year, with both the injury and death figures on a scale equivalent to any war.[18]

Direct action started almost immediately with EF! blocking roads in Brighton town centre on the last shopping Saturday before Christmas 1991. An attempt to disrupt the opening of the Dartford road bridge was aborted by the police in high-speed boats. An EF! anti-car campaign meeting in April led to the formal launch of the RTS campaign. On 15 May 1992, around 70 EF! activists sat down and blocked traffic on Waterloo Bridge during an RTS action. In 1993 the Motor Show at Earls Court was disrupted and cycle lanes were painted on to a number of London's roads. While activists such as Torrance were ignorant of Bakhtin's legacy, aesthetics was married to politics from an early stage. On 1 August a Mini that had been disassembled and transported on the underground was put back together at Hyde Park and smashed while the EF!ers read extracts from Heathcote Williams' poem 'Autogeddon'. The RTS campaign soon halted, however, as activists became involved in the No M11 campaign against motorway construction in Wanstead and Leytonstone.

Again art was blended with politics. Such an articulation was strengthened by the Criminal Justice and Public Order Act, which criminalized rave music. At Claremont Road, a row of houses were squatted and large free parties held at weekends. For those of us who visited, and more so for its inhabitants, it was a magical autonomous zone. Nets crossed the street, large sculptures stood outside the houses and murals were spread across the walls. Resistance was linked to beauty in the form of a high metal tower that was used to resist the demolition of the street. But in the end the road was built.[19]

From the No M11 campaign RTS re-emerged to run a series of street parties. Key activists had been recruited including a series of serious and imaginative political thinkers. Alliances were built with community groups, socialists, ravers and many more beyond the initial orbit of radical environmentalism. The first party at Camden was rather modest but saw a couple of thousand people occupying the road and excluding cars. The next at Upper Street, also in London, was much larger and impressive. In 1996 around 7,000 people occupied the M41, holding a massive party. Under the curve of the skirt of a giant dancing figure, jackhammers were used to dig holes in the tarmac and plant a tree.[20]

RTS, drawing on anarchist traditions, rejected the idea of direct action as a means of influencing the policy process. Their action was literally direct and unmediated. It did not aim to generate publicity or influence politicians, but directly to change society. Taking cars off the streets to open up social space was an immediate goal. In turn, the party concept was used to encourage participation.

> Direct action enables people to develop a new sense of self-confidence and an awareness of their individual and collective power. Direct action is founded on the idea that people can develop the ability for self-rule only through practice, and proposes that all persons directly decide the important issues facing them. Direct action is not just a tactic, it is individuals asserting their ability to control their own lives and to participate in social life without the need for mediation or control by bureaucrats or professional politicians. Direct action encompasses a whole range of activities, from organizing coops to engaging in resistance to authority. Direct action places moral commitment above positive law. Direct action is not a last resort when other methods have failed, but the preferred way of doing things.[21]

For RTS, as time went by, the great car economy was increasingly perceived as just one manifestation of a capitalist order. To liberate the earth and restore social space, capitalism had to be fought. RTS argued, 'our streets are as full of capitalism as of cars and the pollution of capitalism is much more insidious'.[22] Such a realization was accompanied by formal alliances with working-class groups, most notably the Liverpool Dockers who held a long strike to resist casualization. RTS noted:

> We're saying that the power that attacks those who work, through
> union legislation and casualization, is the same power that is attacking
> the planet with over-production and over-consumption of resources;
> the power that produces cars by 4 million a year is the same power that
> decides to attack workers through the disempowerment of unions, re-
> ducing work to slavery.[23]

Contact and common campaigning with a range of militant union activists was developed, including sacked Magnet workers, cleaners from
Hillingdon and tube drivers. Not only were alliances made with the working class in the UK, but RTS also networked into a global coalition of
revolutionaries. Indeed, the 'Carnival against Capitalism' of 18 June
1999 was launched under the slogan 'Our resistance is as global as capital.' The global dimension was strengthened as RTS was one of the
elements that constituted People's Global Action. This international
movement, which rejected participation by political parties and pressure
groups, was established by the Zapatistas, who had risen in armed revolt
against the creation of the North American Free Trade Association in January 1994. The 'Carnival against Capitalism' was just one event among
hundreds held on the same day across the globe.[24]

# On the signal follow your colour

The 'Carnival against Capitalism' was a carefully planned act of chaos.
Fifty thousand gold flyers distributed at clubs and pubs, a global e-mail
discussion list and vigorous fly posting were used to draw 10,000 partygoers to the meeting point at Liverpool Street Station, London. Banners
proclaimed 'Kill capitalism' and 'Global ecology not global economy'.
Coloured masks were distributed and different colours were led off in
different directions. The RTS flags are green for ecology, red for communism and black for anarchy. Earlier a critical mass cyclists' event
blocked the streets around the financial heart of London. Marchers shut
down the Bank of England and surrounded the Treasury.[25] A participant
noted:

> Up around Fenchurch Street, and then suddenly we are all re-united,
> masks of all colours right in the belly of the urban beast – the LIFFE
> building, where computer keyboards send billions of dollars whizzing
> round the globe 24 hours a day. A cobbled street running along the
> building and down to the Thames River has been blocked off and a hy-
> drant opened to free a 40-foot waterspout. The drums beat out against
> the alien buildings, we're dancing and singing in the rain, and under the
> cover of the sound and fury anonymous hands brick up some LIFFE
> entrances and smash others. We block up the drains, flood Dowgate
> Hill and take a rest among other joyous faces on a tiny bit of beach on

the Thames, the Thames that is everywhere enclosed by private capital. We sit there in the sun and smoke a spliff.[26]

According to another activist,

> we got the upper hand with the police, not by throwing bottles but by dancing around a police line and using them as a volleyball net! You won't see this in the news because the police looked very silly and we were being neither criminal nor violent. What can I say; it wasn't the bloodbath brought to you by *The Sun*, it was an expression of resistance and freedom and it was a big party.[27]

Protesters carried giant papier maché heads, representing the countries or regions taking part, and mini sound systems promoted the carnival atmosphere. A punk band played. Company offices were occupied. A McDonald's inevitably was 'trashed'. The LIFFE building was attacked. One participant noted, 'I ran into the LIFFE building, smashed a few mirrors in the foyer and then looked round to see this masked-up figure light a distress flare and hurl it up the escalators towards the offices. Fuck, I thought, this is really full on.'[28] At Cannon Street silver banknotes were dropped on the crowd. Another eyewitness wrote, 'One loony I saw had nicked a fireman's helmet and then proceeded to strap it on tightly and use his head as a battering ram to smash a bank's plate glass window!'[29] Minor fights broke out between drunken partygoers and City workers, while a police van ran over a girl at Liverpool Street. The party went on all day and all round the globe with more modest actions occurring in four continents. This was revolution and for a day Britain's financial centre was brought to a total halt. Even office workers seemed to be drawn in:

> I am one of those poor bastards working in the City of London, not normally involved in demos . . .
>
> On J18 me and a few people from my office skipped work for the day and joined the crowds at Liverpool Street station. We sat in the sun smoking and listening to cool music, chatting to friends and strangers alike. When the aggro started later on, we got caught up in the battles on lower Thames Street. We found ourselves in the middle of the brick-throwing mob just as the coppers baton charged us.
>
> My mates from work were cynical about the Carnival beforehand ('tree hugging hippy crap' they thought) but once they had experienced the police's new steel batons around their heads – for no reason other than being there – they changed their mind. From what I saw, the police violence outweighed whatever a small core of troublesome protesters did.[30]

The financial centre of London was shut for the day and the police admitted to having been caught unawares. Massive damage was done and the carnival came close to taking control of the LIFFE building. Anarchism, Marxism and ecology were combined with a sense of creativity.

The narrative moved on to a series of dramatic May Day protests and in 2003 RTS established a large permanent community based in White-chapel and was campaigning against the new Gulf War. The Carnival against Capitalism prefigured and resourced a rolling series of anti-capitalist protests in Seattle, Prague, Quebec, Gothenburg and Genoa. While Marx inspired such protest, Bakhtin was equally important.

# Rabelais and his world

Medieval Europe was famed for riotous saints' days and other carnival events. Today we might think of civic probity and floats in the shape of large cakes on a single summer's evening in some rural conservative backwater. In the Renaissance, carnival took up as many as three months of the year and occupied considerable energy. Rabelais described and celebrated medieval carnival in his novels. Bakhtin examined Rabelais's world of carnival because he felt that it was politically important as well as providing a rich source of literary metaphor. For Bakhtin the carnival provided a powerful arena for political resistance. In a feudal society dominated by the empire, the aristocracy and above all the church, the carnival provided one rare opportunity for freedom. Within the carnival, ordinary people were in control and the world was turned upside down. Revolution was aligned with pleasure and feasting. 'Carnival is not a spectacle seen by the people; they live in it, and everyone participates because its very idea embraces all the people.'[31]

Bakhtin uses the term 'carnivalesque' to denote the mixing of different and contradictory elements. Religious observance was connected to pagan excess. The poor met with the rich. A joyous mess was the result.

Bakhtin's observations are apparent in RTS events from the first street parties through to the anti-capitalist May Days. The events created social spaces briefly separate from the rest of social reality. Pleasure is a feature, as we can see from the extracts above. Worlds are turned upside down with carnivalesque acts such as the notorious daubing of Churchill's statute, on the 2000 May Day in Parliament Square, where he was also given a green mohican made of turf. The parties are not means to an ultimate revolutionary end, but are celebrations of liberation in the present. Although catalysts are necessary, the parties cannot be marshalled by RTS but spill anarchically into new spaces. They are participant shaped rather than driven by leaders and watched by spectators.

It can be argued that the carnival is a safety valve that prevents revolution, rather than a liberating event. Yet both Bakhtin and RTS argue that the carnival shows that other worlds are possible. Instead of the oppressed letting off steam, the carnival spirit indicates that hierarchy is ultimately impossible because everything is in a state of flux and nothing is fixed. All social systems will pass.

The very seriousness of such forms, though, fuelled Bakhtin's rebellious texts. Terry Eagleton notes that 'in what is perhaps the boldest, most devious gesture in the history of "Marxist criticism", Bakhtin pits against that "official, formalistic and logical authoritarianism" whose unspoken name is Stalinism the explosive politics of the body, the erotic, the licentious and semiotic'.[32]

John Jordan, an RTS activist, told me that several RTS supporters had independently read Bakhtin and decided that he would provide inspiration for their work. Graeme Chesters, an RTS activist and academic, has shown how many direct actions use

> playful, irreverent and performative strategies to disturb, provoke or illuminate. Other examples which come to mind are the arrest of a pantomime cow at Newbury, and the celebrated Fokker bi-plane that was 'crashed' into the upper reaches of a tree at Mary Hare camp, in the same campaign. Elsewhere SHAG (Super Heroes Against Genetics) have invaded Monsanto's offices dressed in their fetching super-hero garb, sculptures have doubled as barricades in Claremont Road on the route of the M11, The Third Battle of Newbury suffered an 'Art Bi-pass' and huge carnival figures hid the planting of trees on the M41, in the middle of a Reclaim The Streets party. In these actions and others the symbolic mixes with the irreverent, the instrumental with the bizarre, theatricality, humour, performance and ritual are merged and the only constraint appears the imagination of those involved.[33]

# Soviet pagan

Carnival as revolution does not exhaust the meaning of Bakhtin's work for green anti-capitalists. We may be mistaken to believe that ending capitalism will be enough to heal the division between humanity and the rest of nature. Anti-capitalism is necessary but insufficient if we are to get to a green society. Long before capitalism, humanity was degrading the environment: for example, in the Palaeolithic era, mammoths and other varieties of furry mega fauna were hunted to extinction. In turn the first farmers in the British Isles wiped out around 70 per cent of the existing wildwood. The Romans suffered from soil erosion and lead poisoning, and slaughtered masses of wildlife in their attempts to maintain imperial hegemony.[34] Thus radical greens have argued that even when capitalism has been abolished the ecology crisis will be far from over. We need to find a way of interacting with the rest of nature that minimizes resource use and the exploitation of other species if we are to maintain our own species into the future. Numerous commentators have argued that if we downgrade the material and celebrate the unnatural, environmental destruction fuelled by the exercise of instrumental reason will result in catastrophe.

As well as economic needs and political motivations, ecological destruction may be accelerated by philosophies that see the material world as fallen and profane. There is a Gnostic tradition which chimes with the Christian notion of original sin that sees the world we have as flawed. Religion in many guises often champions the Platonic view that we live in a realm of shadows and that there exists a really real 'spiritual' realm. If what is, is corrupt, why nurture and conserve it?

Bakhtin did not specifically deal with the ecological crisis, but he has been seen as advocating a green social theory because of his celebration of the gross material aspects of life, which rejects the division between mind and matter. He has no time for those who downgrade the world of physical matter. Sex, shit, birth, death, eating, etc. are part of the cycle of life; they are the holies. Haram, so to speak, is halal! Most shockingly to those of a Gnostic sentiment, his scatological celebration of excrement was based on an affinity with fertile life. Thus Bakhtin's Rabelais text celebrates a rough-and-ready paganism. The carnival is seen as having its origin in the old religions, and the material rather than the spiritual is raised to the position of the sacred. Food, sex and shit are all seen as essential to life and the festivities raise life.[35]

# The battle for language

It is difficult to exhaust Bakhtin's potential contribution to anti-capitalism. A significant area of additional discussion must be his notion that language is an arena of political conflict, where we battle over meanings right down to the level of individual words. For him, words are not fixed; nor are they free-floating signifiers that mean nothing.

Social movement theorists argue that political activists have to exploit structural conditions, utilize pre-existing networks, gather resources and frame their message to create mobilization.[36] Framing is a process developed from Goffman and Bateson by Snow and Benford to show how activists create movements through discursive practices. A problem must be identified, a cause of crisis illustrated and a course of action flagged up if successful mobilization is to take place. An environmental pressure group might seek to show that road building is a problem, government action is the cause and participation in lobbying a solution. Anarchists may frame the state as a cause of crisis and identify participation in the Black Bloc as a solution. Leninists see the solution in terms of the disciplined party and advocate party activism as the appropriate course of action. The innovative social movement researcher Marc Steinberg rejects the notion that frames are relatively stable discursive resources and draws upon Bakhtin to argue that the words used in the framing process are politically contested.[37] Colin Barker cites Bakhtin at length to show that words are a site of class struggle.

> When we seek to understand a word, what matters is not the direct meaning the word gives to objects and emotions – this is the false front of the word; what matters is rather the actual and always self-interested use to which this meaning is put and the way it is expressed by the speaker, a use determined by the speaker's position (profession, social class, etc.) and by the concrete situation. Who speaks and under what conditions he speaks: this is what determines the word's actual meaning. All direct meanings and direct expressions are false, and this is especially true of emotional meanings and expressions.[38]

To win, contestants have to challenge the supposedly fixed meaning of words and create new meanings. The RTS actions are used to challenge notions of the capitalist economy as an economy licensed by science, in order to show that the market is a political concept that can be replaced with a new moral economy. The anti-capitalist movement at its most subversive challenges notions of necessity and freedom supposedly enshrined within capitalism. New Labour and the non-governmental organizations increasingly accept the meanings of the multinationals. Bakhtin's celebration of all things 'gross' is a useful reminder that an ecological society will demand that we re-accent words which are seen as denoting the profane in pursuit of a new awareness of our metabolism with the earth.

# Exploiting Bakhtin

Bakhtin champions the multiple but nonetheless rejects capitalism and hierarchy; he values the people and the earth. Meaning is constantly up for debate by the people:

> There is neither a first word nor a last word. The contexts of dialogue are without limit. They extend into the deepest past and the most distant future. Even meaning born in dialogues of the remotest past will never be fully grasped once and for all, for they will always be renewed in later dialogue. At any present moment of the dialogue there are great masses of forgotten meanings, but these will be recalled again at any given moment in the dialogue's later course when it will be given new life. For nothing is absolutely dead, every meaning will someday have its homecoming festival.[39]

Bakhtin's emphasis on polysemy and heteroglossia may seem poststructuralist, but his demand that space be created so that different voices can be heard is a political call not just a celebration of free-floating relativity. Unsurprisingly, his concept of 'carnival' has most directly resourced not just RTS but a whole way of performing anti-capitalism. RTS's exploitation of Bakhtin is an interesting example of how highly sophisticated theory can be used to resource practical change and as such it throws up a number of implications. First, it indicates that it is false to label the 'new' anti-capitalism as a 'new social movement' based on postmodern identity politics. Numerous theorists, most notably Laclau and Mouffe, have argued that the old politics of class is redundant and that a new democratic plural space must be created in society. New social movements have been seen as a rainbow alliance of movements that stress personal identity goals in a postmaterial society rather than strategy.[40] Yet RTS articulates calls for dialogue and pluralism with the supposed 'old' politics of revolution. Like Bakhtin, it argues that dominant power structures shut off dialogue and must be fought. Laclau and Mouffe fail to problematize capitalism as a threat to creativity and the environment. The Communist Party they originated in seemed to swing from Stalinism right through to a politics that, while claiming to speak for diversity, embraced the market. Both Stalin and the market have acted as powerful sources of monologue drowning out different voices.

Second, as we have already noted, it is false to establish a binary division between 'Marxism' and postmodern or anarchic politics. Clearly RTS, in its use of Bakhtin, accepted key elements of Marx's mature works such as *Das Kapital*. It notes that capitalism works by appropriating workers' surplus labour power, creating alienation and, via the productive metabolism between humanity and non-human nature, threatening global ecology.

Third, by opening up a dialogue about how revolutionaries should revolt, RTS has used Bakhtin's insights to indicate how much supposed revolutionary practice has been routinized and normalized. The predictable practices of Leninist political parties such as the Socialist Workers' Party, with their slogans, paper sales, recruitment drives and constant need to reposition in the face of a fast-moving political market, can be defined by the term 'the McDonaldization of protest'.[41] Bakhtin's celebration of shit, sex and text provides a politics that is very difficult to normalize!

Bakhtin is one source of anti-capitalist protest, but RTS reminds us that radical green protest taps into underground streams of alternative Marxism and unorthodox revolutionary traditions. In Britain we have the Diggers and the Ranters of the civil war era; the Romantic poets, especially Blake and Shelley. In 1884 the Social Democratic Federation, Britain's first Marxist organization, was founded and Marxism looked pretty green! William Morris was perhaps the most prominent and charismatic Marxist of the period and ecological concern was a cornerstone of his politics. Equally, how can we forget the almost totally forgotten Edward Carpenter. This Victorian would-be clergyman was an open campaigner for gay rights and lived for decades with his lover George Merrill.[42] Animal liberation was another of his passions. His Sheffield Socialist Society comrades set up stalls in the city to warn of pollution and hiked vigorously through the Yorkshire Dales. War and centralized socialism, in the form of both the Fabians-orientated Labour Party and the Communist Party of Great Britain (CPGB), delivered hammer blows to such ecosocialism, but did not totally destroy it. In 1924 the entire Labour cabinet signed and sent Carpenter an eightieth birthday card. In 1935 the late and much lamented Benny Rothman, a keen direct actionist and Communist Party member, led the Kinder Scout trespass that called for the British countryside to be opened up to working-class walkers and climbers.[43] Fifty years later he spoke on a particularly anarchic rally at Twyford Down to urge direct action against the road builders.[44] During the 1940s, the Commonwealth Party under Richard Acland campaigned for democratic socialism and conservation.[45] The late 1940s is still distantly remembered by some as a green era of squatting and community gardening. After 1956 a wave of disillusioned Marxists left the CPGB in the wake of the Soviet tanks going into Hungary and formed the first British New Left. Most notably we have the late Edward Thompson, the most famous of Britain's Marxist historians, who did so much to reawaken interest in William Morris. By the 1970s we have the Socialist Environment and Resources Association (SERA), which reproduced the work of Morris, Thompson and Raymond Williams, and in turn fuelled the municipal ecosocialism of the Greater London Council of the early 1980s.[46]

Like RTS, many of these diverse ecosocialist figures have emphasized art as a source of revolution, which is the point at which, after a rather long break, we must formally reintroduce our ailing Soviet nicotine addict. Anti-capitalism has its limits, as we noted at the start; it is often far from antagonistic to capital! In turn, protest policing has made it difficult to recreate the carnival. Equally, RTS has been riven by organizational difficulties and the movement has been appropriated to an extent by less radical and imaginative forces. Yet RTS's use of carnival provides a source of inspiration for struggle that at best prefigures future dialogue and at worst thumbs a nose at apocalypse, sterility and silence.

# 6

# Activist Networks in the UK: Mapping the Build-Up to the Anti-Globalization Movement

## Alexandra Plows

> Lots of these different groups which are portrayed within the media as
> single-issue groups, actually are all about capitalism. Actually you
> can't just sum it up in that word – it's this whole system and mindset
> which is fucking up the planet. And it's bigger than any single-issue
> thing, we need to show that we are in communication and all of these
> issues are linked up . . .[1]

## 2001

We are in north Wales. Environmental activists, Kurdish dancers and
members of the Welsh Language Society form a heterogeneous mass,
marking the fortieth anniversary of the creation of a huge dam (Treweryn)
that swept away a local village. The demonstration is also part of the Illisu
Dam campaign run from Oxford, which seeks to prevent the construction
of a similar dam in a Kurdish area of Turkey.

We are outside the fence at Campsfield, a centre for asylum seekers in
rural Oxford. Local greens, anarchists and animal rights activists are incorporated in the monthly demonstration against racist asylum laws. In
the verdant countryside, a prison surrounded by bales of razor wire, security cameras and high fences acts as a holding centre. An American
socialist is talking about marching on the IMF meeting in Prague during
the previous week.

We are in a pub in central London. An ecology graduate and member of
a West of England Earth First! (EF!) group talks of travelling to Brazil
and Geneva to organize anti-capitalist actions involving hundreds of
people worldwide.

We are back in north Wales. EF!ers have just pelted the Development

Minister, Clare Short, with custard pies after her speech on 'making globalization work for the world's poor'.

We are in Manchester. It is May Day 2001 and the police in large numbers are enclosing a group of about 60 activists who are attempting to protest vibrantly against capitalism as part of an international day of action.

# Introduction

This chapter maps what is already part of movement history, albeit an ongoing one. It does not discuss the protests *per se*, but rather sets the scene, tracing the roots of the massive international mobilizations against global capitalism at the turn of the millennium. It does so by examining the UK legacy of previous activist generations, and the complex tangle of a wide variety of current activist networks which provided the discourses, action strategies and – crucially – the people, that formed the base to launch the protests on the streets of London, Seattle, Prague, Gothenburg, Genoa and Evian. The snapshots of action above illustrate that resistance to globalization at grassroots level is multifaceted; activism around issues such as road construction, genetics and capitalism, which is here termed 'environmental direct action' (EDA) as a rough shorthand, is based on loose but dynamic networks rather than formal organizations. In turn, such networks blend together with, and become, other mobilizations and movements. This is the process that has spawned the anti-globalization movement.

The data discussed in this chapter come primarily[2] from a project comparing networks of EDA in three areas in Britain – Manchester, Oxford and north Wales[3] – using participant observation, in-depth interviews and historical analysis of movement documents, including non-violent direct action journals such as *Peace News* and local news letters. This research highlights that pre-existing EDA networks have been crucial to recent anti-globalization mobilizations. The ethnographic examples of UK action, primarily, though not exclusively, focused on the case study areas, give a sense of the complexity of resistance. These snapshots do not, of course, map or explain the anti-globalization mobilizations in full – this is a micro study – but they can highlight the sorts of process, the latent networks and the myriad actions that underlie global protest.

What is significant and new about recent protests is the acceleration of explicit anti-capitalist discourse and actions that increasingly aim to highlight the links between issues and campaigns, symbiotically connected to the rapid acceleration of international protests targeting the 'heart of the beast' – the WTO, G8, etc. Here the significance of previous networks to contemporary struggle is illustrated, showing how networks engage in collective capacity building and identity construction.[4] Further, the chapter highlights how external factors such as the Internet, global environmental problems and the drive to neoliberalism have accelerated activist network formation and mobilizations. All of these themes have been key in producing another notable aspect of the anti-globalization movement: the range, and diversity, of social actors who have come together in (biodegradable) coalitions to demonstrate that they share the same struggle.

To set the scene, the waves of direct action in the 1980s are outlined below to highlight how repertoires of action have diffused down from previous activist generations as successions of movements, networks and actions have cross-pollinated each other. Attention is then given to the more recent direct action mobilizations of the 1990s, which more directly gave birth to the explicitly anti-capitalist and anti-globalization agenda and action from 1998 onwards. The second half of the chapter uses the case studies of local areas to discuss, in a 'micro' context, some of the key issues that have triggered and come to characterize anti-globalization protests, such as the tendency for other social groups, and other campaign networks, readily to join in coalition activity with more 'radical' activist groupings, to demonstrate their opposition.

# The 1980s

> The world we live in, the oppressions we suffer and perpetuate, are phenomenally complex. Class, feminist, race, anarchist and third-world experience and analyses of oppression are all valuable. The oppressions they name and seek to overturn interconnect and mutually reinforce . . . The struggle is at least as complex as the oppressions themselves. One potentially creative and constructive antidote is to form coalitions with those groups whose aims and methods we roughly share . . .[5]

Written as commentary on the UK Stop the City protests in 1984, this editorial could have been taken from recent communiqués from People's Global Action (PGA). The 1983–4 Stop the City events in London and elsewhere, like their counterparts nearly 20 years later, came out of a sustained wave of movement action. Throughout the 1970s and 1980s, the focus for non-violent direct action (NVDA) in the UK was the peace/anti-nuclear movement. In the late 1970s direct action was used to try to prevent the construction of nuclear power stations.[6] These activists against nuclear power helped enrich a renewed campaign against nuclear weapons bases. There were protest camps at Greenham Common, Molesworth, Menwith Hill and other military bases across the UK. Rallies and occupations attracted thousands of people. Discourses on arms sales, the relationship between the USA and the UK, and the legitimacy of nuclear weapons melded with those on human rights and the environment. Connections were made between these issues at an ethical level (oppression, injustice) and also by tracing cause and effect, the role of particular companies and governments, and the movement of capital, leaving snail tracks across all these 'single issues'. The way demonstrations and protest camps were policed triggered discussions on violence and the imbalance of power, and shaped the way activists took action, strategically and tactically.

Interviews with activists from the 1980s have highlighted other key events, actions and discourses shaping UK action. Many were involved with providing support for the miners' strike.

> What really did hit us in March 84 was the miners' strike . . . quite soon into the strike the Neath, Dulais and Swansea Valley Support Group sent people up to this area; they picketed Wylfa [nuclear power station]. I think some Cymdeithas y Iaith [the Welsh Language Society] people first got in touch with them because they went to see them on the picket line and links were made there . . . Again you have the same sort of network that was working with CND, those type of people, you had some people in Bangor, there was quite a strong socialist society at the time . . . there were some Cymdeithas people involved in that . . .[7]

The Economic and Social Research Council (ESRC) research comparing activist networks in three distinct geographical areas has highlighted how local opportunities and circumstances shape the nature and type of political action engaged with. In the example above, it can be seen how in north Wales the NVDA of Cymdeithas y Iaith provided key network crossover, sharing discourses and action strategies with other movements. Then as now, the cross-fertilization of campaigns resulted in biodegradable coalitions that could arise over specific issues (Greenham Common, the miners' strike), strengthening social ties between groups and an appreciation of common themes amongst campaigners. Whilst the influence of Cymdeithas is a geographically specific factor that may not be generalized to UK activism as a whole, it serves as a key example of precisely how campaigns on peace, socialist and human rights, feminist issues, anti-nuclear power, etc. diffuse and deepen their discourses and action strategies. Opposition to Thatcher, unsurprisingly, is another key reference point for 1980s activists. The privatization of public services, a key tenet of the Thatcher project, has continued to be a focus for activist opposition, especially given the escalation of the mandates of GATT (now the WTO).

In England, and in particular the south-west, the clampdown on New Age Travellers (the 'peace convoy') added a further dimension to NVDA in the 1980s. The crossover between traveller lifestyles and the peace camps was considerable and the police violence towards Travellers was seen in activist networks as part of a continuum with the policing of miners and peace camp dwellers. Explicitly international dimensions to 1980s protest included Nicaragua Solidarity and anti-apartheid campaigns. All of these and other issues were disseminated through activist publications, the national media and the learning curves experienced by individual activists taking action and engaging in movement discourses.

## The 1990s

> What we're tackling is so enormous, we're tackling the way the whole world is run, and that's something we have become more aware of . . . You know, a few years ago at the EF! gathering we might be sitting down and discussing how we could challenge the government's road programme – that doesn't happen so much now, people are much more explicit that we're tackling an enormous problem . . .[8]

Interviews and participant observation with current activists highlight that many have links with 1980s campaigners. Some current activists were taken to peace camps by their parents; others simply have strong memories of seeing the miners' strike, Greenham Common and Greenpeace ships on the television. Protests and discourses during the 1980s had diffused into popular consciousness, with postcards of the *Rainbow Warrior* or ones proclaiming 'Think global, act local!' stuck up in kitchens around the country. Tactics and strategies from peace movement camps diffused down into the next wave of protest activity – the road protests of the early and mid-1990s. This was also a time of new energy and ideas, particularly the influence of US Earth First! (EF!) on the new generation of UK activists. UK EF! was kick-started in 1991, more or less coinciding with the first road protest at Twyford Down. The environment (and in particular at the start of the 1990s, post-Rio, global warming and related issues) replaced peace issues as the key action trigger, though peace action, against arms sales and nuclear bases, continued and was revitalized by the new activist generation. Again, it should be emphasized that the categorization of movement waves into (for example) 'peace' and 'the environment' is an over-simplification.

The first EF! national actions were rainforest action related, with mass demonstrations outside hardwood importers; super quarries in the UK, such as Whatley Quarry, were also the site of mass actions. Activists stopping the bulldozers at Twyford Down, Newbury and other road protests quickly became aware of how the construction companies they were opposing were linked to environmentally destructive construction projects globally. More recently, activists targeted Balfour Beatty (a major UK British road builder) because of its construction role in the Turkish Illisu Dam. The Oxford-based Corporate Watch keeps track of such multinational corporations (MNCs), charting their vested interests, and their effects, across the globe.

Activists were also quick to link the environmental destruction, population displacement and human rights abuses caused by oil drilling in Nigeria, Columbia and elsewhere to their opposition to road building. Road protesters thus targeted (as they continue to target) companies like Shell Oil, holding forecourt blockades and disrupting annual general meetings (AGMs). Examining the operations of MNCs again highlighted how international monetary policy was contributing to enable and actively promote the plundering of natural resources globally. The tangled web of IMF loans linked to, for example, mining/resource extraction by RTZ was traced back home to the UK, where activists targeted involved companies and highlighted the connections between issues. Solidarity with indigenous struggles worldwide has been a key theme in 1990s EDA.

As mentioned briefly above, arms sales continue to be a target for current EDA activists, building directly on earlier peace networks which are still active, such as the Campaign Against the Arms Trade. The human rights abuses perpetrated in Tibet and East Timor, for example, are causes championed by UK activists, who highlight the role of the UK government and UK companies in providing military hardware and weapons of torture for military dictatorships. When I first gave a version of this paper at a conference in Helsinki in summer 2001, I highlighted that local groups of UK activists were preparing for a four-day protest at an arms fair (DSEI – the largest in Europe) in London in September 2001; a bitter irony that the first day of DSEI would be the infamous 9/11. The shared discourses of the EDA, anti-globalization and peace movements – literally the same people in many cases – around arms sales, the mandates of global capitalism fuelling the oil economy and the attendant human rights, environmental and peace issues, have been well established.[9] These issues are returned to in the conclusion of this chapter. As before, such discourses were disseminated and strengthened through underground publications – for example, the EF! *Action Update* (AU) – as well as gatherings, workshops and interaction on actions and protest camps.

By the late 1990s there had been a decline in the number of road protest camps, and opposition to genetically modified organisms (GMOs) replaced transport as a major national focus for direct action. Activists had woken up to the growing role of the WTO, trade agreements, patenting/TRIPS (trade-related intellectual property rights), etc. as MNCs pushed their agenda further. In this global context, GM issues have been very closely linked to globalization in activist discourse. Thus, for example, the patenting of the Basmati rice gene, opposition in India to the commercial growing of crops, the roles of companies such as Aventis and Monsanto, and the influence they have on WTO policy committees, are standard activist reasons for opposition to GMO together with more standard opposition to GMOs on health and environmental grounds. The *explicit*[10] linking of a 'single issue' – GM crops – to issues of globalized economic structures highlights a significant step in the movement's 'cognitive praxis'.[11] Previously, such connections would have formed a more implicit part of activist discourse when explaining their opposition to specific issues. It is a feature of protest from the late 1990s onwards that campaigners strive to articulate the bigger picture as an integral part of their campaigns. Simultaneously, there appears to be more of a focus on common bond coalitions, the coming together of interconnected groups and campaigns over specific issues. Whilst coalitions are in themselves nothing new (see 1980s action above), the underlying theme being constantly made explicit, that globalization mechanisms are the common enemy, signifies a new dimension to activist resistance. But whilst global market mechanisms were targeted in the 1980s (via the Stop the City and other similar protests), it is with the rise of the WTO and other free market agents' powers and agendas that activist discourse and action has gathered shape and pace. While this is not the place to theorize changes in contemporary capitalism, it is clear that activists react to the changing shape of capitalism, and strategize accordingly.

# Consolidating a decade of activity: J18

Anti-capitalist activity was already a significant force in 1998, when anti-WTO and anti-G8 protests occurred in Geneva and Birmingham.[12] These actions helped build capacity for the better-known, and better-attended, protests of 18 June 1999 in London. Whilst this was not the first specifically anti-globalization mass mobilization in the UK or internationally, J18 benchmarked a moment in the development of EDA discourse and strategies. We can get a sense of the diversity and scale of 1990s protest, just before the J18 anti-capitalist action in 1999, by examining the contents of that month's EF! *Action Update*:[13] nine GM test sites were reported as destroyed in one night. A GM 'crop squat' in Norfolk took place with Indian farmers from the 'Intercontinental Caravan' present. Biotech company AstraZeneca's AGM was disrupted. Last-minute details of the 18 June 'Carnival against Capitalism' protest in the City of London were given. Cycle 'critical masses' took place in Norwich and other towns nationwide. URGENT, a coordinating network for the many anti-greenfield housing campaigns, advertised an action. Faslane peace camp had two 'very successful' actions against the Trident submarines. A mass direct action at the Valley D'Aspe road scheme in the Pyrenees was reported. Leeds protestors targeted Tesco on several occasions over GM food. Activists in Sheffield held a series of 'hit and run' mini-actions on one day, targeting a BP garage, a 'cat torturer', a Shell garage, Reed Employment Agency, Midland Bank and McDonald's. A squatted church in Leeds – 'A-Spire autonomous zone' – was evicted. A mini 'opencast mine' was opened by opencast protestors inside the Millennium Dome. A new road camp was set up in Essex. There was news from other protest camps – the Birmingham Northern Relief Road, Arthur's Wood at Manchester Airport, the Avon Ring Road. Tarmac's AGM in Birmingham was disrupted. Proactive actions, such as 'Diggers' land reclamations, permaculture courses, people growing organic vegetables, being vegan, setting up food/land cooperatives and performing educational environmental theatre, are apparent too. All in all, this single snapshot from the *Action Update* gives some sense of the energy and activity of the EDA movement at this time. This is the more latent power-base of a myriad campaigns and networks out of which the international anti-globalization actions were launched.

# Assessing the contribution of grassroots activist networks in the UK

> We now call for sympathetic communities, grassroots groups, and individuals around the world to organise their own autonomous actions, protests, and carnivals against the capitalist system on November 30th . . .[14]

Some more specific detail about some of these local and/or 'single-issue'[15] networks is given in the following sections. Schlosberg, discussing environmental justice networks in the USA, argues that such loose, heterogeneous and informal radicalism provides flexibility, mirrors a capitalism that is also increasingly de-centred and is prefigurative of a more just and democratic society.[16] In this context, it is significant that People's Global Action (PGA) emphasizes the need to develop grassroots resistance at a local level. Demonstrating resistance in the streets of Gothenburg and Genoa is vital, but the counterpoint to this is the hard work of making the framing discourses behind such protests relevant in local-level demonstrations against the privatization of public services, or emphasizing the WTO's potential role in social and environmental dumping.

It is possible that in the long term, the strength of the international protests will be revitalization of and increased networking between the multiple grassroots campaigns around the globe. Whilst the PGA, for example, indisputably consists partially of key figures who are forging links and helping to coordinate resistance internationally, its strength also lies as a networking tool, an information and contact point for activists worldwide. An explosion in online networking is enabling geographically distanced activists to interact and exchange information and ideas on an unprecedented scale, and the PGA e-mail lists and website are one part of a rash of e-groups and connected Internet sites where online activists are interacting. As with the continuity of ideas and discourses inherited from previous activist generations, the interaction on the Internet is an extension of what has been happening in the movement for years, albeit more slowly and with less scope, through workshops, gatherings and underground publications produced by this prolific movement.

## Local opposition – global implications

> Local grassroots campaigning, explaining to people what the issues are, shoring up support in our communities, explaining (for example) the connections between bad bus services, privatization and GATT, we do this a lot and we need to do more of it. We need to redouble our efforts to contextualize the global locally, otherwise people will feel increasingly disconnected from what we are doing and why. We recently had an action at Bangor McDonald's making the links between McDonald's, MNCs, agribusiness, globalization, the WTO, and promoting local production as the sustainable alternative . . .[17]

The global implications of local protests have been an implicit feature of the movement over many years. That these connections are now often explicitly made the central focus of protest is the end result partially of years of collective capacity building, partially of the impetus provided by events themselves. The e-mail above, like the examples of action given at the start of this chapter, highlights the diversity of activist resistance to globalization. Local environmental activists in the research project's three areas of study – Manchester, north Wales and Bangor – have been strongly involved in global resistance to capitalism at a local as well as a national level.

The research has also highlighted that from the mid-1990s onwards,[18] the EDA movement consciously made an effort to build up grassroots community resistance and proactive projects, partially in recognition of the limitations of maintaining high-cost national protest camps. Such projects were (and are) also a contact point for activist groups like EF! who, due to worries about security, are often hard to locate. 'Squat cafés', such as the Anarchist Teapot in Brighton, were opened.

> I think that we also need to keep our feet on the ground and be involved in things that are bringing about change in communities . . . say, a squat café, where we only serve food that is GE free, and having lots of information, having talks, having videos about GE, saying this is why we're doing this, and giving people a very gentle way into it, showing them a whole spectrum of things they can do in their own lives. The number of squat cafés and social centres is rocketing; people are getting really into doing those sorts of community actions . . .[19]

Activists who have successfully attracted over £1 million of funding to promote community regeneration and sustainable development set up the

Manchester Environmental Resources Association Initiative (MERCI) centre in Manchester. These activists are simultaneously involved in direct action that is more confrontational locally, nationally and internationally. It is precisely this more hidden picture of activity at a local level, and the conventional nature of much of this submerged activity (meetings with local councillors, funding bids, etc.), which currently needs emphasizing, given the tendency of the media to paint one-dimensional pictures of activist resistance in terms of 'violent black-clad eco-terrorists and anarchists' on the streets of Genoa.

Arising out of this perceived need to conceptualize the global locally, activists have organized solidarity actions in their local area during global days of action. On 30 November 1999 (N30 Seattle) there were several solidarity actions around the UK (see the appendix), including actions in the three case study areas. A Lloyds Bank was occupied and shut down by 50 EF! activists in Manchester. A rally was organized in Oxford, and other activists travelled to London for another N30 protest. In Bangor, north Wales, a coalition of groups including EF!, Plaid Cymru, Cymdeithas yr Iaith and NGOs such as Christian Aid held a colourful protest march in the High Street. The leaflets on the Bangor demonstration made the connections to events in Seattle and highlighted how globalization affected people in Wales. All these locally based actions were networked on activist e-mail lists and websites along with dozens of other solidarity actions across the globe. In all three case study areas there were many activists who had travelled to – and helped to organize – international protests. To paraphrase a Greenham Common slogan, 'Seattle was everywhere.'[20]

# Loose coalitions, biodegradable networks, other voices: the alliance patterns of the anti-globalization protests

The nature and scope of activist alliances is perhaps the most notable aspect of the anti-globalization mobilizations, whether at local, national or international level. Alliances at a local level as well as at an international level are affected by a number of variables, notably political opportunities,[21] the issues at stake, geography, previous political cleavages and actor agency. At the time of study, among the three case study areas north Wales had the most obviously diverse alliance patterns, with many 'weak ties' links to more conventional actors such as NGOs. Here the pattern of coalitions and demonstrations, with more conventional actors and campaigns demonstrating resistance to the WTO, is similar in substance, if not in scale, to the coalitions of radical and conventional actors that have characterized Seattle and similar protests.

Sustained participant observation in north Wales highlighted that local activists (Gwynedd and Mon EF!) had been proactively working to attract a range of allies. At the same time, other groups have been far more likely to frame their grievances centrally in terms of global capitalism. Equally, ranges of issues during a single protest event are dealt with to cement alliances and provide an anti-capitalist bridge between network frames. Thus the Welsh anniversary demonstration in 2001 over the building of the Treweryn Dam was used as an opportunity to highlight Welsh language and community issues together with support for the Illisu Dam campaign, and raised a myriad issues: human rights, environmental damage, the economic mandate pushing the dam, the World Bank, etc. A demonstration at McDonald's in Bangor, organized by EF! in 2001, had local farmers attending and Cymdeithas y Iaith support. The Welsh nationalist community has increasingly come to see the globalization of economic forces and institutions as a threat to the sustainability of their culture and environment, and EF! activists have been quick to make links. Bringing together all groups and individuals opposing and suffering from the effects of globalization and/or making the global connections between local protests on planning issues, public transport, etc. is an articulated goal of north Wales activists. Many social theorists, including Foucault, suggest that power can be conceptualized as a network – a contention 'illustrated most forcefully by the fact that most local environmental justice organisations may begin with a single issue in mind, but most often begin to relate issues and various forms of domination'.[22]

Whilst these loose networks are highly conducive to the diffusion of information, resources and tactical repertoires, leading to an uptake in mobilization,[23] diversity can also lead to contradictions that are potentially both productive and a source of conflict. At Genoa, NGOs condemned violent activists, and Black Bloc anarchists came into conflict with the moderate Ya Basta. In the case study localities, such tensions are also apparent. When UK Development Minister, Clare Short, was custard pied during a visit to Bangor in March 2001, the action shocked many of the NGO groups that Gwynedd and Mon EF! had been forging ties with. The limits of alliance-based protests (at a local level, at least) for activists are simply that such actions tend on the whole to be 'safe', having networking and the realization of commonly held critiques as the primary end goals. The more radical actions associated with EF! are harder to initiate when working with conventional partners, which is possibly why, in areas such as Manchester, where the radical activist community is large enough to mobilize on its own, such coalitions are rare.

Without going too far outside the remit of this chapter, the parallels with events on the international stage can be made. The tensions caused by the violent[24] tactics of individuals or groups within loose coalitions are a strategic problem for those helping to organize, or attending, anti-globalization actions in Prague, Genoa and elsewhere. It is a credit to those involved that these international alliances have so far resisted impulses to fracture permanently. It may well be that the death of Carlo Giuliani during the Genoa protests will shore up a commitment to non-violent (but proactive) protest; or conversely, these alliances may degrade, leaving a more hard core of radical actors to carry on mobilizing. The many issues, pros and cons surrounding the variety of alliances at local, national and international level could form a chapter in themselves; to summarize, the biodegradability of these alliances – the shape and nature of the EDA movement – allows for rapid change. If it is not working, the energy driving these network patterns will dissipate and move on.[25]

# Triggers for alliances

The study of UK EDAs suggests that radical actors tend to have many more ties to conventional actors, actions and strategies than might appear,[26] and that conventional actors and NGOs, in particular Third World-focused charities such as Christian Aid and Oxfam, correspondingly have an (apparently increased) radical agenda and are prepared to form coalitions in some cases. Clearly there is much action being taken at a local level with a range of actors, arising from the simple fact that there are a massive number of groups of people – public sector workers, people using these services, and so on – who are being hit by the accelerated knock-on effects of the neoliberal economic agenda.

In the UK, the threat posed to working conditions by the WTO has been one trigger leading to a revitalization of the 'Old Left', with disparate strands united in opposition to the agenda set by globalization. The Private Finance Initiative (PFI) and foundation hospitals, in essence the internalization of private market mechanisms into public health, a diffusion down of WTO mandates, have triggered not only hard-line union opposition but also sustained – and successful – opposition within the heart of the Labour Party.[27] At Prague, a number of anti-IMF activists, including the former Czech Communist Party, organized actions. Revolution, the youth group of Workers' Power, also promoted the May Day 2001 action. Unions in the USA were key players in the Seattle protests.

Interaction between social movement actors and the *organised* 'Old Left' is seen as extremely problematic by many in the UK EDA movement, who feel that the Socialist Alliance-driven Globalise Resistance is a front for their own political goals, rather than a genuine social movement for grassroots change.[28] I would agree with this analysis. However, overall it is significant that mobilization has been triggered in this group of actors, and as a whole the anti-globalization movement has been strengthened by the fact that other groups outside the EDA movement, such as workers in the public sector, are also opposing these mechanisms. It has been a strongly articulated argument within the radical activist movement that the support of civil society is necessary for there to be sustained change. There is evidence that this is happening.

Again in the UK, there was some evidence during the research that farmers are also starting to make connections and perceive globalization as a threat. Jose Bove and Indian farmers opposing the growing of GM crops have, of course, already set the precedent. Farmers in the Third World have long opposed WTO and MNC involvement in agribusiness, and highlighted the detrimental effects on their livelihoods; it is possible that UK farmers may be catching up a little. Activists in Norwich invited the Intercontinental Caravan of farmers opposed to globalization to their GM 'crop squat' in 1999.[29] With motives and discourses similar to those used by north Wales activists, Norwich campaigners have organized weekend workshops, bringing together EDA actors and ordinary farmers. EDA activists and Greens have been attempting to win over farmers[30] to their cause by highlighting the importance of sustainable farming methods and systems over agribusiness. Oxford-based networks such as Pruning Hooks and Rural Futures have arisen to network information to farmers and make the links between green arguments and the farming crisis, combining such discourses with critiques of WTO policy. As evidenced earlier, activists in north Wales have been successful in creating 'weak ties' links to the farming community, where small sheep farmers have been hard hit by the farming crisis. Nationally, organic and small farmers have been quick to join such coalitions; the harder task is to convince the farming community as a whole. As the recent UK fuel protests have shown,[31] farmers are a potent force if mobilized; it remains to be seen to what extent they are prepared to break with tradition and work with new allies. As Melucci has long argued, movements continually negotiate their identities, even when they apparently stride on the world stage to make history.[32] The diversity of the new anti-capitalism, as reflected in the micro study of local EDA networks in the UK, enhances such an emphasis. Farmers, the 'Old Left' and conventional NGOs are just three examples of the way in which civil society groupings have joined in with radical activist discourse, and often action, to oppose neoliberalism.

The many tensions which are ingrained within these coalitions, in particular the likelihood that such 'weak ties' links will often contain elements – frames, long-term strategies for change, prejudices[33] and so on – which run contrary to the more sustained radical critique and tactics of the direct action movement, will have to be, as Melucci puts it, 'negotiated'. This is possibly the greatest challenge currently facing the direct action movement – whether to dissolve these ties, postpone the moment of action that coalesced divergent groups, and focus again on taking radical action within a core 'strong ties' base, or to try to work through the difficulties of working in 'weak ties' networks in the medium to long term. My suspicions are that movement 'biodegradability' will provide the answer, as it has in the past.[34]

# Sources of accelerated global protest

The evidence given in previous sections indicates that activism over several decades, in local towns and cities, on a huge variety of interlinked single issues, has involved movement capacity building. Thus, the diffusion of activist repertoires and discourses via the cross-fertilization of networks and movements has contributed to UK involvement in the current wave of anti-globalization. Beyond the teargas-filled streets of Gothenburg and Genoa, it is the local grassroots networks and single-issue campaigns that continue to provide the substantive weight of UK movement action and discourse. That these campaigns and networks tend nowadays explicitly to emphasize the global implications of their protests and the interconnectedness of many issues (through cross-movement actions and alliances, for example) is in no small way due to decades of activist diffusion, the learning curve of an ever-changing movement.

In turn, other significant factors have accelerated anti-globalization protests both in the UK and internationally. Movements in other countries have been engaged on similar cognitive and strategic journeys, for example, and their contributions to anti-neoliberalist discourse and action, whilst outside the scope of this chapter, can at least be acknowledged in passing here.[35] Interaction between protestors worldwide and UK activists has, as highlighted in previous sections, been ongoing for decades. This section highlights several further sources of accelerated global direct action. Many of these issues have been mentioned in passing in previous sections – the increasing role of the Internet, the macro trigger of global political opportunities. Constraints of space mean that these factors are addressed in an overview fashion rather than being subject to in-depth analysis. Further, these are simply some key examples.

## Global implications of environmental problems

> We are absolutely, completely and utterly devastating the planet we live on . . . we're totally dazzled by capitalism running away with itself, technology too, and not thinking about the consequences which are exploitation and oppression and damage to the environment . . .[36]

Over the past few decades, environmental problems have come to be seen as global in nature. Problems such as low-level radiation, the greenhouse effect, the thinning ozone layer, loss of biodiversity and acid rain pollution know no state or sub-state boundaries. For activists worldwide, the potential for GMOs set free in the environment to alter the planet's genetic heritage in ways as yet undreamed of is one more nail in the coffin of an already (possibly irrevocably) damaged earth.

Environmental campaigners have long recognized the global implications of locally produced pollution. To take an example, following years of campaigning by different groups, the international community has woken up to the issue of global warming. The Rio Summit in 1991 addressed the issue, but despite pressure from environmental campaigners little has changed in terms of policy over the last decade, whilst in the same period the effects of global warming have become more widely felt. The Kyoto Accord is seen by campaigners as a minimal step in the right direction; however, radical activists remain sceptical about the implementation of its principles, pointing, for example, to continued road building, greenfield development and the underfunding of public transport in the UK as evidence of a 'business as usual' policy (again linking such discourses back to the development agenda set by MNCs).[37] The issue of carbon emissions was on the agenda during the UK road protest mobilizations of the early/mid-1990s, and there is evidence that similar networks are re-emerging, boosted in part, arguably, by intergovernmental accord on the issue. Other mobilization triggers include the revitalization of the road-building programme under New Labour, and worsening climatic conditions. In 2001, the Rising Tide network in the UK, coordinated by activists in Manchester and Oxford, undertook a series of actions focused on issues of public transport, global warming, etc.; local groups are encouraged to undertake their own actions, a standard being a mass non-payment of train fares, with a statement saying that for a 90 per cent reduction in carbon emissions to become possible, there should be a 90 per cent reduction in train fares. EF! groups in Manchester and north Wales had '90 per cent' actions. Such action networks have many direct links to 1990s anti-road protests.

Global warming is a good example of how globally perceived eco-risk can link campaigners, highlight links between geographically dispersed issues, and boost international understanding and action. Local pollution or resource extraction campaigns around the globe are perceived not just by activists, but increasingly by the general public, as affecting everybody's backyard. The ramifications of local pollution for the planet as a whole have been boosted by scientific research on cause and effect. The human fallout caused by 'natural' eco-disasters such as floods and landslides, linked to global warming and resource extraction issues, very quickly brings in other discourses on human rights, for example. Again, the interconnectedness of issues can be highlighted by campaigners.

## Global political opportunities: accelerated neoliberalist agenda

Activists from diverse groups and movements around the world are discussing, networking and organizing for an international day of action on November 30th. On this day, officials of 150 governments will meet in Seattle for the 3rd conference of the World Trade Organisation (WTO), at which they will decide on new policies that will further escalate the exploitation of our planet and its people by the global capitalist system. Thus there will be attempts to push through a new version of the Multilateral Agreement on Investment (MAI), strengthen intellectual property rights, and further neoliberalization through a new round of free trade talks.[38]

Capitalist accumulation has been seen as a significant source of both environmental and social problems increasingly supported by transnational companies and institutions. Institutions such as the European Union (EU) and the WTO see forms of environmental protection as potential barriers to free trade. The Single European Act of 1992, which was designed to create a single market, typically swept away the German beer purity laws that made it illegal to use a range of chemical additives in beverages. The WTO forced the EU in turn to import US beef despite the existence of growth hormones. US environmentalists have been horrified by the fact that Americans cannot reject imported shrimps from Asia caught with nets that trap endangered turtles. Free trade means more goods travelling long distances, leading to the creation of more pollution, and disrupting farmers and producers who use low technology and low environmental impact techniques. Increased trade competitively forces countries to lower standards of labour protection and leads to cultural homogenization. Free trade is seen to lead to the McDonaldization of the planet, with low wages, increased exploitation of nature and the death of cultural diversity. Privatization and TRIPS mechanisms are perceived as dispossessing millions of their heritage and shared resources.

Thus the expansion of neoliberalism through mechanisms such as the WTO has been the trigger for the recent wave of anti-globalization actions, with campaigners and affected groups across the globe coming together to demonstrate opposition to these policies. WTO and G8 summits, where such policies are made, are thus the primary target for internationally coordinated actions. There has long been an appreciation of how such mechanisms underpin the single issues with which the EDA movement is involved. As the WTO's mandate has grown, activists have kept up to speed with policy. Workshops at UK activist gatherings since the mid/late 1990s have included many briefings on WTO policy, with the accumulation of such knowledge being passed on to other activists. Such responses are clear examples of the process of movement cognitive praxis, and of the way global political opportunities trigger mobilization.[39]

There can be no doubt that power has been de-centred from the national state to some extent. At the very least, the global economic forces and institutions noted above mean that the global political opportunities are at least as significant as the national. 'Think globally, act globally' could be a genuinely new slogan of green social movements. Again, the UK EDA movement has boosted its own understanding of these issues through cross-movement networking with international campaigners. Similar patterns of activist responses will no doubt hold true for other countries, although it is outside the remit of this chapter to do more than highlight this here.[40]

A number of commentators have convincingly argued that neoliberal capitalist accumulation has progressively reduced state autonomy and restricted political opportunities at a national level. So to be effective, activists have had to exploit developing international political opportunities. The recent history of dramatic international protest from Seattle to Genoa shows the potency of such an approach.

## Accelerated IT communication

Activists worldwide are using e-mail and websites to plan actions, network information, and provide a space for activist discourse on a massive scale. During the Genoa protests, activist and alternative media websites provided up-to-date accounts of events on the streets, together with press releases, eyewitness accounts, etc. Similar sites were utilized during the J18 and Seattle protests. As discussed earlier, interaction between groups and individuals is not new; but the process has been radically speeded up and become more widely diffused through information technology. For those with access to IT and the resources to use it cheaply, communication and networking has drastically improved. It is possible to network information about actions worldwide, increasing activists' sense of connection. It has become cheaper and easier to plan and advertise actions. Activists can e-mail leaflet texts and accounts of local action, and advertise forthcoming events on websites and e-mail lists.

The Internet is thus a resource for activists and provides a crucial network base. Participant observation and research has highlighted how activists use the Internet as a discussion tool. Activist discourse on familiar themes – violence/non-violence, long-term strategies, firsthand accounts and arguments over the 'how and why' of political action – can all be found in new settings. Movement praxis is facilitated through instant communication between geographically dispersed actors. Gwynedd and Mon EF! set up two e-group chat lists in 2000, linking Welsh campaigners across the country. These lists have become a vital resource as activists across Wales network actions and discuss ideas. While information overload is a common problem for online activists, it is evident that IT has radically reshaped the opportunities and resources available to activists globally. It is hard to imagine how the anti-globalization protests would have fared without the input of IT; though it would be wrong to surmise, as the national media did, that these protests were solely triggered through online activity. Rather, pre-existing networks of activists used IT to mobilize a fast-expanding base of online potential activists.

# Conclusion

I wrote an earlier draft of this conclusion[41] as the USA and the UK were bombing Iraq; a move that seemed inevitable the moment the Florida chads made Bush president. This chapter has charted a recent movement history that has already been overlaid with memories of the many mobilizations post-9/11. To focus on more recent events briefly, it can be clearly seen how the 'movement of movements'[42] has continued to build capacity throughout this key period of history. The media claimed, post-9/11, that the anti-globalization movement was effectively silenced, as if being anti-capitalist made the movement pro-Osama. In Bangor, November 2001, an anti-WTO demonstration timed to coincide with the Qatar WTO conference was the biggest local anti-capitalist protest yet seen; speaker after speaker made the links between global capitalism, oil, arms sales and war – with the inevitable human and environmental fallout.

The anti-globalization discourses were galvanized post-9/11; never were these analyses more crucial to any discussion of a global peace. Peace, environmental and anti-capitalist protestors – again, the same people, the same networks, to a large degree – have come together to revitalize the peace movement, triggering the most incredible mobilizations of the general public in opposition to the Iraq war. Here we have true signs of a 'social movement society'[43] – not least in the form of the many thousands of schoolchildren skipping school to take part in demonstrations against war with Iraq, who learned on 9/11 that today's wars, today's deals, are part of what triggers tomorrow's terrorism. This is perhaps one of the positive effects of a globalized society – an increased sense of connection and global citizenship.

To summarize the main points of this chapter – opposition to globalization is not new; the networks of international activists seen on our television screens did not suddenly erupt from nowhere. Discourses and repertoires diffused downwards from previous movement cycles and across a series of contemporary networks as activists came together to oppose perceived global threats. Historical developments in terms of global ecology, global political economy and the work of generations of previous activists are accelerating novel features of old struggles for democracy, sustainability and social justice. These factors are not only galvanizing pre-existing activist networks, but are triggering new, and in some cases unusual, allies into action. Whether these strange bedfellow coalitions thrive or biodegrade, this is civil society (as well as social movements) engaged in capacity building – a process seeded by decades of direct action and radical discourses, which have stood the test of time.

This chapter has stayed deliberately focused on how, within the UK, local activist networks contributed to, and partially represent the make-up of, international mobilizations. The nature and focus of activist networks, and their 'road to Seattle', so to speak, will have been different in other countries, shaped by local and national political opportunities, geography and so on. Accordingly, I have not tried to present a coherent explanation of how the international anti-globalization movement came to be or what it is, but rather to shine a torch on some ethnography from within my own networks which attempt a local explanation for UK involvement and international interaction. That being said, perhaps people are not so different. Across the globe, accounts of actions, and stories of how communities of activists came into being, seem to have common elements. For me, one of the most inspiring parts of the anti-globalization movement was encountering the strong voices of other people who told me not only that we shared the same struggle, but that in our different ways, we were telling the same story about how we had come to be there.

# Appendix: 30 November 1999, UK (Seattle – N30 solidarity protests)

In Halifax a Nestlé factory is occupied and an anti-WTO banner is dropped outside; 16 are arrested. In Leeds city centre, around 50 protestors leaflet outside scummy companies. In Manchester, Lloyds Bank is occupied and shut down by 50 activists, who then proceed to block the street outside. A disused garage and an old Toll House, soon to be luxury apartments, have been squatted in Totnes, South Devon to draw local people's attention to the WTO. In Exeter a coalition of activists protest against the WTO and global capitalism. An anti-WTO procession marches through downtown Cardiff, Wales. In Bangor, north Wales, a coalition of groups hold a non-violent and colourful protest march in the high street.

London. In the morning people distribute leaflets and stickers designed to raise awareness of capitalism and the WTO. At noon, construction workers protest. Students picket a bank to highlight globalization-induced student loan debt. Nigerians and British environmentalists hold a street theatre 'People's Court'. A rally at 5:00 p.m. at Euston Station draws nearly two thousand people to support public transport workers and to highlight the links between the free trade agenda of the WTO and the privatization of public transport in the UK. There were also speakers covering a wide array of issues linked to the WTO and the system it governs. Afterwards, protestors make an attempt to block a busy intersection but confrontations with the police result in an overturned burning police van, 38 arrests, and several casualties. A pirate radio station replaces a yuppie one on 106.9 FM across London until it is shut down at 4:00 p.m.

From http://www.n30.org.

# 7

# Keyboard Protest: Hacktivist Spiders on the Web

## Paul A. Taylor

> The world-market [has] given a cosmopolitan character to production and consumption in every country . . . it has drawn from under the feet of industry the national ground on which it stood. Industries . . . no longer work up indigenous raw material, but raw material drawn from the remotest zones; industries whose products are consumed, not only at home, but in every quarter of the globe . . . And as in material production, so also in intellectual production. The intellectual creations of individual nations become common property. National one-sidedness and narrow-mindedness become more and more impossible, and from the numerous national and local literatures, there arises a world literature.
>
> Karl Marx and Frederick Engels[1]

Hacktivism refers to the phenomenon that has arisen in recent years of political protest that involves some of the techniques of hacking. It should be pointed out immediately that the term *hacking* is contestable. In recent times it has come to be predominantly associated with illicit computer intrusions when in fact the term has a much richer and more ambiguous history.[2] This chapter describes the way in which hacktivism has served to reclaim an original and relatively ignored aspect of hacking, namely its essential focus upon the ingenious reappropriation and re-engineering of *any* technology or system. Opening up the concept of hacking in this way allows us to see more clearly the continuity between hacking and hacktivism, and the evolution of the former to the technologically mediated political protest of the latter. As the above quotation from Marx implies, the nature of the global capitalist system is double-edged. On the one hand, its material productive ability assumes the status of a transnational power, but on the other hand, so does its intellectual production. The same capitalist circuits that circulate commodities can, in the true hacker style, be rejigged to circulate oppositional struggle. Hacktivism's close association with computing techniques assures it a global reach that offers the potential to turn it into an important element of the political world literature that Marx foresaw.

## Hacking – access is all and the loss of the hacker ethic

> All information should be free
> Mistrust Authority – Promote Decentralisation
> Hackers should be judged by their hacking, not bogus criteria such as degrees, age, race, or position.
> You can create art and beauty on a computer.
> Computers can change your life for the better.[3]

Whilst there are exceptions (for example, Abbie Hoffman's Techno-logical American Party (TAP) and the German hacker group Chaos Computer Club (CCC)), in general, early hacker culture was not noted for the outward-looking nature of its political values.[4] Levy produced the above quotation as part of the *hacker ethic* and it illustrates the tendency of hackers to privilege access to information and computing hardware above more focused political aims. There is also a strong tradition within the hacking community that 'true' hacking refers to a curious approach to technology in general rather than just a single particular artefact. This is important for our later consideration of hacktivism's origins in opposition to the capitalist system. The 'hack' represents an ingenious re-engineering of any technology or system so that it can be used in a way or for a purpose not anticipated by its original designers or subsequent owners.

Levy identified three main hacker generations:

1. *'True' hackers*: during the 1950s and 1960s, these were the pioneers of the earliest days of computing. They experimented with the capabilities of the room-filling mainframe computers of such US universities as MIT.
2. *Hardware hackers*: in the 1970s these were the innovators behind the development of the much smaller computers that made the personal computing revolution possible. They played a key role in bringing computing hardware to the people.
3. *Game hackers*: making use of the previous generation's hardware in-novations, in the 1980s these were the creators of popular software applications for gaming.[5]

A fuller schema of hacking's evolution[6] is obtained with addition of the following three generations:

4.  *Hacker/cracker*: from the mid-1980s to the present day, depending upon the perspective of the labeller, both these terms are used to describe a person who illicitly breaks into other people's computer systems.

5.  *Microserfs*: this is the phrase used in Douglas Coupland's novel of the same name,[7] to describe those programmers who, despite sharing the programming ingenuity of hackers, betrayed the 'information should be free' ethic in favour of the corporate structure of Microsoft.

6.  *Hacktivists*: from the mid-1990s, hacking techniques were adopted by groups with a more overtly political stance and often with close links to the anti-gobalization movement.

The various generations of hackers (but particularly the first two) have contained hackers who have applied their skills not only to a diverse range of artefacts (for example, model railways, parking meters and general electronics) but also to *systems* (phone phreaks and their love of the phone system were early precursors of hackers). Whilst, over time, hacking tended to get bogged down in technical minutiae, hacktivism has resurrected its concern with systems, particularly the overarching one of capitalism. To varying degrees, the first five of the above categories subscribed to the normative assertion of Levy's hacker ethic that 'all information should be free' and privileged the freedom of information above all else. Throughout the hacker generations, however, any aspirations that such freedom of information was a means for creating greater social liberation tended to be short lived. It was swamped either by a myopic fascination with technological means over social ends or by the inevitable profits to be made from information freely circulating within the confines of a profit-making capitalist system.

At times, early hacking culture and its precursors' technical obsessions provide vivid manifestations of the Frankfurt School's notion of instrumental reason[8] and the inherent inability to see beyond the technical particularities of the dominant system. Adorno, for example, scathingly describes the pathological, immature conformity and essential conservatism of the archetypal radio ham:

> At twenty, he is still at the stage of a boy scout working on complicated knots just to please his parents. This type is held in high esteem in radio matters. He patiently builds sets whose most important parts he must buy ready-made, and scans the air for shortwave secrets, though there are none. As a reader of Indian stories and travel books, he once discovered unknown lands and cleared his path through the forest primeval. As radio ham, he becomes the discoverer of just those industrial products which are interested in being discovered by him. He brings nothing home that would not be delivered to his house.[9]

The nadir of such conformity and conservatism is vividly described both in *Microserfs* – Douglas Coupland's 'factional' account of the workers at Microsoft's headquarters – and Paulina Boorsook's scathing account of techno-libertarian excesses in California's silicon valley. *Microserfs* describes 'the first full-scale integration of the corporate realm into the private'[10] and the alienating effects upon the individual and society that accompany the living out of the hacker's dream to be totally immersed in computer code. Ironically, Boorsook's non-fictional account is more dramatically judgemental and provides a contemporary update of Adorno's portrayal of the hacker as underdeveloped social animal:

> the most virulent form of philosophical technolibertarianism is a kind of scary, psychologically brittle, prepolitical autism. It bespeaks a lack of human connection and a discomfort with the core of what many of us consider it means to be human. It's an inability to reconcile the demands of being an individual with the demands of participating in society, which coincides beautifully with a preference for, and glorification of, being the solo commander of one's computer in lieu of any other economically viable behavior. Computers are so much more rule-based, controllable, fixable, and comprehensible than any human will ever be. As many political schools of thought do, these techno-libertarians make a philosophy out of a personality defect.[11]

The above examples of hackers' absorption within the system show how the counter-cultural promise of the originally subversive *hack* have been lost in hackers' inability to gain a critical distance from the artefacts and over-arching systems they manipulate. From this perspective, rather than representing a deviation from hacking's core activities, hacktivism marks a return to its purest concern of ingenious reappropriation and re-engineering. In contrast to the tendency of hackers to adopt an access-is-all attitude that produces a much more heavily circumscribed, instrumental and apolitical mindset, the hacktivist movement has no such ends–means confusion. Its *raison d'être* is based upon the ingenious use of various artefacts and systems for a political purpose. The key significance of hacktivism is thus the unique manner in which it seeks to draw upon a conventional tradition of political resistance using new technology-based techniques. It does so in order to reassert counter-cultural values in the face of the pervasive and invasive commodified values of the global economic order.

# Hacktivism

> The vocabulary of resistance must be expanded to include means of electronic disturbance. Just as authority located in the street was once

met by demonstrations and barricades, the authority that locates itself in the electronic field must be met with electronic resistance.[12]

Hacktivism has two main forms: direct online action and satirical performance.

## Direct online action

In what can be termed a form of anti-capitalist ju-jitsu, rather than just merely railing against the iniquities of 'the system', hacktivists have taken a much more proactive approach by asserting themselves both within and by means of the same system they oppose. Two hacktivist groups exemplify this particular form of anti-capitalist resistance. In 1998 the Electronic Disturbance Theatre (EDT) coordinated a series of web sit-ins in support of the Mexican anti-government group, the Zapatistas. They transformed traditional forms of civil disobedience such as peaceful sit-ins into new forms of *electronic civil disobedience*. One of their most notable performances was the use of an automated piece of software revealingly called *Flood Net*. When this piece of software is downloaded on a user's computer, it connects the surfer to a pre-selected website, and every seven seconds the reload button of that site is automatically activated. The combined effect of such a large number of activists using *Flood Net* all on the same day can significantly disrupt the operations of a particular targeted server. The second group, ®™ark, used similar techniques in the etoy campaign of 1999. This campaign took the form of a hacktivist action to object to a commercial company's attempt to remove an art collective's website domain name through the court system just because of its similarity to the company's own name eToys.[13] 'The Brent Spar of e-commerce', as it was called,[14] combined Internet and media public relations stunts that eventually forced the company to retreat from its original, litigious position. By means of its action, ®™ark effectively *hacked* the stock-market and corporate public relations systems. The result was a 70% decline in the company's NASDAQ stock value.

## Satirical performance

The second form of hacktivist reclamation of the hacker ethic, *satirical performance*, seeks to reappropriate the notion of performance and return an element of the dramatic to its now largely commodified status. Such an aim is explicit from the names of such groups as the Electronic Disturbance *Theatre* and the actions of such groups as the Yes Men and their various satirical attacks upon the ethos of the World Trade Organization.[15] If sufficiently subversive and thought-provoking, the advantage of such drama-informed protest is that it tends to be less easily co-opted back into the society of commodified spectacle that it is protesting against. The performative element of hacktivist actions is designed to parody and provoke, to the extent that it becomes more difficult subsequently to gloss over the political point being made.

In their different ways, both approaches undermine the passive reception of capitalist messages. Direct online action consciously eschews the technical methods that would allow one single skilled hacker to cause disruption, in favour of technically unsophisticated but labour-intensive actions that require mass solidarity. Satirical performances, meanwhile, are in keeping with Baudrillard's claim that 'The symbolic consists precisely in breaching the univocality of the "message," in restoring the ambivalence of meaning and in demolishing in the same stroke the agency of code.'[16] It is to specific examples of this promotion of ambivalence and the destruction of code that we now turn.

# ®™ark and 'performance stocks'

> ®™ark felt it had to offer, perceptually if not actually, an alternative to the endless flow of bounty provided by the stock market. Much as the National Endowment for the Arts, even with its slim offerings, provided the illusion of an alternative to corporate systems – an illusion more important than the actual sums (and which has now vanished, along with the NEA's influence) – ®™ark hoped to provide a similar illusory but conceptually powerful alternative to the 'bottom line' of corporate power.[17]

Whilst at times engaging in mass action (such as the previously cited etoy campaign), the hacktivist group ®™ark tends to concentrate upon the satirical performance element of hacktivism by promoting anti-capitalist projects based upon an imitation of the stock-market model.[18] Typical examples include the setting up of a website entitled Voteauction.com. This acted as a clearing site purporting to buy votes from people in order to highlight the democratic deficit in the USA and the everyday corporate-sponsored buying of votes that takes place in less overt but nevertheless effective forms. Other projects involved the setting up of a fake WTO site in order to satirize the organization's aggressive free trade stance. Finally, the group funded the Barbie Liberation Organization, which switched the voice boxes in 300 Talking Barbie dolls and Talking GI Joe dolls during the 1989 Christmas period to highlight the issue of gender-based stereotyping in children's toys.

®™ark's projects are designed with four key elements: worker, sponsor, product and idea: '®™ark is a system of workers, ideas, and money whose function is to encourage the intelligent sabotage of mass-produced items . . . ®™ark is essentially a matchmaker and bank, helping groups or individuals fund sabotage projects.'[19] With its aim of 'intelligent sabotage' the group manifests aspects of the original 'hack', but by focusing such sabotage against mass-produced items, and by extension the system that produces them, it is overtly and intrinsically political. In *Understanding Media*,[20] McLuhan uses the myth of Narcissus to describe the numbing effect of modern media, whilst in *The Society of the Spectacle*,[21] Debord describes the pervasion of spectacular commodity values throughout society. ®™ark recognizes the mutually reinforcing effects of both the narcotic media and a social environment saturated with consumption. It refers to the way in which aesthetics have been transformed by corporate capitalism into a commodity-based *anaesthetic*. To counter such anaesthetic effects, ®™ark actively reinterprets the term 'curation' from the art world. 'Curates' can be translated as a form of influence with which the groups seeks to counter capitalism's tendency to pervade the social and the cultural with commodity values – a process that Hardt and Negri label *biopolitics*.[22] ®™ark projects reject and react to the formulation of citizens as 'input mechanisms' for consumerist values to the exclusion of non-commodified values.[23] It promotes the alternative conceptualization of citizens as performers in a social drama. The activities of the Electronic Disturbance Theatre share certain satirical elements of ®™ark but are also frequently subversive in a much more direct, performance-orientated fashion that explores this notion of the social drama to its fullest extent.

# Drama and the Electronic Disturbance Theatre

The Electronic Disturbance Theater (EDT) is a small group of cyber activists and artists engaged in developing the theory and practice of Electronic Civil Disobedience (ECD). Until now the group has focused its electronic actions against the Mexican and US governments to draw attention to the war being waged against the Zapatistas and others in Mexico. But ECD tactics have potential application by a range of political and artistic movements. The Electronic Disturbance Theater, working at the intersections of radical politics, recombinant and performance art, and computer software design, has produced an ECD device called *Flood Net*, URL-based software used to flood and block an opponent's website. While at present a catalyst for moving forward with ECD tactics, the Electronic Disturbance Theater hopes to eventually blend into the background to become one of many small autonomous groups heightening and enhancing the ways and means of computerized resistance.[24]

The EDT is perhaps most noteworthy for the way in which it combines the previously explored re-engineering aspect of the 'true hack' with a highly developed sense of the hack's performance element. For example, when an unobtainable request is made on the Internet for a particular web-page, the 404 error message informing the user of its unavailability comes up on the user's screen. In the Digital Zapatista protests against the Mexican government, this technical 404 feature was turned into a form of artistic protest:

> We ask President Zedillo's server or the Pentagon's web server 'Where is human rights in your server?' The server then responds 'Human rights not found on this server' . . . This use of the 'not found' system . . . is a well known gesture among the net art communities. EDT just re-focused the 404 function towards a political gesture.[25]

We have already touched upon the way in which hacker culture can be criticized for privileging access to the technical over more generally political issues. For the EDT, in contrast, the social form of the protest takes precedence over its technological content. One example of this is the way in which elements within the hacker community object to the resource hungry nature and technical inelegance of such programmes as *Flood Net* and argue that the rationale for political protest does not justify the disruption of users' bandwidth. This 'digitally correct' position holds that protest then becomes a form of censorship because it interferes with people's access to the Internet.

For the EDT, the digitally correct are nerdishly missing the point. The fact that the relatively technically inefficient program required large numbers of people clogging up the Internet was precisely its strength. The technical aspects of political protests are the least important part of a larger and more significant three-act social performance. Dominguez calls this a *social drama* and in various public performances and presentations has expressed his concern that the digitally correct tendency seem to view Internet rights as more important that human rights. The social drama's first act involves stating the political purpose of what is going to happen, the second is the actual act itself, and the third act is the dialogue or, perhaps, afterlife of the event as it generates discussion. Dominguez thus argues: 'A virtual plaza, a digital situation, is thus generated in which we all gather and have an encounter, or an Encuentro, as the Zapatistas would say – about the nature of neo-liberalism in the real world and in cyberspace.'[26] Digital Zapatismo has added an additional transgressive and, in the age of constant media noise, an unusual element to such social drama. Tactical silence is used where, literally in Mexico and metaphorically for online supporters, activists retreat back into the jungle to reflect upon events.

## Performance as the hacktivist ethic

> In technological forms of life, not just resistance but also power is non-linear. Power itself is no longer primarily pedagogical or narrative but instead, itself performative. 'Nation' now works less through

'narrative' or 'pedagogy' but through the performativity of information and communication. Power works less through the linearity and the reflective argument of discourse or ideology than through the immediacy of information, of communications.[27]

In *Perform or Else*,[28] McKenzie critically explores the transformation and subversion of the concept of *performance*. Its primary connotation of the dramaturgical is now overwhelmingly dominated by a commercial sense of efficiency. Lash uses similar analysis to trace the way in which information has become the dominant entity within global capital. For both McKenzie and Lash, performance in anything other than the efficient, commercial sense becomes increasingly difficult, if not impossible. Due to the immanence of information and communication technologies, more and more of our social meanings are disproportionately mediated through the prism of immediate data so that functionality overrides more substantive considerations (the basis of Hardt and Negri's biopolitics). It is as a reaction to this pushing out of the traditional notion of performance that the Digital Zapatistas purposefully shape their actions. For example, in contrast to the performance values of the capitalist mass media, after an action they may use periods of silence and non-action to promote reflective and analytical thought. The Latin American influence upon hacktivism has provided a useful store of alternative cultural resources. Hacktivism is thus informed by a sense of 'practical magic realism' and the Digitial Zapatistas regularly adopt performance techniques heavily influenced by Mayan culture.[29]

Eco addresses head-on the problems faced by political protest in a media-dominated age.[30] He identifies two main forms of response: the strategic and tactical approach. Strategic responses attempt to fill the existing communication outlets with fellow-travellers, so that radical views can be prominently displayed. Tactical approaches, in contrast, involve overtly confrontational techniques. In Eco's view, however, the strategic approach has the least long-term promise because beyond any short-term success it may have, 'I begin to fear it produces very skimpy results for anyone hoping to restore to human beings a certain freedom in the face of the total phenomenon of Communication.'[31] Using the example of the French student protests in 1968, Baudrillard further underlines this pessimism about the fate of high-profile protest in the media age by providing a variation upon McLuhan's aphorism: *the medium is the message*. He suggests that even the tactical approach risks being subsumed by the regime of total communication: 'transgression and subversion never get "on the air" without being subtly negated as they are: transformed into models, neutralized into signs, they are eviscerated of their meaning ... there is no better way to reduce it than to administer it a mortal dose of publicity'.[32]

Whilst hacktivist acts will continue to receive press attention whether it is wanted or not, two things offer at least some immunity from

Baudrillard's 'mortal dose'. In the first place, hacktivist methods such as online acts of civil disobedience have a *mass* quality to them, as we have already seen in their rejection of technical elegance for its own sake. This answers a concern of Baudrillard's about attempts to re-engineer capitalist communication methods through the widespread attainment of individual technical expertise. In so far as the early hacker community had a political agenda, it was premised upon such a technical approach. However, the essential political problem of the passive nature of the individual's reception of the mass media's output, is not solved by simply trying to turn more people into skilled transmitters. Baudrillard dismisses this notion as in essence a deeply conservative move far too similar to Adorno's previously cited ham radio operator:

> this 'revolution' at bottom conserves the category of transmitter, which it is content to generalize as separated, transforming everyone into his own transmitter, it fails to place the mass media system in check. We know the results of such phenomena as mass ownership of walkie-talkies, or everyone making their own cinema: a kind of personalized amateurism, the equivalent of Sunday tinkering on the periphery of the system.[33]

Political action in the mass media age constantly risks losing its subversive edge. The difficulty is illustrated by the fate of grafitti, an example of a transgressive anti-capitalist act cited approvingly by Baudrillard. He talks of 'the graffiti reversal of advertising after May '68',[34] but failed to foresee the various ways in which modern advertising is more likely to co-opt the appearance of urban graffiti to give it 'street cred' than to be undermined by it.

# Hacktivism's peace with pace

> Constant revolutionizing of production, uninterrupted disturbance of all social relations, everlasting uncertainty and agitation, distinguish the bourgeois epoch from all earlier times. All fixed, fast-frozen relationships, with their train of venerable ideas and opinions, are swept away, all new-formed ones become obsolete before they can ossify. All that is solid melts into air, all that is holy is profaned.[35]

Marx recognized the great creativity, productive capacity and essentially iconoclastic nature of bourgeois industry, whilst criticising its exploitative basis. In contemporary times, engagement with this pace and the iconoclastic nature of the change it ushers forth has tended to be dominated by its evangelical commercially minded promoters (pejoratively referred to as the 'corporate salivating of business pornography').[36] Many of the writers referred to in this chapter, however, are now more actively seeking positive ways to deal with this disorientating flux. McKenzie, for example, shares Hardt and Negri's recognition of the simultaneously pervasive and invasive nature of the flux's cultural consequences:

> performative objects are unstable rather than fixed, simulated rather than real. They do not occupy a single 'proper' place in knowledge; there is no such thing as the thing-in-itself. Instead, objects are pro-duced and maintained through a variety of sociotechnical systems, overcoded by many discourses, and situated in numerous sites of prac-tice . . . the mechanisms of performative power are nomadic and flexible more than sedentary and rigid.[37]

The novel potential of hacktivism's anti-capitalist transgression rests upon the way in which it readily accepts the instability, the 'everything melts into air' quality, of capitalist-induced change. We have seen how the subversive potential of early hacker culture was lost, as much of the hacker ethic became quickly assimilated into the capitalist system. We should not forget, however, the potential embodied in such figures as Chip Tango, an archetypal early hacker who

> looks at the future with enthusiasm. His trust in humanity is inexhaust-ible. He takes for granted that computer technology is out of control, and he wants to ride it like a surfer rides a wave. The opportunities for fouling up the world through computer power are unlimited, but he thinks that people like him are useful agents in establishing a balance, a sense of humaneness and humor . . . when presented with a scenario of a world which increasingly uses information in an oppressive Orwell-ian manner, [he] replied, 'I'm not worried for a minute about the future. If the world you describe is going to happen, man, I can fuck it up a lot faster than the world we live in now!'[38]

Hacktivism seeks to rectify hacking's failure to build upon this early promise of intuitive ease with the fluidity of digitally inspired environ-ments. It represents a strongly anti-capitalist movement that seeks to resurrect Chip Tango's ethos from the mentality of the microserf. It revels in disorientating change and the ability to alternate between real and vir-tual sites of protest.

# Hactivists within the Empire – spiders on a web?

> The terminals of the network society are static. The bonding, on the other hand, of web weavers with machines is nomadic. They form communities with machines, navigate in cultural worlds attached to machines. These spiders weave not networks, but webs, perhaps elec-

tronic webs, undermining and undercutting the networks. Networks need walls. Webs go around the walls, up the walls, hide in the nooks and crannies and corners of where the walls meet . . . Networks are shiny, new, flawless. Spiders' webs, in contrast, attach to abandoned rooms, to disused objects, to the ruins, the disused and discarded objects of capitalist production. Networks are cast more or less in stone, webs are weak, easily destroyed. Networks connect by a utilitarian logic, a logic of instrumental rationality. Webs are tactile, experiential rather than calculating, their reach more ontological than utilitarian.[39]

Much opposition to globalization trends is based upon its tendency to treat culture as a form of Heidegger's *standing reserve*: a commodifiable resource to be exploited like any other. Hacktivist acts, however, provide some practical examples of the increasing theoretical attention being given to ways in which the same communication channels responsible for the facilitation of globalization are now also its potentially most fruitful sites of political protest. Lash, for example, argues that: 'With the dominance of communication there is a politics of struggle around not accumulation but *circulation*. Manufacturing capitalism privileges production and accumulation, the network society privileges communication and circulation.'[40] Similarly, Dyer-Witheford sees new contested sites of circulation: 'the cyberspatial realm . . . increasingly provides a medium both for capitalist control and for the "circulation of struggles"'.[41]

There is an increasingly common call amongst radical thinkers for oppositional groups to match the nomadic flows enjoyed by corporations due to their own 'global-webs' of capital,[42] and to counter-colonize this global web with their own values. New social movements use a sophisticated intuitive *a priori* sense of circulation's importance and thereby put practical flesh on the theoretical bones of such commentators. Information about struggle from the EDT, for example, spreads 'via a strange chaos moving horizontally, non-linearly, and over many sub-networks. Rather than operating through a central command structure in which information filters down from the top in a vertical and linear manner . . . information about Zapatistas on the Internet has moved laterally from node to node.'[43] Thus the call for the 'counter-populating' of 'the global multitude' has been answered by various groups of hacktivists seeking to develop new web-based tactics to better confront capital in the age of the matrix. They re-engineer the binary-based circulation systems of capitalism for their own more web-like, non-binary purposes.

# Conclusion

In times of constant effervescence, certain stimulating impertinences are required.[44]

> Spiders . . . the image strikes me as a fitting one for this Web-age global activism. Logos, by the force of ubiquity, have become the closest thing we have to an international language, recognized and understood in many more places than English. Activists are now free to swing off this web of logos like spy/spiders – trading information about labor practices, chemical spills, animal cruelty and unethical marketing around the world.[45]

To recap, it is worth considering the meaning behind the neologism 'hacktivism'. The 'hack' part of the term refers us to a fundamental aspect of the true 'hack', namely the hacker's innate desire to re-engineer or reverse the original and primary purpose of an artefact or system. The 'ism' part of the term refers to the political activism that motivates its various acts and events. We have seen in this chapter how hacktivism has kept faith with both of its constituent parts. Rather than making the empty gesture of Canute-like opposition to an unstoppable capitalist tide, hacktivism imaginatively reinterprets the functions of capitalism's informational channels. It is empowered, not threatened, by the speed of the capitalist system it operates within. The new social dramas that result are thus given additional bite because they achieve their effects from within the system rather than from a 'pure' intellectual distance. The danger of replicating through online actions the abstract capitalist rationalism of the market is avoided because hacktivists remain mindful of the grounded world beyond code. Their eventual success or failure is obviously unknown at this point, but at least new online activist groups are sensitive to the factors that dampened previous forms of protetst. The hacktivist development of various tactical semiological performances and events designed to shock people from the passivity of Eco's regime of total communication makes them promising candidates to fill his request for 'communications guerrillas'. They may yet avoid the 'subtle negation' that Baudrillard identifies as the conventional fate of media-based protest. Hacktivism provides the beginnings of a practical strategy with which to move amidst modern capitalism's abstract, yet nevertheless circumscribing networks: like spiders on a web.

# 8

# Consuming Heresy: Theoretical and Practical Problems of Challenging Consumerism in Contemporary Protest Cultures[1]

## *Jonathan Purkis*

The British political commentator George Monbiot recently suggested that the people who currently run capitalism are behaving as though they were a millenarian cult, such is the forcefulness of their self-delusion that the drive for more consumption will ensure some kind of eventual global parity of quality of life.[2] His argument that quality of life for North American and western European nation states peaked sometime in the early to mid-1970s is a powerful one, supported by considerable research. Ironically, however, in searching for a convenient metaphor, Monbiot has unknowingly passed up an ideal opportunity to talk about millenarian traditions that are as far away from glamorizing material acquisition as is possible. Deluded and self-destructive the rulers of the world might be, but it is actually those at the radical end of contemporary anti-capitalist movements who are embracing the heretical tradition.

This chapter suggests that the millenarian association is more than just a convenient label and is actually an important touchstone for understanding the theory and practice of contemporary struggles against globalization, social injustice and ecological destruction. Whilst clearly the diversity and complexity of these movements mitigates against such a generic reading, it is possible to make this claim by concentrating specifically on the anarchist aspects of these social and political forces, and especially those areas concerned with consumerism. One of the classic features of a millenarian movement has been its apparent exclusiveness, in terms of both critique and practice, particularly around issues of what we would now call 'lifestyle politics', 'self-actualization' or individual 'empowerment'. More importantly, it is the anti-authoritarian context within which these characteristics appear that is crucial for constructing a genealogy of anticonsumerism.[3]

The discussion is therefore not really concerned with lobbying organizations but rather with the radical cultures of this particular anti-capitalist milieu. What all movements do have to address, however, are strategic considerations as how best to advocate for more responsible, ethical or, crucially, less consumption. The general public can and have often been found to support a number of issues, including the cancellation of Third World debt, ending sweat-shop labour, opposing ecological devastation to tropical and temperate old growth rainforests, and reclaiming the streets for urban communities. Campaigning on the issue of reduced consumption and appropriate lifestyle changes has been something that the major environmental and development non-governmental organizations have consistently been reluctant to do, despite producing excellent literature on the problems in question.[4]

Issues of lifestyle changes therefore exist as a kind of political 'dark matter',[5] underpinning most of the current concerns that unite anti-capitalist and anti-globalization activists. Fundamental changes are clearly needed to the global economic system (and the suggestions for these vary considerably), but understanding how people define, experience and organize their lives around the things that they consume remains pivotal on both theoretical and practical levels for activists and academics alike.

How one theorizes consumption therefore impacts on the strategic campaigning of activists and the extent to which they are successful or not. In the present context, the philosophies subscribed to by many anti-capitalist activists and their advocacy of lifestyles radically different from those experienced by the 'consumer classes' of the western world pose strategic problems for campaigning. This applies not only to how messages are conveyed to the general public, but also to how campaigning on these issues can be sustained. Sociologists of social movements call this the problem of 'capacity building',[6] and not only does this continue to be a complex set of issues within any protest culture, but it is particularly difficult with regard to challenging dominant ideas about consumption.

Nevertheless, the general integration of environmental values into public policy debates does provide sufficient conceptual ground for the existence of 'discursive bridges' between radical anticonsumerist campaigners and the general public. The manner in which protest itself takes place can be seen to assist these processes, particularly where imaginative theatrical techniques are employed or spaces not normally perceived as contested are temporarily occupied.

Firstly, however, we need to consider the political and sociological background to the emergence of the kind of critiques of consumption that underpin contemporary protest. This is required in order to differentiate the organizations that are trying to reduce the impact of consumerism through existing societal structures and those that believe the structures within society are inextricably interconnected with the destruction of the social and natural environment. It is this latter, more anti-authoritarian trend that can be linked to the history of millenarian movements at the level of theory and practice.

# Framing contemporary opposition to consumerism

Understanding the potential impact of consumer societies on both human and natural ecosystems is central to ecological political thought. Andrew Dobson suggests that this means rethinking energy use, trade systems and travel, our use of technology, agricultural practices, ways of working, population levels and political structures.[7] In order to develop a truly 'green' society, a fundamental shift in thought is needed on all of these levels, requiring a 'deep green' world-view rather than a 'light green' one. Such a perspective is one that is informed by a non-instrumental philosophy of nature where non-human ecosystems are given value in their own right. Accordingly, more decentralized, bioregional and sustainable methods of living are advocated, planned on a local level with maximum participation from the local populace; a view Dobson argues as fairly akin to anarchist models. The problem, he maintains, is that sociologists and political thinkers are often incapable of linking environmental issues with an appropriate and consistent political perspective. Instead, decisions on policy tend to follow authoritarian methods, such as green taxes, centralized planning and increased interference in everyday life, as opposed to devolution of power and ecological economics.

A useful way of understanding some of these issues is to consider the influential sociological thesis of 'reflexive modernization', which argues for the existence of more progressive attitudes within social policy towards the environment. Developed by sociologists Ulrich Beck,[8] Anthony Giddens[9] and Scott Lash,[10] 'reflexive modernization' theory suggests that contemporary societies are beginning to face up to the contradictions of modernity, thinking in new ways and adopting strategies to prevent damage to social and ecological systems. Such developments have emerged due to the increasingly unmanageable nature of modernity, particularly the way that economic and technological systems now impact on human and non-human ecosystems, across time as well as space. These processes create both new forms of inequality and new forms of political action. 'Risk' rather than wealth begins to define the organizational basis of everyday life, with 'risk winners' (such as chemical companies) and 'risk losers' (Third World populations). As a consequence of these developments, individuals in risk society begin to employ a 'long distance morality', therefore placing [themselves] in the position of potentially having to take a continual stand'.[11] This, for the reflexive modernists, constitutes a radicalization of modernity.

On the face of it, these claims for a more reflexive society help to explain the emergence of ethical and green consumption in the 1980s as well as international agreements such as the Local Agenda 21 commitments at the 1992 'Earth Summit' in Rio de Janeiro. These theories also help to explain the manner in which campaigners have forced many multinational companies to issue codes of conduct concerning their work practices, develop environmental policies and be accountable in terms of some of their marketing practices. However, they do not tell us very much about the movements involved in these campaigns, their histories, participants, strategies or methods of organizing. Similarly, there is less commitment to locating these struggles within pre-existing political or intellectual traditions. The fact that many of the characteristics of the 'risk society' thesis can be traced back to nineteenth-century concerns about the value of science to society suggests that Beck's claims for this 'new' awareness being equivalent to a Second Reformation are probably overstated.[12]

It is important, therefore, to locate notions of reflexivity and reflexive modernization within a wider historical debate about the long-standing interests of state and capital. There must, for instance, be degrees of reflexivity and it must benefit some groups more than others.[13] Consequently, it is probably better to think of many of these advancements as limited notions of reflexivity based upon activity within particular 'expert systems' and policy-making bodies, as opposed to a more fundamental set of changes.[14] As even politically moderate sociologists have noted, dominant social, political and economic spheres are used to adapting to contradictions within capitalist society.[15] Reflexive processes might also be seen in the light of the emergence of what Klaus Eder[16] has called a new alternative 'masterframe' whereby the achievements of the environmental movements of the 1970s and 1980s have resulted in the formation of a more ecological public sphere. This, he claims, has implications for the mobilization of subsequent environmental grassroots campaigns, since their frames of reference can be easily incorporated within the assumptions of ordinary policy. Put another way, as Chesters and Welsh note, amidst all of the policy talk around ecological modernization and sustainability, there remains the question of whether it is the environment that is being sustained or the capitalist system itself.[17]

Mobilization around consumption therefore needs to be seen in the light of the institutionalization of environmental critiques, but also in terms of the emergence of the radical environmental direct action movement of the early 1990s in the UK. The boom of green businesses, ethical consumption and fair trade politics certainly indicated a level of public acceptability of green issues as well as facilitating appropriate lifestyles based around alternative consumption. Yet the incorporation (and softening) of the radical messages of 1970s environmentalism into the discourse of official policy left the non-governmental organizations of that era with less room to manoeuvre. Hard-hitting concepts such as 'zero growth', 'appropriate technology' and 'environmental limits' began to coalesce instead around 'sustainable development'. However, the emerging direct action movement of the early 1990s – including networks such as Earth First! and Reclaim the Streets – began to draw on a new wave of institutional research that not only reinforced the message of the 1970s but went even further. Central to this was a revamped *Beyond the Limits of Growth* (1992), the work of the World Watch Institute (including its annual *State of the World* reports) as well as Alan Durning's *How Much Is Enough?*,[18] which argued that the consumer classes of the world (about 20 per cent of the global population) were consuming a staggering 80 per cent of the planet's resources. More public, however, have been the findings of the 1990 United Nations International Panel on Climate Change (IPCC), which served up some sobering statistics about the amount of carbon emissions that would have to be reduced in order for global warming to stabilize. The IPCC recommended reduction in emissions was 60 per cent, although more recently Friends of the Earth has estimated that the practical reductions needed in the UK are around 88 per cent, given its position as one of the largest consumers of resources.[19]

These studies and projections are often useful scientific resources for radical campaigners to draw upon to provide something of a 'discursive bridge' between their own views and those of the general public. Moreover, although these messages are often articulated within the language of ethical and green consumerism for particular strategic reasons, the anticonsumer message has become increasingly prevalent in contemporary anti-capitalist and anti-globalization movements. The mobilizations around international trade conferences, whether of the World Trade Organization, the World Bank and International Monetary Fund, the Group of Eight leading industrialized nations or the World Economic Summit, have all demonstrated that, to use an activist phrase, 'another world is possible'.

The utopianism of this message provides a link to the past and to locate contemporary protest within a longer historical tradition that has focused on particular lifestyles, philosophical outlooks and organizational strategies. In short, consumption can no longer be treated as an epiphenomenon of the production process, as the left has sometimes been guilty of doing, but as an area of protest that has its own distinctive areas of analysis that need to be conceptualized in their own right. Indeed, it is possible to argue that categories such as 'production' and 'consumption' are themselves far from mutually exclusive categories. This is especially the case, I argue, when considering some of the aspects of lifestyle politics that are particular to the contemporary milieu, where these distinctions become blurred.

Before discussing consumption within the context of a radical political tradition, a number of definitional matters require resolving. Thus far in the argument there has been a *laissez-faire* attitude to using 'consumption' and 'consumerism', as though the distinction were obvious or the categories synonymous. Indeed, some commentators[20] have suggested that sociologists of culture and cultural studies theorists tend to subsume studies of consumption into analyses of consumerism, with a concentration on the more glamorous aspects of symbolic activity such as shopping mall behaviour. This is to by-pass the important question of needs and the practicalities of everyday forms of consumption, especially collective consumption of services. Although important, this is hardly a new point,[21] and it is a particularly difficult one when projected into a more idealized political context. A useful distinction therefore might be one that suggests 'consumption' to be the social organization of particular material necessities, whereas 'consumerism' is the way that these needs have been translated into specific cultural and ideological forms. Williams notes the way the word 'consume' has changed its meaning over time, from emphasizing wastefulness to a positive beneficial activity and back to wasteful again.[22] The notion of needs and necessities has also moved away from simple definitions based around food, water, shelter and clothing to embrace more ontological issues such as physical security, appropriate education and non-hazardous work and living environments.[23] It is debates about the organization of such needs and where the divisions between consumption and consumerism, necessity and excess are perceived to lie that underpin much of the rest of the chapter.

Firstly, however, we need to locate some of these notions of needs, lifestyle and the organization of social provision into a broader social and historical context.

## Millennial moments

In previous publications[24] I have suggested that contemporary anti-consumer activities can be located within the millenarian tradition.[25] To attempt this, two steps are required. The first is to depart somewhat from the classic text on millenarian history, Norman Cohn's *The Pursuit of the Millennium*.[26] The second is to interpret history from a more unorthodox methodological point of view than is usually followed.

In the former instance, Cohn gives a systematic and vivid assessment of the visionary sects and 'mystical anarchist' of the Middle Ages, which were influential on the counter-cultures of the 1960s. Briefly put, the argument that Cohn offers towards the end of his book – that the utopian visions of the millenarian tradition resulted in fascism and Stalinism – misunderstands the essentially anti-authoritarian and self-organizational nature of the millenarian tradition.[27] It is precisely this type of position which both Chomsky[28] and Maffesoli[29] see as a methodological problem within historical research. According to them, writers frequently interpret turbulent periods of history from a liberal-bourgeois perspective, reflecting many of the assumptions about power and authority that their own political systems produce. The consequences of these assumptions are that self-organized, non-hierarchical 'tribal' formations are not credited with shaping events, with more 'visible' authoritarian structures acknowledged instead. Even the socialist historical tradition can sometimes be susceptible to this.

In his book *The Ecology of Freedom*,[30] the social ecologist Murray Bookchin[31] locates these millenarian movements within an anti-dualistic philosophical tradition. Although there is not space here to do justice to his full argument, the key point is that he sees these movements as trying to break down the 'epistemologies of rule' which serve to distance people from nature and from each other. For all of their contradictions, Bookchin sees these millenarian movements as articulating the language and culture of 'freedom', and because of their anti-hierarchical tendencies and self-organization, he sees them as offering a glimpse of how society might be.

This is an important differentiation from the more popular associations of millenarian movements solely as prophets of the end of the world. Such pessimistic views were evident in the thinking of sixteenth-century groups such as the Brethren of the Free Spirit, the Anabaptists and the Hutterites throughout Europe, but these groups succeeded in doing more than just popularizing this idea in the context of natural disasters, plagues, famines or war. These movements succeeded in uniting the landless, the religiously marginalized or persecuted, beggars, itinerant traders and sections of the intelligentsia, albeit for short periods of time. Moreover, notions of social and theological liberation began to merge into a belief in the possibility of 'immediate, collective, total, this-worldly salvation'.[32] Many of these characteristics were evident within groups such as the Ranters, Fifth Monarchists, Diggers and, to some extent, the Quakers, during one of the most fruitful periods of millenarianism, the English Revolution of the 1640s and 1650s.[33]

These millenarian movements can be seen as distinctive in terms of the way in which they linked their anti-authoritarian theologies with practical realizations in their ways of living. This tended to manifest itself in the need to create a 'heaven on earth' and to achieve a 'state of grace' through individual actions and contemplation. Such ideas involved subverting the dominant religious separation of people and nature from God and opposing the mediation of religious experience by church hierarchies. This sense of prefiguring the society that one wished to create by trying to live in ways consistent with one's beliefs is perhaps an example of the later anarchist argument for equating the means of an action with its ends. Some examples of this included: the claiming of towns or 'common land' for one's own use (Anabaptists and Diggers respectively), disrupting church services or organizing them non-hierarchically (Flagellants and Quakers respectively), rejecting fasting and penitence for pleasurable eating and spiritual purification through sexual promiscuity (Brethren of the Free Spirit) and writing blasphemous pamphlets and performing them in the streets (Ranters).[34] The use of the body as a political weapon can also be seen as an ancestor to the kind of politics of consumption that are more familiar to the contemporary theorist, even if there were massively different issues at stake.

This tradition of radical anti-dualistic thought can be traced into the nineteenth-century 'practical utopias' of small collectively run communities, predominantly (but not exclusively) in the north of England. Hardy notes that a significant characteristic of these communities was the consistency of their organizational and lifestyle practices.[35] Influenced by mid-century American utopian movements, the writings of Peter Kropotkin and Leo Tolstoy, a mix of rural communities (the Norton Colony near Sheffield and Clousden Hill near Newcastle) and their urban counterparts (the Blackburn and Leeds Brotherhoods) sprang up. Experiments with abandoning money, producing newspapers, cultivating crops and redefining the traditional sexual division of labour took place throughout these communities. Arguing that there was a degree of holism in their analysis of the world, Hardy points to progressive attitudes to the relationship between means and ends of the community's commitment to particular lifestyles that did not involve the exploitation of others and, in some instances, animals. Such communities needed to be considered 'as a method of social change and an end in themselves'.[36] The existence of such communities as part of a radical tradition is something that has been recognized in the sociological literature on 'new social movements'. Paul Bagguley and many others have found examples of the kind of themes often associated with post-1960s feminist and environmental movements throughout the nineteenth century.[37]

The importance of identifying these millenarian groups and their marginal and oppositional lifestyles and politics is that it helps to uncover a genealogy of resistance to dominant philosophical traditions, not necessarily articulated within even liberal opinion of the particular time. Whilst the roots of contemporary environmentalism and the history of non-instrumental attitudes towards nature are well documented,[38] the anti-authoritarian attitudes towards consumption are not. In this respect, the connection between radical religious beliefs, attitudes towards material possessions and societal organization is a crucial prehistory to the politics of contemporary anti-capitalism.

# Dualistic thought and the radical consumer critique

In the light of the above discussion, a number of observations can be made as to how one frames a contemporary 'millenarian' position. This can be achieved by looking at both the critique of consumerism and the organizational philosophy of the groups in question.

In terms of prefiguring the society one wishes to live in, one can look for a consistency between the critique of consumer societies and the critique of hierarchical structures. This is largely because the ethos of accumulation and pursuit of fulfilment through material gratification can be seen to be central to and continually reinforced by the competitive and hierarchical organization of society. In order to address this, from an anticonsumer perspective, there has to be a move away from the dominant assumptions about social structures as much as from the assumed psychological benefits of consumerism. To place this in the context of the reflexive modernization thesis, for an organization to be truly reflexive, it must be as critical about its structure as its policy content. The reflexive modernization thesis appears not to factor the question of power and vested interests into its equation – a position more consistent with liberalism. One way of differentiating organizations campaigning on consumption and the environment, therefore, is to talk about their levels of reflexivity. Here we can use Lawrence Cox's useful distinction between groups who can consume social relations reflexively but not produce them reflexively.[39] This is the difference between being able to identify particular problems and contradictions within the social world and not necessarily being able to organize in a manner that irons them out. It is essentially a position that derives from the anarchist adage that the means of an action must be commensurate with its ends. Therefore, to produce reflexive social relations, a move away from top-down, expert-led forms of decision making and problem solving to more participatory and self-organized structures is required. This explains the resistance within the contemporary milieu to embracing non-governmental organizational strategies that simply involve retaining much of the existing social structures and economic rationales.

Secondly, in order to pursue more consistent strategies for action, a number of anti-dualistic philosophical positions require embracing. As has been suggested, it is at moments of radical political and social upheaval that one can best observe the undermining of dominant 'epistemologies'. In recent years, the critique of dualistic thought has become central to radical political theory as well as many areas of the social sciences and humanities. These critiques have moved away from the 'classic' dualism identified in philosophy – the Cartesian mind/body split – towards identifying the way in which power is maintained through the reinforcement of other categories of opposition. These extend from assumptions about sex and gender such as male/female and heterosexual/homosexual, to self/other, civilized/primitive, culture/nature, biological/technological and many others. These categories also define the practices of consumption and politics of consumerism and can be seen to be relevant as helping to define the world-view of the most radical elements of contemporary anti-capitalist protest.

In particular, the impetus of the 1990s radical environmental movement has helped carry a much 'darker' shade of ecological theory to the understanding of the impact of globalization. Here we see an implicit rejection of the anthropocentric perspective ascribed in the opposition culture/nature, whereby the needs of humans are put above the long-term needs and sustainability of non-human ecosystems. Such instrumentalism is seen to have fuelled the ecological crisis and exposed the futility of economic philosophies based upon a 'grow or die' principle. Consequently, more ecocentric models of organization, use and distribution of resources and political culture have begun to appear (not necessarily from radical organizations) and to impact on perceptions about instrumentalism. Associated with these developments are controversial debates about the role of science and technology in the shaping of a new society and the validity of critiques that are informed by psychology and psychoanalysis or even spirituality. There is not space to do justice to these sizeable areas of study, but they signify an important departure from many progressive attitudes on the left, which have traditionally adopted instrumental attitudes towards nature.[40]

This instrumental attitude operates on a number of different levels. For instance, within the ideology of western consumer societies, the formation of the contemporary self depends to some extent on the exploitation of the other, principally through the consumption of natural and social resources. This is particularly the case with respect to the manufactured identities that people are encouraged to consume through changing fashions within mass culture. Whilst this alienated and instrumental process has been discussed before, there are ecophilosophical issues that are worthy of note. McBurney suggests that there is an irreverence which comes with being separated from the procurement of the resources that sustain us, and that this has repercussions for how we think about ourselves and the environment.[41] The campaigning that takes place on consumer-related issues within the current milieu can therefore be seen to 'render power visible',[42] identifying the various ways that everyday lifestyles are implicated within complex power relations, from car culture to genetic seed technologies. The places of production and consumption become collapsed into the same conceptual space, whether in the occupation of the offices and retail floors of multinational companies or through the processes of empathy and solidarity with indigenous cultures such as the Zapatistas in Mexico and the Uwa in Columbia. Contemporary anticonsumer identities therefore require a deconstruction of existing dualisms between self and other, First and Third World and probably 'civilized' and 'primitive' cultures. This realizes itself on practical grounds in terms of trying to be more reverent towards what is being produced and consumed, and how those things might be brought under the auspices of a more participatory form of local organization.

As I argued in the previous section, millenarian movements manifested a number of characteristics, such as aspiring to a 'state of grace' through adopting a morally consistent course of action prefiguring the society that was aspired to. Three ideas assist this. The first is that there has to be a connection between lifestyle choices and the drive to remove exploitative relations; thus the critique is a lived one. The second is to embrace the notion that 'happiness' can be linked to non-material things – such as family, community and security – and it is these things which help form a more balanced self.[43] Thirdly, these things can be facilitated through the blurring of the boundaries between work and leisure and production and consumption. This inevitably requires a much more participatory approach to living than the individualistic and divisive nature of existing capitalist relations: in short, a renegotiation of one of the oldest tensions in political theory, that of the individual and the collective, is required.

Therefore, in order to construct an effective genealogy of anti-consumerism, one has to link the rejection of materialism with a number of other factors, notably an anti-dualistic, non-anthropocentric world-view that believes in the consistency of means and ends of actions. It also depends on identifying instances of a removal of the boundaries between consumption and production. This then is the philosophical base for understanding contemporary radical opposition to consumer capitalism, and an important way of linking the millenarian movements of the Middle Ages through to the nineteenth century. To complete the genealogy we must consider examples of twentieth-century activist communities that can also demonstrate an anti-dualistic theory and practice.

## Practical utopias

The kind of utopian communities described by Hardy during the late nineteenth and early twentieth centuries have, of course, existed in a variety of different contexts throughout the subsequent decades. Radical educational experiments such as Summerhill School in Suffolk and Dartington Hall School in Devon (both begun in the 1920s) have always worked as alternative communities, practising participatory decision-making structures and self-actualization activities for the children.[44] The work of anarchist writer Colin Ward has constantly documented the historical role of the allotment, squatting and tenants' groups, making the links between land ownership, community participation and self-organization.[45] Indeed, anarchist commentators are fond of pointing out that these types of co-operative activity are not exclusive to radical communities but in fact exist in normal life amongst ordinary people and are frequently brought to light during sudden disasters or crises.[46] The kinds of community organization that were practised during the 1984–5 miners' strike, the sharing of resources and the politicizing of women have sometimes been argued to mirror the political mobilizations and self-organization of large areas of Spain during the revolution of 1936–9.[47]

The countercultures of the late 1960s managed to link anarchist politics with a rejection of the consumer society, resulting in a new wave of communal experiments, especially in places such as north Wales and the West Country, and the growth of associated free music festivals in the 1970s.[48] During the 1970s and 1980s, struggles against nuclear weapons and nuclear power were firmly connected in the public imagination with the protest camp. Media representations were frequently problematic, especially when the Thatcher government declared war on 'new age travellers', thereby ensuring much more vigilant policing of any attempt to establish alternative communities.[49] Nevertheless, not only has the protest camp managed to manifest alternative attitudes to work, consumption and decision making, but in the 1990s the wave of opposition to road building led to much more sympathetic relationships between local communities under attack from such schemes and the 'full time' anti-road activists. Although not exclusively, this tended to be more successful the more urban was the context of the development, especially at the Claremont Road/'Wanstonia', East London, site of the M11 extension and at the Pollock Park site of the M77 extension in Glasgow (both 1994–5). Commenting on the latter campaign, Seel notes the importance that such protest spaces (frequently referred to as autonomous zones) have for the transformation of identities and experimentation with alternative ways of living and thinking.[50] This was especially the case with the relatively high-profile example of ecological living and anticonsumer practices at the Wandsworth eco-village squat in London, started in May 1996 by the group This Land is Ours, who took over an empty plot of land owned by the Guinness company. A crucial aspect to the relative success of this project, notes Lawley, was the way that the village dwellers were able to integrate themselves with the surrounding community, especially on play areas for children, as well as impressing the local authorities with their compost toilets![51]

In some British cities and towns, more established enclaves of activists attempt to recreate some of the same ideals of Hardy's nineteenth-century 'practical utopias'. Doherty, Plows and Wall document some of those based around the environmental direct action politics.[52] They observe that in Oxford and the Hulme area of Manchester, it is possible to see small examples of participatory community ideals, whether through tenants' associations, alternative economics such as the Local Exchange Trading Systems (LETS),[53] multi-purpose activist spaces or arts projects. Such enclaves can be seen to coexist alongside more formal green businesses and networks.[54]

The presence of alternative (and even temporarily autonomous) zones has been particularly pertinent to the coordination of alternative globalization movement activities in recent years. Many of these actions have addressed the question of western lifestyles, corporate power and the impact of neoliberal economics around the world a little more directly than through a particular issue, but the momentum had been growing for some time. Central to this has been the identification with the Zapatista struggle against multinational business incursions into the Chiapas region of Mexico backed up by lethal military force. New alliances such as the People's Global Action network, Globalise Resistance and the World Social Forum have emerged to contest the neoliberal agenda of the World Trade Organization, the World Bank and International Monetary Fund, the Group of Eight industrialized countries and the World Economic Summit. At each of the international conferences by these trade organizations, activists have formed their own alternative spaces, food distribution centres, training and education programmes, and independent media. These have to be seen as more than just the support structures for the protests themselves; they are microcosms of the 'other world' that 'is possible'. The boundaries between production and consumption, means and ends, leader and led, become blurred. Many of the participants in these events are from British networks which a decade ago were often focused on solely environmental agendas, and which have become increasingly broader in their critiques and linking of issues.[55]

It is important not to regard all of the aforementioned 'practical utopias' as necessarily conforming to the same anti-dualistic and anti-authoritarian traditions. Most of them do, however, exist outside of the formal economy and experiment enough with alternative structures as to have convincingly undermined the dualistic assumptions about work and leisure, production and consumption. Many prefigure the society that they wish to create, although sometimes with limited success. However, some contemporary ecological writers have suggested that this kind of eco-village model of alternative politics can be comfortably brought within the auspices of the present dominant system and is hardly threatening to it.[56] Whilst this is a moot point, one needs to balance this kind of assessment against the way that alternative communities can easily become the source of institutional wrath. The work of the Exodus Collective in Luton, which ran free raves for disaffected local youth, a city farm and a number of restoration projects in the mid-1990s, is a case in point.

The collective's widely praised work in the community was repeatedly questioned by a handful of vindictive local and national politicians, who tried unsuccessfully to evict the collective.

The eulogizing of 'purer' radical communities and projects and the ridiculing of those which do not have the same ecological and political credentials is an old tactic within the libertarian left and, apart from its divisiveness, also assumes that societal change happens in easily identifiable ways. Given the complexity of the issues involved in changing people's consumption patterns in the consumer societies of the West, contingency as opposed to determinism might well be a more useful watchword. It is to the communication of radical ideas beyond the familiar comfort of the immediate social group that I now turn.

# Problems of campaigning to reduce consumption

Despite the groundswell of practical examples of alternative economic, political and social structures that have emerged in recent years, the translation of these experiments into viable options for the general public still remains remote at best. As suggested earlier, the general public have shown themselves to be favourable to certain environmental and development-related issues. Yet, if major non-governmental organizations shy away from campaigning on reducing levels of consumption, what are the hopes of a broad section of the public embracing these ideas? In order to answer this question, we must address two different sets of issues that inform this very old political dilemma: what is being communicated and how is it being done?

## Constructing 'discursive bridges'

The message that the whole economic and political system that we live under is destroying the planet is a difficult one to communicate, especially when what is being advocated are huge changes to lifestyle, including work, mobility, and social and political structures. As Ted Trainer has noted, 'hardly any of the hundreds of millions of people who live in rich world cities have any idea of an alternative to the consumer way and their settlements have no provision for anything but maximising the throughput of resources'.[57] Given the seriousness and extensiveness of the problems that confront us, any communication must be rooted in identifiable and 'commonsensical' strategies[58] and, perhaps contrary to expectation, I would suggest that these are not inconsistent with the anti-dualistic philosophies that I have been detailing in the previous pages.

To accomplish this, let us return to a point raised earlier: Klaus Eder's notion of environmental politics constituting an alternative 'masterframe'.

The idea that environmental discourse has had an ideological impact on civil society and the public sphere during the last decade and a half is a potentially useful one. Despite the aforementioned moderating of many of the radical ideas of the 1970s into the language of government during the late 1980s, it should be acknowledged that a considerable percolation of the practical implications of ecological thinking for public policy has occurred in British society. At some level, then, a moderate ecological discourse now constitutes part of a 'commonsense' view of the world. Although this is a 'light green' and largely anthropocentric version of ecological thought, it can be considered to be one side of a 'discursive bridge' where particular political terms are shared with those of a much more radical disposition.

The idea of a 'discursive bridge' can be practically linked to Szerszynski's notion that within protest culture there is a sense of actions fulfilling a 'dual-legitimacy' with two or more functions taking place at the same time.[59] Thus political movements can be seen to be negotiating their political performance and group identity depending on the context in which they are being perceived. This approach is particularly true of protest discourse and the tactical use of language for particular situations. Thus an 'ideal speech situation', as Habermas would have it,[60] takes place at the level of 'common sense' rather than within the reference points of the anticonsumerist world-view. Within the remit of 'commonsensical' discourse, for instance, there are a number of possible conversational resources that activists can draw upon. Peer pressure and the obligations that exist in the run-up to Christmas as well as the commercialization of particular dates in the year, such as Valentine's Day and Mother's Day, are relatively unproblematic topics. Similarly, the reality of stress in the workplace, longer working hours and increasing rates of unhappiness in proportion to material security in western societies are useful reference points to open up discussions about 'downshifting'. The uneven system of trade, where fruit and vegetables from Australia and New Zealand can undercut the prices of those grown in the UK or France, opens up questions of sustainability, need and the impact of transportation and a critique of neoliberal economics. These discussions can often be assisted by the research carried out by more formal organizations such as the World Watch Institute or the New Economics Foundation, which adds legitimacy to the campaigner's claims. The chances of a favourable outcome to any of these potential exchanges are, as I argue below, very much determined by the time and space of the campaigning situation itself.

However, alongside the debate about the effects of consumer society, another discourse must run, emphasizing the validity of participatory forms of decision-making, self-organization and local action. On the face of it, this appears to be a more difficult bridge to cross, yet the increasing disaffection with parliamentary politics, recent disasters in the UK farming community, rural and urban poverty, and frustration with national transport policies are just some of the potential areas for discussion. The anti-progressive People's Fuel Lobby of autumn 2000 might well have failed to connect itself to more enduring political problems, but it illustrated how quickly and effectively grassroots mobilization can occur. The potential for what Chomsky calls the 'theory of spontaneous organization' is, of course, central to the anarchist argument of self-organization being central to the natural evolution of human societies.[61]

In this respect, on the issue of farming, it is worth considering the effectiveness that farmers' markets have had on local businesses and communities in the wake of the foot-and-mouth disaster of spring 2001. Many lessons about intensive agriculture and the long-distance transportation of animals have been learned by communities already extremely aware of the way that foreign imports undercut locally produced goods in the large supermarkets. While the media concentrate on the hunting-dominated Countryside Alliance campaigns and the big business agendas of the National Farmers' Union, opportunities for change are already being taken by people 'on the other side' of our metaphorical bridge. Given the importance of food politics, these are fruitful areas for campaigners against genetically modified crops and on related issues.

## Overcoming discursive barriers

A number of years ago I interviewed a community activist involved in promoting the LETS scheme on a poor estate in Greater Manchester. One of the most significant things to emerge from the discussion was the observation that people in the community thought that there must be 'a catch' somewhere; surely one could not really get something for nothing. Such distrust of political activists generally and politicians in particular makes the identification of barriers to communication all the more important. In this respect, the temporal and spatial context for discursive bridging is a vital factor and here we can turn to an internal debate within the activist milieu itself for inspiration.

Following the 'Carnival against Capitalism' of 18 June 1999 in London, an activist publication called *Reflections on June 18th* was quickly put together and distributed through the participating political networks. One specific article entitled 'Give up activism', influenced by the radical French communist writer Jacques Camatte, argued against the exclusiveness of the 'professional activist' who failed to communicate effectively with the general public, so distanced were they in terms of their commitment to the cause. The intensity of 1990s campaign agendas had led to a situation where 'professional activists' moved from protest camp to protest camp without really engaging with the wider world. Camatte's metaphor for this behaviour was that of the gang. Moreover, according to the author(s), protest tactics were also suffering from a 'spectacularisation', reinforcing divisions of active protestor and passive bystander, rather than breaking these divisions down.[62] The drift towards more and more theatrical extravagance, sometimes to legitimate the non-violent nature of the protest event, was seen to be breeding its own contradictions. When conducting my own doctoral research in the early 1990s, it was clear to me that the tendency for groups such as Friends of the Earth and Greenpeace to concentrate more on media-friendly actions than on actual communication or effective protest strategies was a reason why people joined Earth First!.[63] Deconstructing the barriers between protestor and general public is therefore vital, if hierarchies are once more establishing themselves in 'radical' organizations.

One of the most effective campaign strategies on consumption matters since the mid-1990s has been the way that groups promoting Buy Nothing Day (No Shop Day in the UK) focused on people's obligations in the run-up to Christmas. The use of 'shopping-free zones' in the midst of a city centre plaza, providing free cups of tea, a comfy chair and a leaflet, offers a non-intimidating psychological space for discussion in such a way as to facilitate conversation. Many campaigns used by Earth First! in the UK over the last decade have utilized strategies that facilitate communication in places not popularly conceived of as spaces for protest. The practice of 'ethical shoplifting' for instance, whereby protestors liberated illegally logged mahogany from superstores to take to the police, provided ample opportunities for protestors to engage with a variety of different groups within society – store managers, the general public and security guards. Sometimes these tactics involved campaigners posing as members of the public to assist the process of communication.[64]

Given the seriousness of the messages being articulated by anti-capitalist and anticonsumerist groups, the role of humour has become central to conveying the complex interconnections between big business and everyday life. As observed by commentators such as Goaman and Graeber, the strange juxtaposition of dress, play and self-parody is now mandatory at anti-capitalist and anti-globalization events.[65] The May Day Monopoly Game in London in 2002 managed to combine all of these factors as well as preventing activists getting hemmed into easily contained spaces by the police. Both these writers note the deliberate attempt to break with predictable left-wing protest aesthetics and strategies, in order to provide more accessible activities.

Whilst it would be possible to provide many further examples of these kinds of 'bridging' moment, it is important to note that their success depends on how the general public are perceived by the activists themselves. One of the problems that afflicts activists of all political hues is the belief that the general public behave as an uncritical mass suffering from 'false consciousness', and in this sense consumption can bring out the worst in everyone's analysis. For anticonsumer activists to be effectively offering a view of the world reminiscent of Frankfurt School Marxists such as Adorno, Horkheimer or Marcuse is to reproduce the zealousness of earlier millenarian movements. Whilst it is important not to celebrate consumer creativity as postmodern liberation, as has been the trend in some areas of cultural studies,[66] the processes of complicity with the 'system' are complex and indicate that power is perpetuated in multifaceted ways. In addition, prescriptive rhetoric about what people do and do not need is frequently inextricably connected with these kinds of problem. This revisits one of the methodological questions raised in the discussion of millenarianism, that how we look at the organization of society and history determines our interpretation of it. Just as millenarian movements need to be seen in the context of their time, so too do production and consumption practices. This impacts on the types of theoretical position adopted by activists as well as how they carry them out in practice. In particular, one of the contingent issues generated by this debate is the extent to which radical ideas can sustain themselves enough to be effective.

## Building anticonsumerist 'capacity'

How social movements generate momentum over time has become a matter of concern for sociologists trying to understand the relationship that movements have with the dominant political structures within a society as well as in their own terms. There has been a tendency for writers to assume what movements are 'for' and to consider how effective they have been at influencing corporate and governmental powers. Often this has meant overlooking the cultural side to movement dynamics, questions of identity formation and experimenting with alternative methods of organization. It is worth acknowledging here the emergence of theories that attempt to understand social movements on their own terms and to account for the transmission of ideas over time. Ian Welsh's work on protest against the nuclear power industry is important in this respect: he tries to understand how movement action resources future movement action, particularly direct action strategies.[67] 'Capacity building, then, is the process whereby a social movement culture manages to facilitate the diffusion of ideas within wider society such that they are taken up by other groups and networks. These processes take place in localized contexts where experimentation with ideas and action helps to generate symbolic and practical resistance of the sort that does not take place within institutional politics (although these may be touched by the ideas).

It can be claimed that capacity building has been very evident with respect to the relationship between the anti-road movements of the 1990s and the more recent alternative globalization movement. As I have suggested, there are continuities between millenarian movements and similar themes that manifest themselves differently in specific eras, yet building capacity around reducing consumption and forging systemic short- and long-term changes is deeply problematic. This is true for all of the aforementioned tactical and theoretical problems around building discursive bridges, but it is also true with respect to the structure of the movements themselves.

Something of a classic problem within anarchist practice is a resistance to having any kind of 'blueprint' for the shape of a future society, lest that become constraining in itself. This becomes linked to fears of institutionalization, something which the radical environmental and alternative globalization networks have largely avoided. The anti-authoritarian sentiments of this milieu can diffuse into more moderate political campaigns, but the form of the opposition to consumerism is as problematic as the content when consistency of means and ends is being advocated. In this respect, Derek Wall's adaptation of Welsh's model to include the idea of 'capacity destruction' – how movements can tear themselves apart – becomes a useful addition to the discussion around the future of anticonsumerism.[68]

Moreover, although discursive bridges are established, it is easier to maintain these when specific and achievable goals are set, such as the encouragement of permaculture, transport sharing, reducing and refusing packaging, shared housing and widening community participation. Advocating boycotts of certain countries or companies without a rationale for how this could fit into the practical transformation of the world poses problems. Equally, expecting people to become part of the aforementioned 'practical utopias' is not a useful course of action. It is in these situations that radical networks utilize their cultural capital, networking with ecological economists and political scientists who can provide workable projections that utilize concepts of 'localization', 'ecological protectionism' and so forth.[69] In this more general public context, we can see the importance of the interplay between notions of 'capacity building', 'discursive bridges' and 'dual-legitimacy'.

# Conclusion

What I have suggested in this chapter is that there is an important historical relationship between movements commonly identified as 'millenarian', the questioning of material accumulation for its own sake, and political actions that challenge dominant epistemologies. Whilst there is a long history to this relationship, in recent years these issues have converged within the radical environmental milieu and movements against capitalism and globalization have begun to constitute a critique of consumerism. Although some sociologists have suggested that these developments can be regarded as a radicalization of modernity, where individuals and institutions are more reflexive about the consequences of their actions, this is to misunderstand the nature of the problem. Reflexive critiques of both capitalism and modernity are not new and more importantly need to be addressed at the level of form as much as content, since some of the destructive qualities of these systems involve the hierarchical nature of the organizations involved. The liberalizing forces are just that – liberal organizations charged with solving the contradictions of consumer capitalism by reproducing the methods of domination through their own limited systems.

To be completely reflexive, political action needs to be at the level of production as well as consumption. This can be understood in terms of the anarchist adage that the means of an action has to be commensurate with its ends, and non-hierarchical systems need to be adopted. In the context of the 1990s, this effectively separated out the greener and ethical forms of consumerism from the more radical anticonsumer aspects, whereby questions about material acquisition *per se* were asked and alternative social structures and economics advocated. I suggested that this was why it was possible to trace a genealogy of anticonsumerism through looking at millenarian movements and social experiments from the fifteenth to the twenty-first centuries. These 'practical utopian' movements were self-organizing and anti-hierarchical, and attempted to undermine dominant epistemological and ideological systems. Contemporary protest enclaves can be seen to inherit this tradition, from protest camps against road building, to communal living in a handful of UK cities, to support centres at anti-globalization protests.

Questioning consumerism as an ideology is no longer sacrilege and on an intellectual, moral and ecological level, many of the arguments have been won in terms of contesting its alleged benefits. However, just as with the anti-road movements, the translation of these small 'victories' into public policy and into widespread individual lifestyle changes is a different matter altogether. One could argue in sweeping ecopsychological terms, that much of western society is in a state of denial about what really needs to be done to create a truly sustainable, just and equitable society. However, the practicalities of campaigning on these issues are incredibly complex. An important tactic, which avoids patronizing the general public, is to look for 'discursive bridges' that link the 'light green' philosophies established in social policy during the last decade and the beliefs of radical anticonsumer activists. There are more opportunities for this than might be immediately realized, and these can be utilized to begin to 'build' movement 'capacity' beyond the exclusiveness of the anticonsumer networks.

An increasingly important aspect of the building of these discursive bridges is to draw on the resources provided by popular culture. It is interesting to note the proliferation of ironic and 'subversive' media texts about consumerism within even commercial culture: mainstream cinema articulating the emptiness of retail therapy in the form of films such as *Fight Club* (1999) and *American Beauty* (2000). 'Subvertising', the guerrilla art tactic invented by the Situationist International through their concept of *détournement* and pioneered by Adbusters, has become so widespread that it is in danger of becoming the tool of the advertising industry instead. Naomi Klein's critique of globalization, *No Logo*, has become one of the most popular political books of the last few decades.[70] Meanwhile, the alternative globalization movement has found ways of successfully linking diverse cultures around the globe and articulating interrelated struggles in a way that their 1960s counterparts – fighting against the Vietnam War and the sterile postwar boom – were unable to achieve.

An interesting occurrence in recent years is that, apart from the movements discussed already, some of the groups who have most directly addressed the issue of consumerism and all of its consequences have been religious in nature. There is a nice symmetry here in that the only surviving seventeenth-century millenarian group – the Quakers – have with their ongoing 'Living Witness' project pushed far more radical agendas than many of the existing environmental non-governmental organizations.[71] The 'Living Witness' programme attempts to address consumerism in terms of personal carbon usage, challenges individualistic aspects of consumer culture by asking questions about the roots of oppression, and encourages personal development in non-material (but not necessarily religious) ways. Moreover, the Quakers practise extremely participatory and quasi-anarchist structures in terms of their worship and decision-making processes. As with many contemporary alternative globalization movements, there is a sense of organizational evolution and the diffusion of ideas into the mainstream that is unrestricted by political parties and government policies. And, as a final point of differentiation from groups who maintain something of a business interest in the ecological crisis, the Quakers do not offer VISA facilities or sell Christmas catalogues of environmentally friendly gadgets that you never knew you needed.

# 9

# Anti-Capitalist Resistance in Genoa: A Personal Reflection

## *Anonymous*

It became obvious when I got to Genoa that, like in Prague, the protests had a fair degree of mainstream acceptance. The convergence centre had a huge marquee that must have cost a fortune to hire and a big stage with a giant PA and lighting rig, together with lots of over-priced hot-dog vendors and a bar. It was like being at the Glastonbury Festival. These people obviously had some money.

And indeed this turned out to be true. The Genoa Social Forum (GSF), which was the official organizing body for the protests, was a coalition of about 700 different non-governmental organizations (NGOs, i.e. charities, pressure groups, etc.) and other 'civil society organizations'. It enjoyed a fair degree of mainstream support, including that of the lefty Genoa City Council, which had let it have the space for the convergence centre, as well as a school building for its media centre and several sports stadiums for all the demonstrators to stay in. Apparently this even extended to the police as well. Someone told me that the Polizia Municipale, under the control of the city council, was more sympathetic to us than the Carabinieri or any of the other nationally controlled types of police present in Genoa. So we even had lefty police!

## The left in Italy

This is a situation hard to imagine in present-day Britain. In Italy the left and institutionalized social democracy exist to a far greater extent than in Britain. The closest we get to this is 'Red' Ken Livingstone and some local lefty councils. If you imagine a return to the glory days of the 1980s when Ken was at the height of his power as head of the Greater London Council, Militant ran Liverpool and loony left councils were declaring nuclear-free zones across the country, then you are getting closer to what it is like in Italy. Even though Ken has on occasion cautiously expressed his support for anti-globalization protestors, it is still difficult to imagine in Britain a city council supporting the anti-G8 protests, or those protests having the involvement of major unions.

So in Italy the left is still alive and well (and far more Leninist than it ever was in Britain) and the whole political culture of the left is far more widespread and ingrained than in Britain. On the immigrants' march on the Thursday in Genoa, the band struck up the 'Internationale' and everyone (except the Brits and the Americans) knew all the words and was singing along with clenched fists in the air. They proceeded to play a whole bunch of other classic left songs to which everyone also seemed to know all the words. Another thing that you cannot imagine in Britain.

The reason for these differences is partly that the whole intergenerational culture of the labour movement which did exist in Britain has been destroyed over the last 20 years or so of Thatcherism. With the decimation of heavy industry and the restructuring of the economy, most of the old strongholds of the workers' movement no longer exist, such as mining, shipbuilding, the docks and the nationalized industries. It is partly also because this ingrained leftism was never as strong in Britain as in Italy anyway. The Communist Party has never been a very significant force in British politics, whereas in Italy it has dominated the postwar period, if only by virtue of the fact that no effort was spared to keep it out of power. In Genoa you could see more hammer and sickle flags in one day than you would see in Britain in the rest of your life. The Communist Party drew much of its prestige in the postwar period from the fact that it was the only organized group to fight the fascists. The partisans of the resistance movement were dominated by the Communists and in Genoa they succeeded in liberating the city from Mussolini's forces without the help of the Americans (this last part being especially important). The memory of the partisans is obviously still alive and well even among young Italians – whenever a band struck up the partisan song 'Bella Ciao' all the Italians went crazy, singing and jumping around and punching their fists in the air.

Understanding the power that the traditional left still has in Italy will give you some idea of how they managed to get 200,000 people to Genoa – 20 times more than were in Prague! The vast majority of these were Italian, and it was the Italian left of parties, unions and various different sorts of Leninists that made up the bulk of the numbers.

# The plan

The basic plan broke down like this – Thursday the 19th was the day of the immigrants' march for illegal workers and asylum seekers and against 'Fortress Europe' and its policies of exclusion. This was to be entirely peaceful, as the immigrants themselves were to be on the march and could not risk getting arrested because they would then be sent back to whatever country they had just escaped from, with who knows what consequences. Then Friday the 20th was to be the direct action day, when different groups would take all sorts of action against the G8 summit and the Red Zone protecting it. The idea was, similarly to previous summit protests, that different groups would take different positions around the perimeter of the Red Zone and carry out their various different forms of action, therefore in theory allowing pacifists to take action along the north edge of the Red Zone, while the Black Bloc attacked the eastern edge of the Red Zone, for example. This scheme was supposed to keep everyone happy because it allowed everyone to do their own thing unimpeded by people who wanted to do something different. How this actually worked out on the day will be seen below. Saturday the 21st was planned as the big united march of everyone, including all the parties and the unions and obviously including everyone who was working and could not come during the week. This, like Thursday, was supposed to be entirely peaceful and just a straightforward march from point A to point B, with a rally and speakers and no violence.

# The Black Bloc

When foreign anarchists arrived in Genoa, they found that the Italian anarchists had not organized anything. Apart from the workers' march, there was no Black Bloc meeting point organized for the Friday. In the long run-up to the Genoa protests, most Italian anarchists seemed to have spent their time denouncing the GSF for being a bunch of liberals and had expended their energy doing this rather than organizing anything themselves. Many had decided that the whole thing was completely compromised by liberal reformist ideas and that it was all a waste of time. So when the international anarchists started showing up in the few days prior to the protests, they had to run around trying to organize an anarchist meeting point. To the extent that the Black Bloc was organized at all, it was organized by international anarchists at the last moment. The main debate was over where the anarchists were going to go on Friday, and it seemed that no one wanted the poor old Black Bloc. It was eventually decided that we would all meet at the same meeting point as the Cobas (a coalition of grassroots unions) because their politics were in some ways the closest to our own and they also seemed to be up for some action and for trying to get into the Red Zone.

In Europe, it is usually not just the Black Bloc which is a bloc – *everyone* is in blocs. A normal lefty demo on the continent will be composed of all the various parties and unions arranged in blocs, one after the other, each marching in a group behind their banner. It is normal for the anarchists (whether by choice or compulsion is unclear) to bring up the rear of the march, forming a Black Bloc at the end of the demo, often trashing things along the route of the march or fighting the police. As the concept of the Black Bloc has travelled around the world, to Britain and America and elsewhere, it has left behind this original social context from which it came.

Another thing that needs sorting out is the identification of the Black Bloc with anarchists. In Genoa on Friday and Saturday there were lots of anarchists who were not in the Black Bloc and lots of people in the Black Bloc who were not anarchists. Although on the Friday anarchists did organize a pre-arranged meet-up point for the Black Bloc, many more people were engaged in Black Bloc-esque street fighting than simply the anarchists. And on the Saturday there was no pre-arranged plan at all – it was simply that people who wanted to fight went where the fighting was and people who did not tried to stay away.

Against some on the left who have tried to present the Black Bloc as something uniquely anarchist, even tracing the origins of the Black Bloc back to Bakunin's fondness for clandestine plotting and secret cells, and also against those anarchists who have tried to present the Black Bloc as something uniquely anarchist, it needs saying that there is nothing uniquely anarchist in the origins of the Black Bloc. As far as I understand it, the technique of the Black Bloc originated mainly in the 1980s Autonomen scene in northern Europe, which was at least as much anti-imperialist/Leninist as it was anarchist. This was clearly to be seen in Genoa as well, for all that the media made much of the 'anarchist' Black Bloc. If you look at photos of those engaged in the rioting, there are many red hammer and sickle flags in amongst the black-clad people, probably more than there are anarchist flags. As an example, I saw people from the Kurdistan Workers' Party (PKK) and Basque nationalists in with the Black Bloc.

And in response to the various left groups, with their very obvious self-serving agendas, all jostling for the best position in order to exploit the fame of the Genoa protests, it needs to be said that the Black Bloc is no sort of organization, no sort of group. It does not exist outside the demonstration and is united only on that demonstration by some minimal unity of tactics – people who are up for property destruction and for fighting the police. Basically, to cut through all the mythologizing bullshit, it is as simple as this – on a big demo like in Genoa, everyone wants to hang out with people who are up for the same thing they are. Even without any prior organization at all, if a fight starts with the police, people who want to fight the police will move to the front to be a part of it, and those who do not will move in the opposite direction. Therefore, just by default, effective groups will emerge. Given that quite a lot of people have been on a few demos over time, some collective ideas have emerged – masking up being one and trying to wear similar-looking clothing being another. Both for very straightforward practical reasons. That is all the Black Bloc is.

Some accuse the Black Bloc or those who engage in more militant activity in general of being 'elitist'. This is an absurd distortion. The point of being an elite is that you try to exercise power over other people. The point about the Black Bloc is that people simply want the autonomy to be able to express their anger as they see fit. There is nothing elitist in that. Accusing the Black Bloc of being a vanguard or an elite when no one ever tries to tell anyone else what to do is ridiculous. In the case of the Leninist party organizations that criticize the Black Bloc for this reason, their motives are pretty clear: the mode of organization they favour is 'democratic centralism', where everyone would be subjected to some huge democratic process of deciding what would and what would not be allowed on demos; a decision, when made by our 'representatives', would then be enforced. Now that really would be elitist.

Despite all of this, there may be a positive side to the way anarchists are always credited with all the most militant activity. So, rather than always complaining about how anarchists get demonized by the media as violent troublemakers, perhaps we should try looking at the positive side to this. When the name of anarchist has become synonymous with the most militant section of the protest movement, that gives us a certain advantage. If a larger social struggle does kick off at some point in the future, this may put us in a position of having a certain amount of street cred, if nothing more. And people attracted to the militancy, and hearing that it is all anarchists, may want to learn more about the politics. And it must really annoy the PKK et al. that whenever they engage in militant activity they get called anarchists.

## Police tactics

The Thursday immigrant march went pretty smoothly – it was noisy, musical, colourful and completely non-violent. It was at least half anarchists, a situation that was not to be replicated on any of the following days. At one point where the march turned a corner and passed a line of cops someone threw something at the cops and they were ready to charge into the crowd, but anarchists formed a line between the cops and the crowd to stop this and in order to stop any further violence. Not a scene that you will often see, admittedly, but one that goes to disprove the image of anarchists as simply violent troublemakers and mindless hooligans. People quite clearly recognized that the immigrant march was not the time or the place for any fighting to happen and stopped it from happening.

Friday's direct action day was, of course, the day that saw the most militant fighting and the most violence. Many anarchists involved in the FAI (like the Italian version of the Anarchist Federation in Britain) had spent a long time organizing with a group of workers who were on strike in the west of Genoa to have a march on the Friday; it would march from the site of the strike, around the perimeter of the Red Zone. They had promised the workers that there would not be any violence on this march, as some of the workers would have their families present. So on the Friday, a fairly substantial section of anarchists did not join the Black Bloc, but joined the workers' march in the west of the city. Then to the north of the Red Zone was the area where several different pacifist organizations would be holding their actions. The Tute Bianche (White Overalls) groups would be marching directly from their stadium in the east of the city to the Red Zone and attempting to break in on the eastern side. Then the Cobas and the Black Bloc were slightly to the south of the Tute Bianche, and other groups, like Globalise Resistance, ATTAC and the Pink and Silver group were marching on the Red Zone from the south side. In fact these neat distinctions pretty soon broke down as soon as anything actually kicked off, as the Black Bloc was split in half and forced in different directions, the Tute Bianche were repulsed by the police and various other groups all mingled together. Later on in the day you could see Tute Bianche, Black Bloc-ers, people from the social centres, Cobas, etc. all side by side. And as some of the padded-up Tute Bianche shed their armour and others donned theirs, people rapidly became indistinguishable.

The police strategy for the day seemed to rely mostly on hitting everyone with huge amounts of tear gas, almost regardless of who they were or whether they were doing anything. As hardly anyone had proper gas masks, this had a large effect. The idea seems to have been to try and disperse the crowds, and to slowly drive them away from the Red Zone and off into the suburbs of Genoa. People panicked and ran far too easily when the police started firing tear gas; they had to be restrained by some individuals calling for them to calm down and not to run. When people in a crowd start running, everyone else starts running too, and with a large crowd in a confined area, people can get trampled and squashed because everyone is being shoved on by the stampeding masses behind. In this sort of situation, the panicking crowd is easily more dangerous than the tear gas. And in any case, people were picking up the tear gas and throwing it back at the cops, which seemed to work quite well.

The result of these police tactics was that the protests and all the fighting on Friday amounted to a large and not particularly organized retreat lasting several hours. We started off relatively close to the centre and to the Red Zone, and then as soon as any fighting kicked off, the police fired huge volumes of tear gas and advanced, scattering and dispersing the crowd. Elements of the crowd attempted to slow the retreat and to buy some time by erecting barricades and attacking the police, but by and large the day consisted of the demonstrators being split into smaller and smaller groups, and being pushed further and further from the town centre and out into the suburbs.

This had several results. It is worth noting that from the beginning almost everything really worth attacking was already sealed away inside the Red Zone, which looked like it had been extended to include the main boulevard of posh shops. Therefore from the outset the demonstrators were only left with the outskirts of town to smash up and as the police advanced and pushed people further away and off into the outlying areas of town, the potential targets became more and more mundane (a corner shop, a newspaper kiosk, etc.).

# Mindful destruction

Hence some people's complaints that the Black Bloc destroyed a lot of minor property – small shops, ordinary cars and so on. A lot of the time this was the only sort of thing around. Which maybe should have meant that people did not smash anything at all, and certainly setting fire to a bank underneath a whole set of apartments seemed like a pretty stupid thing to have done – especially considering the locals had been overwhelmingly supportive, giving demonstrators/rioters food and water, allowing them to hide in their houses from the cops, cheering them on, giving them rides, etc.). However, sometimes coming under attack from the police, you have to use whatever is to hand. And if you need to use a car or a litter bin to barricade the street with, then so be it. Some of the complaints I heard just seemed to me to be remarkably petty, when people were complaining that phone boxes or bus shelters got destroyed. OK, so they did. And, yes, it is true that the rich do not generally use these things. But on the other hand it is a *riot,* and riots generally contain a fair amount of chaos and disorder. OK, maybe if everyone was acting with perfect good order and discipline then these things would not have happened, but really in the great scheme of things, does it really matter? For fuck's sake, phone boxes get smashed up every day of the week anyway. Riots have historically proven to be a very effective way for the dispossessed to make their voices heard and to enforce their will. Does anyone really imagine that in the French Revolution, or the Peasants' Revolt, or the bread riots of the nineteenth century or the anti-structural adjustment riots in the Third World today, no random stupid shit happened? Of course it did, and if there is ever going to be any sort of revolution then it will probably involve a whole lot more random chaos and disorder and fucked-up stuff happening, so get used to it.

However, that said, it does not mean that we should not try and minimize this and conduct ourselves with as much good order as possible –

which, to their credit, people were doing. Contrary to the stereotypes of anarchists thugs engaging in mindless and uncontrolled destruction, everything I saw (maybe the burning bank excepted) seemed very soberly done and thoughtful. Walking down the Corso Torino in the aftermath of some of the fighting, it was completely clear to see – every single bank was smashed to pieces and *nothing* else was. There were also numerous examples of people questioning each other during the fighting about what they were doing and attempting to stop people doing especially stupid things – of the crowd policing itself in a way. Crowds and riots are almost never as wild and uncontrolled as the media would have you believe. Most people involved know very clearly what they are doing and can tell you why.

But there were some people doing fairly silly things during the fighting. One friend of mine said it seemed like rioting by numbers: there were lots of young people there who may have been attracted to the protests by coverage of other similar things they had seen on television, and they were doing what they had seen on television – what they thought you were *supposed* to do during riots. So people were building barricades in the streets when there was no need to, and then when they were needed to hold the police back, they would be deserted as everyone ran away. Lots of people seemed keener on smashing things up than on defending the space against the police. And people were smashing up random things that made no sense. On one occasion, a group raided a little corner shop and dragged a crate of cola or something into the street and then smashed up all the bottles with hammers.

It is worth noting that the police response to the demonstrators did not seem to be related to who was 'violent' and who was 'peaceful'. They used violence and tear gas and water cannon against everyone – against the pink and silver dancers, against the Trotskyites, against the Tute Bianche and against the Black Bloc. This clearly shows the falsity of the idea that militant sections of the crowd provoke the violence of the police, and that if only we were all pacifists then the police would leave us alone. It is a ridiculous presumption to believe that we can 'decide' how the police will react to us. We had ensured that we were going to get a violent response by gathering in the streets in such large numbers and announcing our intention to get inside the Red Zone. That is a provocative and confrontational stance to take, whether or not you are throwing Molotov cocktails. Then the Black Bloc get all the blame for the violence on account of being the only people actually prepared for the violence that the *entire* demonstration has inevitably provoked. The police strategy was clearly to attack everyone equally, to punish and scare off the non-violent people on the protests from future participation in these sorts of event. The police respond to the level of violence you threaten and to your effectiveness. If you are ineffective but violent, you will probably get a response from the police; if you are ineffective and non-violent, you will probably not get much response from the police; but if you begin to be effective, whether you are using violence or not, then you will be met with a violent response. This was true in Seattle and it was true in Genoa.

Some people have complained about how the trashing of the town detracted from the aim of getting inside the Red Zone. This is self-delusion really. Most people made a fairly realistic assessment that we were unlikely to get inside the Red Zone in any large numbers and that, if a substantial number of people did manage to breach their defences then the police would probably open fire anyway. After all, the police had known the exact day we would attempt our attack for several months, and giving them that much time to prepare, you are unlikely to be able to get past them. Under these circumstances, trashing the town was potentially the best thing to do. The police were too busy protecting the Red Zone, we had effective control of the streets, and this level of destruction will send out an effective message to the whole world, but especially to any other cities that are thinking of hosting summit meetings, that if they do then this is what will happen to their city too. This is making these kinds of summit meetings harder and harder to hold. As the *Guardian* reported, 'there is a shortage of cities queuing up to be turned into a war zone'.[1]

This is one important thing to remember about Genoa – because it was a G8 summit, all the world's media were there, and the news and the images of the rioting will have been carried back to almost every country in the world. The value of this, especially in much of the Third World, is inestimable. Many people in other countries in the world imagine that everyone in the West lives a life of indolent luxury. Remember that *Baywatch* is the most popular television programme in the world. This is the image that many people across the world have of life in the West. It is very valuable for them to be able to see images of things they are familiar with – poor people fighting the police – taking place in the 'rich' West, leading them to realize that the image they have been fed of the western lifestyle is not all it is cracked up to be, and that there are people like them in the West fighting for the same things they are fighting for. The riots in Genoa will send a message of hope to people all over the world that right inside the belly of the beast there are thousands of people who are against the system and are prepared to risk their own life and liberty to fight it.

## Infiltrators, provocateurs, fascists and cops

So there were quite a few people within the Black Bloc who did some stupid things. Well, nothing new there then. Some people have said that the Black Bloc split fairly early on and a whole bunch of people left and went off and did their own thing because they got fed up with the stupid shit that some people were doing. Some people have suggested that the

Black Bloc which was going around doing the more fucked-up anti-social stuff then moved off to the area where the pacifists were and started attacking the police at those points, leading the police to pile in and attack the pacifists. Apparently, this anti-social Black Bloc then moved away from both the Red Zone and the police, and started just randomly destroying ordinary people's property. For these and some other reasons, some people have suggested that this more fucked-up segment of the Black Bloc was composed of police.

Some Leninist and left-liberal groups have gone further than this and have put about the story that the Black Bloc and the police acted together, 'orchestrating' the violence. Apparently, the police allowed the Black Bloc to act unhindered and did not stop them or arrest them when they could have done, but instead used them by driving the Black Bloc into some other sections of the crowd on purpose to give them a reason to attack the peaceful parts of the demonstration. Now there may or may not have been police infiltrators in the Black Bloc, I do not know. But I do know for sure that the police did not orchestrate anything with the Black Bloc as a whole; the Black Bloc had no 'plan' to work with the police to disrupt the peaceful demonstrators, as some of the paranoid rubbish put about by some of the left-liberal groups would suggest. For one thing this would be impossible, as the Black Bloc had no 'plan' of any sort at all. And as for allowing us to go about 'unhindered' . . . well, apart from all the tear gas, baton charges, water cannon, tanks being driven at us, and being shot at, yes, we were pretty much unhindered.

And while we are on the subject of infiltration, lots of the left-liberal groups who have been accusing the Black Bloc of being cops and fascists act is if they are somehow magically immune to infiltration themselves. The finest example of this nonsense is *Socialist Worker* claiming that the Black Bloc's methods and use of masks open them up to police infiltration. How exactly are non-masked-up, non-violent groups any less easy to infiltrate? It is certainly entirely plausible that the cops would infiltrate the Black Bloc – that is exactly the sort of thing they would do. But so also would they infiltrate all the other organizations, including all of those now attacking the Black Bloc. Indeed, is it not just as likely a cop tactic to place cops within the left-liberal organizations to ensure that they denounce the more militant elements of the crowd as it is that the cops would attempt to infiltrate the more militant sections? I am not saying it is true, but that it has about the same likelihood of being true as the Black Bloc being infiltrated by cops and fascists.

Whether or not it actually happened in Genoa, it is certainly entirely possible for the police to infiltrate the Black Bloc and to try and antagonize other protesters and the general public against the more militant elements of these protests. So regardless of whether it actually happened in this instance, we need to be aware that it easily *could* happen and we need to develop some mechanisms to guard against this, if possible.

Probably the best way of doing this would be to develop better collective solidarity and self-policing, allowing people to challenge others in the crowd who are engaging in counterproductive behaviour.

## Saturday and after

After Friday when we had all heard that a guy had been shot dead, we were wondering what Saturday was going to be like. Would it be really angry as a result or would everyone be scared? As it turned out, Saturday was in many ways a re-run of Friday's rioting, with the difference that there was greater antagonism towards the Black Bloc from some of the other demonstrators, some blaming them for the shooting the previous day and some accusing them of being cops or fascists. There were probably more people on the streets, but with numbers this large it is in any case almost impossible to estimate whether you are talking about 100,000 or 200,000. Although Saturday was supposed to be peaceful, this had never been agreed to as unanimously as for the Thursday event and it pretty much kicked off immediately. However, groups like the Tute Bianche, which on Friday had been all padded up for direct action, were now picking on people who had any padding and were forming lines to keep the main bulk of the march separate from the people engaged in fighting the police. Most of the people on the march probably did in fact complete the designated route without being caught up in any street fighting, although they might have got gassed a bit. The rioting on Saturday carried on into the evening, culminating late in the night with the police raid on the GSF media centre and the school where many people were staying.

The main bulk of the crowds that had filled the streets on Saturday left very quickly on Sunday. It was amazing how quickly everyone melted away. Partly this was due to fear of a police crackdown, but the dissipating numbers strengthened this process because the more people left town, the more vulnerable the remaining few felt. The GSF laid on special buses and trains to whisk people out of the area as swiftly as possible.

## The numbers game

On demonstrations like these, two main factors are constantly argued over – militancy and numbers. One group of people are worried that certain levels of militancy will reduce the numbers on protests, and the others are worried that large numbers mean nothing if no one does anything. Both points of view have some truth to them. Clearly numbers in themselves mean nothing. If those people are threatening nothing and are so well policed and disciplined that there is no danger of them getting out of hand, then you can have demos as big as you like and it means nothing. Lots of people were on the streets to celebrate the millennium or for the Golden Jubilee, for example. Of course, even in situations like these there is usually some potential for things to get out of control. But on the other side, militancy without numbers is also clearly a losing game, ending up as isolated, easily repressed and with no connection to anyone else. The numbers on a demonstration and the militancy of the demonstrators can compensate for one another. In Prague the militancy of the demonstrators made up for their relatively small number. In Seattle the reverse was the case, with large numbers compensating for relatively little militancy.

Being in essence a political protest movement, the anti-globalization movement has a limited constituency and it is not so easy to expand numerically on that basis. There seems no especially easy or obvious way for the movement to 'go forward' except in terms of increasing militancy. In a way, the shooting of Carlo Guiliani in Genoa, although in the grand scheme of things nothing that remarkable, demonstrates the bottom line to this movement. If the movement progresses in terms of escalating violence alone then we will lose because they have guns and we do not. This demonstrates that perhaps the movement is reaching the limits of a separate political protest movement with no particular social base.

In terms of developing the sort of generalized social struggle that will allow us to go beyond just being a political movement and to begin to be a real anti-capitalist *social* movement, we may have an advantage in Britain precisely because the left does not exist here in the same way that it does in Italy. The whole neoliberal project has had a headstart in Britain, in that after 20 years of Thatcherism, the left has been destroyed and the power of the unions broken to an unprecedented degree. Of course, the fortunes of the left in general are tied to the fortunes of the class struggle. The left is weak at the moment because the class struggle as a whole is weak. An upsurge in class struggle may see a corresponding upsurge in the left, as the various left parties and unions attempt to ride the new wave. If this is so, they will try to control and rein in any upsurge in struggle and it may well come to nothing. After all, probably the main reason for the failure of the closest thing we have come to a revolution in modern times, in France in 1968, was that workers failed to break with the unions and the unions were successfully able to contain the revolt.

On the face of it, the greater strength of the left there may make it seem like more is going on in Italy, but the potential for some sort of revolutionary activity could be greater in Britain because, if there is any sort of upsurge in struggle here, it could stand a greater chance of escaping the control of the left. The whole Thatcherite project was a gamble – they were betting that they could dismantle the whole postwar social-democratic consensus, increasing insecurity, cutting wages and increasing work, without provoking the sort of class struggle that necessitated the introduction of the whole apparatus of the postwar state in the first place. This gamble could go wrong and the whole thing could blow up in their faces. Britain is perhaps in a better situation for this to occur than Italy, and it is precisely this sort of social crisis that could provide a basis for the anti-capitalist movement, allowing it to avoid becoming trapped in an escalating cycle of increasing militancy.

# Notes

## Introduction

1. F. Fukuyama, *The End of History and the Last Man* (London: Hamish Hamilton, 1992).
2. D. Bell, *The End of Ideology* (New York: Free Press, 1965).
3. C. Hay, *The Political Economy of New Labour: Labouring under False Pretences* (Manchester: Manchester University Press, 1999).

## Chapter 1    Anti-Capitalism: Are We All Anarchists Now?

1. E. Birchman and J. Charlton (eds), *Anti-Capitalism: A Guide to the Movement* (London: Bookmarks, 2001), pp. 340–1.
2. N. Klein, *No Logo* (London: Flamingo, 2001).
3. G. Debord, *The Society of the Spectacle* (New York: Zone Books, 1994), p. 24.
4. Anon., 'Friday June 18th 1999: confronting capitalism and smashing the state', *Do or Die*, 8, 1999, pp. 1–12.
5. G. McKay, *Senseless Acts of Beauty: Cultures of Resistance since the Sixties* (London: Verso, 1996).
6. The dsei protests were a series of creative actions against a government-sponsored death fair held in London's Docklands in 2003.
7. An attack by police on a group of travellers seeking to get to Stonehenge. After cornering them in the Beanfield, they assaulted the convoy and smashed up the vehicles. One ITN reporter said these were 'police tactics which seemed to break new grounds in the scale and the intensity of their violence'.
8. Subvertisers' website can be found at http://www.adbusters.org/home.
9. The Campaign for the Accountability of American Bases website is at http://www.caab.org.uk.
10. Details and reports on the 2003 May Day can be found at http://diy.spc.org/ourmayday/index03.html.
11. The Indymedia site is at http://www.indymedia.org.uk.
12. The Schnews site is at http://www.schnews.co.uk.
13. Urban75's protest discussion boards are at http://www.urban75.net/vbulletin.
14. 'Vampire Alert', an account of the SWP's parasitic relationship to the anti-capitalist movement, can be found at http://www.anarchopunk.free-online.co.uk/reb/leftist.html. We believe that this may originally have been produced by Leeds Earth First!.
15. A. Callinicos, *An Anti-Capitalist Manifesto* (Cambridge: Polity, 2003).
16. Klein, *No Logo*, ch. 3.
17. See Schnews' characterization of the ACM at http://schnews.org.uk/mr.htm.

18. M. Bookchin, *Social Anarchism or Lifestyle Anarchism: An Unbridgeable Chasm* (Edinburgh: AK Press, 1995), p. 10.

19. B. Black, *Anarchy after Leftism* (Columbia, Mo.: CAL Press, 1997), p. 14.

20. C. Belsey, *Poststructuralism: A Very Short Introduction* (Oxford: Oxford University Press, 2002), p. 56.

21. See I. MacKenzie , 'Unravelling the knots: post-structuralism and other "post-isms"', *Journal of Political Ideologies*, 6, 2 (2001), p. 335.

22. A useful discussion of Descartes may be found in B. Russell, *A History of Western Philosophy* (London: Unwin Paperbacks, 1984).

23. T. May, *The Political Philosophy of Poststructuralist Anarchism* (Pennsylvania: Pennsylvania State University Press, 1994), p. 78.

24. H. Bertens, *The Idea of the Postmodern: A History* (London: Routledge, 1995), p. 8.

25. May, *The Political Philosophy of Poststructuralist Anarchism*, pp. 60–5.

26. May denotes social anarchism as a strategic philosophy. See ibid., pp. 8–14.

27. Ibid., p. 11.

28. J. Moore, 'Anarchism and poststructuralism', *Anarchist Studies*, 5, 2 (1997), p. 159. Moore himself was not a subscriber to poststructuralist anarchism. Rather, Moore identified with what he termed the second wave of anarchism that incorporates figures like Debord, Vaneigem, Zerzan and Perlman. This is not a consistent grouping and ranges from situationists to primitivists.

29. May, *The Political Philosophy of Poststructuralist Anarchism*, p. 85.

30. D. Graeber, 'The new anarchists', *New Left Review*, 13 (2002), pp. 61–73.

31. A. Melucci, *Challenging Codes: Collective Action in the Information Age* (Cambridge: Cambridge University Press, 1996).

32. V. Ruggiero, 'New social movements and the "centri sociali" in Milan', *The Sociological Review*, 48, 2 (2000), p. 181.

33. I. Welsh, 'New social movements yesterday, today and tomorrow', *Anarchist Studies*, 7, 1 (1999), p. 79.

34. For a discussion of the role of long-term autonomous capacity building within new social movements, see ibid.

35. May, *The Political Philosophy of Poststructuralist Anarchism*, pp. 10–12.

36. Anon., 'Friday June 18th', *Do or Die*, 8, p. 1.

37. F. Fukuyama, *The End of History and the Last Man* (London: Hamish Hamilton, 1992).

38. See P. Kropotkin, *Act for Yourselves: Articles from 'Freedom' 1886–1907* (London: Freedom Press, 1988).

39. G. Deleuze and F. Guattari, *A Thousand Plateaus: Capitalism and Schizophrenia* (London: Athlone Press, 1988), pp. 103–7.

40. MacKenzie, 'Unravelling the knots', p. 343.

41. Deleuze and Guattari, *A Thousand Plateaus*, pp. 105–6, 469.

42. We refer here to the popular conception of what postmodernism is about: that is, the absence of metanarratives and organizational structures, unifying ideologies and other foundationalist discourses and practices.

## Chapter 2   Time to Replace Globalization: A Green Localist Manifesto for World Trade

This chapter is one of a series of publications produced by Caroline Lucas in areas such as GM foods, animal welfare, aviation and transport, the work of the WTO and the future of Europe. It originally appeared as a report and is reproduced here in slightly adapted form with thanks to Caroline Lucas and Colin Hines. The report was written in 2001 and anticipated a number of issues and controversies that were raised at the WTO ministerial meeting at Cancun in 2003, attended by Caroline as a member of the EU delegation. The authors gratefully acknowledge the help of Cherry Puddicombe and Lucy Ford.

1. W. Sachs (ed.), *The Development Dictionary: A Guide to Knowledge as Power* (London: Zed Books, 1992).

2. A. Simms, *Collision Course: Free Trade's Free Ride on the Global Climate* (London: New Economics Foundation, 2000).

3. *White Paper on International Development* (London: Department for International Development, 2000).

4. See Myth 4 on the theory of comparative advantage.

5. G. Palast, 'An internal IMF study reveals the price "rescued" nations pay: dearer essentials, worse poverty and shorter lives', *Observer*, 8 October 2000.

6. Ibid.

7. Centre for Economic Policy Research, *The Emperor Has No Growth* (London: Centre for Economic Policy Research, 2001).

8. UNCTAD, *Trade and Development Report* (Geneva: UNCTAD, 1997).

9. Cited in the *Ecologist*, 'Globalising poverty: the World Bank, IMF and WTO, their policies exposed', September 2000, p. 4.

10. D. Rodrik, 'Trading in illusions', *Foreign Policy*, 123 (2001), pp. 55–62.

11. World Development Movement, *If It's Broke, Fix It* (London: World Development Movement, 2001).

12. M. J. Finger and P. Schuler, 'Implementation of Uruguay round commitments: the development challenge', World Bank Policy Research Working Paper, no. 2215, October 1999.

13. Cited by Vandana Shiva in a speech to the 'Local Food, Global Solution' Conference, London, July 2001.

14. Martin Khor, *Third World Network Information Service on WTO Issues*, Geneva, September 2001.

15. Friends of the Earth, *The Citizen's Guide to Trade, Environment and Sustainability* (London: Friends of the Earth, 2000).

16. J. Gray, *False Dawn: The Delusions of Global Capitalism* (London: New Press, 1998).

17. WTO, *Trade and the Environment in the WTO* (Geneva: WTO, undated).

18. J. Woodruffe and M. Ellis-Jones, *States of Unrest*, World Development Movement Report, September 2000.

19. 'WTO – Shrink or Sink!', The Turnaround Agenda, International Civil Society sign-on letter; emphasis in original.

20. Quoted in Panos, 'Globalisation and employment: new opportunities, real threats', *Panos Briefing*, no. 33, May 1999, p. 5.

21. N. Hertz, 'It's about apathy', *Observer*, 10 June 2001.

22. W. Greider, *One World Ready or Not: The Manic Logic of Global Capitalism* (London: Simon and Schuster, 2000), p. 148; J. Lloyd, 'Will this be the Chinese century?', *New Statesman*, 10 January 2000.

23. A. E. Eckes Jr, *Opening America's Market: US Foreign Trade Policy since 1776* (Chapel Hill, NC: University of North Carolina Press, 1995).

24. Tony Blair, speech to the Labour Party Conference, Brighton, 2 October 2001.

25. L. Wallach and M. Sforza, *Whose Trade Organisation?* (Washington, DC: Public Citizen, 1999).

26. Ibid.

27. D. Korten, *When Corporations Rule the World* (Bloomfield, Conn.: Kumarian Press, 1995); B. Balanya et al., *Europe Inc.: Regional and Global Restructuring and the Rise of Corporate Power* (London: Pluto Press, 2000).

28. Ibid.

29. J. Mander and E. Goldsmith (eds), *The Case Against the Global Economy* (London: Earthscan, 2001), p. 70; B. Barnet and J. Cavanagh, *Global Dreams: Imperial Corporations and the New World Order* (New York: Simon and Schuster, 1994), p. 423.

30. *Johannesburg Business Day*, 20 February 1997.

31. Tony Blair, speech at 50th Anniversary WTO Ministerial Meeting, Geneva, 1998.

32. D. Keet, 'Globalisation and regionalisation: contradictory tendencies? Counteractive tactics? Or strategic possibilities?', The Foundation for Global Dialogue, Occasional Paper, no. 18, 1999.

33. Ibid.

34. C. Hines, *Localisation: A Global Manifesto* (London: Earthscan, 2000).

35. The Greens/EFA (European Free Alliance) is a political alliance in the European Parliament consisting of ten EFA and 35 Green Members.

# Chapter 3  The Watermelon Myth Exploded: Greens and Anti-Capitalism

1. From *The Fifth Sacred Thing: A Visionary Novel* (New York: Bantam, 1993).

2. In this chapter I have focused on what we can do within the present legal structure to undermine and avoid capitalism. As a political party, the Green Party's objective is to change that political structure at both the national and international level. Policies such as the citizens' income scheme, removing the pressure to work, the land value tax, shifting the burden of tax from income to ownership, and making inheritance tax dependent on the wealth of the inheritor, would have important consequences for our economic system. More details of these and other Green Party policies are available in the Manifesto for a Sustainable Society, online at www.greenparty.org.uk: click on 'policies'.

3. D. H. Meadows, D. L. Meadows, J. Randers and W. W. Behrens III, *The Limits to Growth: A Report for the Club of Rome's Project on the Predicament of Mankind*, 2nd edn (New York: Universe Books, 1974).

4. K. E. Boulding, 'The economics of the coming spaceship Earth', in H. Jarrett (ed.), *Environmental Quality in a Growing Economy* (Washinginton, DC: Johns Hopkins University Press), p. 303.

5. The foremost proponent of the infinite availability of resources is Julian Simon: see his article 'Resources, population, environment: an oversupply of false bad news', *Science*, 268 (1980), pp. 1435–6.

6. For further discussion of this point, see my paper, 'Absolute limits to a relative definition of poverty', presented to the International Sustainable Development Conference, Manchester (March 1996), and published in conference proceedings.

7. See my book about social research that I conducted in the South Wales Valleys, where my respondents held dustmen, plumbers, nurses and midwives to be much more socially valuable than chief executives – or university professors!

(*The Pit and the Pendulum: A Cooperative Future for Work in the South Wales Valleys*, Cardiff: University of Wales Press, 2004).

8. This may seem a rather unfair and one-sided attack on entrepreneurs. To balance it a little I should point out that the evening of the day I wrote this passage was spent at a fabulous party thrown at her expense by my own favourite entrepreneur: the manager of our local wholefood shop, the Treehouse, Jane Burnham. She is a beautiful, statuesque and powerful woman, who has spent most of her life growing organic vegetables and now sells them through a shop. She removes from me the need for all sorts of complex decisions about seasonal and ethical shopping, and has greatly enhanced the quality of my life. Perhaps a more useful approach to the entrepreneur than full-frontal assault is what Len Arthur refers to as 'deviant mainstreaming' – reinventing the entrepreneur to fit our model of how the economic system should look. There are many entrepreneurs in the social economy whose aim is increasing human well-being rather than making a profit. They are the model for entrepreneurship we should use to replace the mainstream model.

9. New Economics Foundation Conference on Localism, 16 May 2003; see: www.neweconomics.org. For more detail, see J. Madeley, *Hungry for Trade: How the Poor Pay for Free Trade* (London: Zed, 2000).

10. *UNCTAD Report on Trade*, 1997, Part Two, chap. IV, sect. B.1; World Bank report: M. Lundberg and L. Squire, *The Simultaneous Evolution of Growth and Inequality*, December 1999. Grateful thanks to Richard Douthwaite for both these references.

11. C. Lucas, M. Hart and C. Hines, *Look to the Local: A Better Agriculture Is Possible!* (2002), produced by the Greens in the European Parliament and the Small and Family Farms Alliance.

12. A. Simms, *Collision Course: Free Trade's Free Ride on the Global Climate* (London: New Economics Foundation, 2000).

13. T. Eagleton, *Marx and Freedom* (London: Phoenix, 1997), p. 28.

14. First statistic from 'Stress prevention in the workplace: assessing the costs and benefits to organisation', by Prof. Cary L. Cooper and Dr Susan Cartwright (both of Manchester School of Management, UMIST); Prof. Paula Liukkonen, Dept of Economics, University of Stockholm, Sweden, published by the European Foundation for the Improvement of Living and Working Conditions; second and third from Rory O'Neill, Background Document for TUC Conference on Stress, October 1996.

15. I have written at greater length on this issue in a short book called *Seven Myths About Work*, reprinted online as *Arbeit Macht Frei* in 2001. For a pdf version contact the author at: molly@greenaudit.org.

16. The results were reported in a BBC article: http://news.bbc.co.uk/1/hi/uk/2951625.stm.

17. H. E. Daly, *Toward a Steady State Economy* (San Francisco: W. H. Freeman, 1973).

18. According to Hazel Henderson, 'Economists are familiar with the top two layers of the cake, in which money is the major ingredient. The icing (top layer) is the private sector where most of the innovation goes on. But it rests on the public sector . . . and these two layers are all the economists see' (from her book *The Politics of the Solar Age* (Totnes: Green Books, 1988)). Maria Mies's iceberg analogy illustrates the invisible economic activity that is outside the realm of measurement of GDP, including women's work, homeworking, subsistence work, the unpaid work of the colonies, and the work of nature herself (see the figure in

'Women in the world economy', chapter 5 in M. S. Cato and M. Kennett (eds), *Green Economics: Beyond Supply and Demand to Meeting People's Needs* (Aberystwyth: Green Audit), pp. 48–62).

19. K. Marx, *Grundrisse* (1858) in R. C. Tucker (ed.), *The Marx-Engels Reader*, 2nd edn (New York: Norton, 1978), p. 479.

20. See C. Hines and T. Lang, 'Time to protect jobs', in M. S. Cato and M. Kennett (eds), *Green Economics: Beyond Supply and Demand to Meeting People's Needs* (Aberystwyth: Green Audit, 1999).

21. My own paper developing the theme of trade subsidiarity, *Trade Subsidiarity: Reducing the Movement of Goods for the Benefit of People and Planet* (Aberystwyth: Green Audit) is available from me on request.

22. M. Tewdwr-Jones and N. A. Phelps, 'Unsustainable behaviour? The subordination of local governance in creating customised spaces for Asian FDI', paper presented to the Regional Studies Association Conference, Bilbao, September 1999; more details about LG can be found in my forthcoming book, *The Pit and the Pendulum: A Cooperative Future for Work in the Valleys* (Cardiff: University of Wales Press, 2004).

23. http://www.bioregional.com/lave/lave1.htm. See also the book by Bioregional directors Pooran Desai and Sue Riddlestone, *Bioregional Solutions for Living on One Planet*, Schumacher Briefing no. 8 (Totnes: Green Books, 2002).

24. K. Morgan and A. Morley, *Relocalising the Food Chain: The Role of Creative Public Procurement* (Cardiff: Regeneration Institute, 2002).

25. This concept, which originated in Quebec, is being developed by the Welsh Institute for Research into Cooperatives, at UWIC Business School, Cardiff: see L. Arthur, M. S. Cato, T. Keenoy and R. Smith, *Pamphlet on Cooperatives* (Cardiff: Welsh Institute for Research into Cooperatives, 2003).

26. On the barter clubs, see R. Pearson, 'Argentina's barter network: new currency for new times?', *Bulletin of Latin American Research*, 22, 2 (2002), pp. 214–30; *Ambito nacional*. 'Es Ley Ya Moneda Provincial: El San Luis', 4 October, describes the regional currencies; the use of grain to pay for GM pick-up trucks was reported in *Ambito Financero*, 'Por mejora del camp, venden mas pick-up', 7 November 2002. Thanks to Heloisa Primavera and Carlos Louge for the story of Argentina.

27. H. Norberg-Hodge, T. Merrifield and S. Gorelick, *Bringing the Food Economy Home: Local Alternatives to Global Agribusiness* (London: Zed, 2002).

28. These ideas are still being developed, but for those who would like more detail see my paper, 'Lessons from the dark ages of capitalism: medieval crafts guilds and worker participation', presented to the Limitation to the Market Conference, Oxford, 15 June 2002.

29. See W. Schwarz, 'Havana Harvest', *Guardian*, 16 January 2002. 'Cuba exports city farming "revolution" to Venezuela', 22 April 2003, by M. Morales, Reuters. Thanks to David Weston for these references and lots of fruitful ideas.

## Chapter 4   9/11 and the Consequences for British-Muslims

1. A. Saeed, N. Blain and D. Forbes, 'New ethnic and national questions in Scotland: post-British identities among Glasgow-Pakistani teenagers', *Ethnic and Racial Studies*, 22, 5 (1999), pp. 821–44.

2. A. Saeed, 'What's in a name? Muhammad Ali and the politics of cultural identity', in A. Bernstein and N Blain (eds), *Sport, Media, Culture: Global and Local Dimensions* (London: Frank Cass, 2002).

3. S. Cannon and A. Saeed, 'Jihad Musical? Musique Hip-hop et musulmans en Grande-Bretagne et France', in A. Hargreaves (ed.), *Minorités ethniques anglophones et francophones: études culturelles comparatives* (London: Avebury, 2002).

4. H. Ansari, *Muslims in Britain* (London: Minority Rights Group, 2002), p. 4.

5. H. Balibar, *Culture, Globalization and the World* (London: Macmillan, 1991), p. 60.

6. A. Abukahlil, *Bin Laden, Islam and America's New 'War on Terrorism'* (New York: Open Media Books, 2002), p. 11.

7. Saeed et al., 'New ethnic and national questions in Scotland', p. 822.

8. *Observer*, 25 November 2001.

9. A. Kundnani, 'In a foreign land: the popular racism', *Race and Class*, 43, 2 (2001), p. 55.

10. A. Saeed, 'A community under suspicion', *Scottish Left Review*, 11, July/August 2002.

11. T. Modood, *Changing Ethnic Identities* (London: PSI, 1994).

12. Kundnani, 'In a foreign land: the popular racism', p. 43.

13. *Guardian*, 21 March 2003.

14. *The Guardian*, 14 May 2002.

15. L. Fekete , *Racism, The Hidden Cost of September 11* (London: Institute of Race Relations, 2002), p. 38.

16. *Sun*, 14 January 2003.

17. Fekete, *Racism, The Hidden Cost of September 11*, p. 2.

18. F. Halliday, *Islam and the Myth of Confrontation: Religion and Politics in the Middle East* (London: I.B. Tauris, 1999).

19. Ibid., p. 161.

20. S. Ziauddin and M. Davies, *Why Do People Hate America?* (London: Icon Books, 2002), p. 49.

21. Halliday, *Islam and the Myth of Confrontation*, p. 2.

22. E. Said, *Orientalism* (London: Routledge and Kegan Paul, 1978), pp. 286–7.

23. Halliday, *Islam and the Myth of Confrontation*, pp. 160–95.

24. Ibid.

25. Fekete, *Racism, The Hidden Cost of September 11*, p. 17.

26. Ibid., pp. 17–18; Halliday, *Islam and the Myth of Confrontation*, pp. 160–95.

27. Ibid., p. 160.

28. F. Halliday, 'Islamophobia reconsidered', *Ethnic and Racial Studies*, 22, 5 (1999), pp. 892–902.

29. Ibid., pp. 898.

30. Halliday, *Islam and the Myth of Confrontation*, p. 194.

31. Fekete, *Racism, The Hidden Cost of September 11*, p. 19. Abukahlil, *Bin Laden, Islam and America's New 'War on Terrorism'*, p. 14.

32. *Guardian*, 14 January 2003.

33. T. Modood et al., *Ethnic Minorities in Britain: Diversity and Disadvantage* (London: PSI, 1997), p. 331.

34. Saeed et al., 'New ethnic and national questions in Scotland', pp. 838–9.

35. *Guardian*, 17 June 2002.

36. The poll was conducted on 23 November 2001.

37. Fekete, *Racism, The Hidden Cost of September 11*, p. 17.

38. T. May, *Social Research Methods* (Buckingham: Open University Press, 1997).

39. Ibid., p. 45.

40. See Abukahlil, *Bin Laden, Islam and America's New 'War on Terrorism'*; N. Chomsky, *9:11* (New York: Open Media Books, 2002); J. Pilger, *The New Rulers of the World* (London: Verso, 2002).

41. M. Parenti, *The Terrorism Trap* (San Franciso: City Light Books, 2002), pp. 35–46.

42. See H. Ansari, *Muslims in Britain* (London: Minority Rights Group, 2002); E. Poole, *Reporting Islam: Media Representations of British Muslims* ( London: I.B. Tauris, 2002).

43. See *Eastern Eye*, 23 November 2001; *Guardian*, 17 June 2002.

44. Ansari, *Muslims in Britain*, p. 2.

45. Runnymede Trust, *Islamophobia: A Challenger for Us All* (London: Runnymede Trust, 1997).

46. Fekete, *Racism, The Hidden Cost of September 11*, pp. 17–19.

47. J. Jacobsen, 'Religion and ethnicity: dual and alternative sources of identity among young British-Pakistanis', *Ethnic and Racial Studies*, 20, 2 (1997), pp. 181–99.

48. Saeed et al., 'New ethnic and national questions in Scotland', pp. 838–42.

49. Halliday, *Islam and the Myth of Confrontation*, pp. 160–95.

50. Ansari, *Muslims in Britain*.

51. See ibid.; Poole, *Reporting Islam: Media Representations of British Muslims*; Runnymede Trust, *Islamophobia: A Challenger for Us All*.

52. A. Saeed, 'The media and new racisms', *Media Education Journal*, 27 (2000), pp. 19–22.

53. Chomsky, *9:11*.

54. Pilger, *The New Rulers of the World*, p. 137.

55. See Saeed, 'A community under suspicion'.

56. Poole, *Reporting Islam: Media Representations of British Muslims*; Runnymede Trust, *Islamophobia: A Challenge for Us All*.

57. Ansari, *Muslims in Britain*, p. 31.

58. Saeed et al., 'New ethnic and national questions in Scotland', p. 826.

## Chapter 5   Bakhtin and the Carnival against Capitalism

1. P. Hitchcock, 'The grotesque of the body electric', in M. M. Bell and M. Gardiner (eds), *Bakhtin and the Human Sciences* (London: Sage, 1998).

2. Anon., 'Friday June 18th 1999. Carnival against Capital!', *Do or Die*, 8 (2000), pp. 18–22.

3. K. Marx, *Capital* (London: Penguin, 1976), p. 742; see also J. Kovel, *The Enemy of Nature* (New York: Zed Press, 2002).

4. Yes, I am being rude about British sociology departments, the Socialist Workers' Party and Workers' Power.

5. I am thinking of the non-governmental organizations such as Oxfam that want a fairer World Trade Organization rather than a fundamentally different society.

6. D. Wall, 'The ecosocialism of fools', *Capitalism Nature Socialism*, 14, 2 (2003), forthcoming.

7. J. Ronson, *Them: Adventures with Extremists* (London: Picador, 2000).

8. D. Wall, *Getting There: Steps to a Green Society* (London: Greenprint, 1990).

9. G. Chesters, 'The new intemperance: protest, imagination and carnival',

*Ecos*, 21, 1 (2000), pp. 2–9; J. Jordan, 'The art of necessity: the subversive imagination of anti-road protest and Reclaim the Streets', in G. McKay (ed.), *DIY Cultures: Parties and Protest in Nineties Britain* ( London: Verso, 1998).

10. M. M. Bell, 'Deep fecology: Mikhail Bakhtin and the call of nature', *Capitalism Nature Socialism*, 5, 4 (1994), pp. 65–84; M. Gardiner, 'Ecology and carnival: traces of a "Green" social theory in the writings of M. M. Bakhtin', *Theory and Society*, 22 (1993), pp. 765–812.

11. M. Steinberg, 'Tilting the frame: considerations on collective action framing from a discursive turn', *Theory and Society*, 27 (1998), pp. 845–72; C. Barker, 'A modern moral economy? Edward Thompson and Valentin Volosinov meet in North Manchester', paper presented to the conference on Making Social Movements: The British Marxist Historians and the Study of Social Movements, Edge Hill College of Higher Education, 26–8 June 2002; M. Gardiner, *The Dialogics of Critique: M. M. Bakhtin and the Theory of Ideology* (London: Routledge, 1992).

12. A good source of biographical detail is K. Clark and M. Holquist, *Mikhail Bakhtin.* (Cambridge, Mass.: Belknap, 1984).

13. Ibid., p. vii.

14. For an excellent summary of these key ideas from a literary perspective, see S. Vice, *Introducing Bakhtin* (Manchester: Manchester University Press, 1997).

15. M. Bakhtin, *Rabelais and His World* (Bloomington, Ind.: Indiana University Press, 1984).

16. D. Wall, *Earth First! and the Anti-Roads Movement* (London: Routledge, 1998).

17. Ibid.

18. Ibid.

19. D. Wall, 'Mobilising Earth First! in the UK', in C. Rootes (ed.), *Environmental Movements – Local, National and Global* (London: Frank Cass, 1999), pp. 81–100.

20. Wall, *Earth First!*.

21. RTS leaflet distributed in July 1996.

22. Ibid.

23. Anon., 'Reclaim the Streets', *Do or Die*, 6 (1997), pp. 1–11.

24. Anon., 'Friday June 18th 1999: confronting capital and the state', *Do or Die*, 8 (2000), pp. 1–12.

25. This account is largely based on Anon, 'Friday June 18th 1999', pp. 1–12.

26. John Barker, 'Carnival against Capitalism', *Vanguard*, online: http:www.vanguardonline.f9.co.uk/1103.htm.

27. Anon., 'J18', *The Loombreaker*, p. 3.

28. Anon., 'Friday June 18th 1999', pp. 18–22.

29. Ibid.

30. From 'Steve Godwin' <steve_godwin@hotmail.com> Date Sat, 6 Nov 1999 16:18:48 -0500 http://www.ainfos.ca/

31. Bakhtin, *Rabelais and His World*, p. 6.

32. T. Eagleton, *Walter Benjamin, or Towards a Revolutionary Criticism* (London: New Left Books, 1981).

33. Chesters, 'The new intemperance', pp. 4–10.

34. D. Wall, *Green History* (London: Routledge, 1994).

35. No doubt Bakhtin would have laughed at the following scatological observation from 18 June 1999: 'I was nicked on one of the actions in the morning so was in a police station as it was kicking off all afternoon. One cop came in

drenched from head to toe in white paint. I really had to control myself to stop laughing – it looked like he'd been shat on by a huge bird.' Anon., 'Friday June 18ᵗʰ 1999', pp. 18–22.

36. S. Tarrow, *Power in Movement* (Cambridge: Cambridge University Press, 1998).

37. Steinberg, *Tilting the Frame*.

38. M. Bakhtin, *The Dialogic Imagination: Four Essays* (Aldershot, Hampshire: Avebury, 1981), cited in C. Barker, 'A modern moral economy?'

39. Cited in K. Clark and M. Holquist, *Mikhail Bakhtin*.

40. E. Laclau and C. Mouffe, *Hegemony and Socialist Strategy* (London: Verso, 2001).

41. See G. Ritzer, *The McDonaldisation of Society* (London: Pine Forge Press, 1995).

42. E. M. Forster, 'Edward Carpenter', in his *Two Cheers for Democracy* (London: Penguin, 1965).

43. B. Rothman, *The 1932 Kinder Scout Trespass* (Altrincham: Willow, 1982).

44. Wall, *Earth First!*, p. 73.

45. A. Calder, *The People's War* (London: Pimlico, 1971), pp. 631–55.

46. Wall, *Earth First!*, p. 22.

## Chapter 6   Activist Networks in the UK: Mapping the Build-Up to the Anti-Globalization Movement

1. Activist in interview, 1999.

2. http://www.esrc.ac.uk/esrccontent/news/november02-9.asp. This chapter thus primarily reports back on the research, and findings, of the project produced by myself and my research colleagues Dr Brian Doherty and Dr Derek Wall. It also draws on my own personal autobiography as an activist throughout the 1990s and my PhD material.

3. Of course, the key issue of these mobilizations was the fact that they were international in character. Focusing on activist networks in the UK and the impact they have had on the anti-globalization movement is obviously far from telling the whole story, but looking at more micro sets of circumstances does enable a more detailed examination of the nature of these global mobilizations.

4. I. Welsh, *Mobilizing Modernity: The Nuclear Moment* (London: Routledge, 2000).

5. Editorial from *Peace News*, 1984.

6. Welsh, *Modernizing Modernity*.

7. Activist in interview, 2000.

8. Activist in interview, 1999.

9. Making final changes to this chapter in October 2003, it is impossible not to highlight the direct action at DSEI which took place in September 2003. Go to http://indymedia.org.uk/en/actions/2003/dsei for full coverage of a week of extremely well-planned and successful action. One of the actions I took part in, and my reasons for doing it, can be found at http://indymedia.org.uk/en/regions/london/2003/09/277046.html – in full rant mode!

10. That is, given as a primary rationale for mobilization on fliers, on websites and so on.

11. R. Eyerman and A. Jamieson, *Social Movements: A Cognitive Approach* (Cambridge: Polity Press, 1991).

12. The first People's Global Action anti-WTO demonstration was in Geneva in February 1998. See http://www.schnews.org.uk/archive/news156.htm. This was followed soon after by the anti-G8 protests in Birmingham. See http://www.schnews.org.uk/archive/news168.htm

13. EF! *Action Update*, June 1999.

14. From People's Global Action literature on http://www.n30.org.

15. As I have emphasized in a number of previous publications, there is no such thing as a 'single issue', but there are main grievances that trigger waves of movement activity, such as roads. The point is, for activists these 'single issues' are almost always seen as interrelated with other issues, over which they also take action; hence the 'multi-issue' nature of all 'single issue' activity. This is the essence of the EDA movement and is, in this chapter, a core argument regarding the genesis of anti-globalization mobilizations. See A. Plows, 'Roads protest/ Earth First! and "multi issue" New Social Movements: beyond the dualisms of the red/green debate', in C. Barker and M. Tyldesley (eds), *Alternative Futures and Popular Protest*, Vol. 1 (Manchester: Manchester Metropolitan University, 1997); A. Plows, 'Earth First! Defending Mother Earth, direct-style', in G. McKay (ed.), *DIY Culture: Party and Protest in Nineties Britain* (London: Verso, 1998); and B. Seel and A. Plows, 'Coming live and direct: strategies of Earth First!', in B. Seel, M. Paterson and B. Doherty (eds), *Direct Action in British Environmentalism* (London: Routledge, 2000).

16. See D. Schlosberg, *Environmental Justice and the New Pluralism* (Oxford: Oxford University Press, 1999).

17. Activist on local north Wales e-group, http://bangor-werdd@ yahoogroups.com, in 2001.

18. It should be highlighted that this was also a key strategy for activists in the 1970s and 1980s, evidenced in the interviews with older activists and in the background searches of publications from these decades. At workshops bringing together activist generations in our three areas (Manchester, Oxford and north Wales), younger activists were often surprised to discover the extent, and radical nature, of earlier community-based activity. In Manchester, the same streets lived in by current generations had been home to a community bakery and a base for 1970s activism, much to the surprise of many of the latest 'micro-cohort'. Recent radical history was known about by some, but not others, in all areas under study; the variability of crossover highlighting that there is as much wheel reinvention as there is reflexive 'capacity building'. I would argue that both are symbiotic, and both are important; that this 'learning from scratch' is also a key process of mobilization.

19. Activist in interview, 1999.

20. Synchronously, but perhaps not altogether unsurprisingly, there is a new collection of activist voices talking about their anti-globalization protests in the publication entitled *We Are Everywhere*. See http://www.weareeverywhere.org.

21. See H. Kreisi, 'The political opportunity structure of New Social Movements: its impact on their structure', in C. Jenkins and B. Klandermans (eds), *The Politics of Social Protest: Comparative Perspectives on States and Social Movements* (London: UCL Press, 1995); S. Tarrow, *Power in Movement: Social Movements, Collective Action, and Politics* (New York: Cambridge University Press, 1998).

22. Schlosberg, *Environmental Justice and the New Pluralism*, p. 137.

23. See M. K. Carroll and R. S. Ratner, 'Master framing and cross-movement networking in contemporary social movements', *Sociological Quarterly*, 37

(1996), pp. 601–25; Mark S. Granovetter, 'The strength of weak ties', *American Journal of Sociology*, 78, 6 (1973), pp. 1360–80.

24. The terms 'violence' and 'non-violence' are subjective, loaded and contentious. This is a highly important topic that cannot be workably discussed in the type of summary this forum would allow. A more detailed discussion formed half of one of my PhD chapters. In essence, 'violence' and 'non-violence', in terms of activists' everyday action taking, are not extreme black and white polarized positions, but occupy a blurred grey area, where context dependency, self-defence and individual bottom lines come into play. The playoff between group responsibility and individual autonomy as key movement ideals is also a key factor shaping the nature of activist debate and action.

25. This in itself has pros and cons – dropped threads of contacts can be picked up at a more conducive time, or they may be impossible to restart.

26. See B. Doherty, A. Plows and D. Wall, 'Comparing radical environmental activism in Manchester, Oxford and north west Wales', paper presented at the European Consortium for Political Research, Grenoble, 6–11 April 2001.

27. October 2003, 'Unions force defeat on hospitals', http://politics.guardian.co.uk/labour2003/story/0,13803,1053815,00.html

28. 'Socialist Workers' Party and Globalize Resistance are trying to do just that. While working closely with "respectable" anti-globalization groups, the SWP/GR increasingly attack those involved in direct action, describing us – just as the gutter press does – as disorganised, mindless hoodlums obsessed with violence. They are willing to make these attacks so they can portray themselves as more "organized" and, therefore, the best bet if you think capitalism stinks and want to do something about it. They are nothing of the sort. They want to kill the vitality of our movement – with the best of intentions, of course – and we need to organize better in the face of this threat . . .' ('Monopolize Resistance? How Globalize Resistance would Hijack Revolt'). The full text of this discussion leaflet can be found at http://www.schnews.org.uk/mr.htm.

29. These are core examples of the diffusion of discourses and even action strategies: north Wales farmers went to London to hear Jose Bove talk in 2001. The impact of these types of interaction, like the Intercontinental Caravan meeting Norfolk farmers, is unquantifiable, but the important thing is that they are happening at all.

30. It should be pointed out that the prime movers in the changing face of farming – the organic farmers and many smallholders – have been highly involved in green campaigns (to the point of taking non-violent direct action) to do with environmental impacts of farming, the importance of organics, the implications of GM crops, the impact of the WTO and the common agricultural policy and so on. Their interaction with more radical activists is less surprising than the seeming tendency of more conventional farmers also to be moving towards similar points of view, especially in areas such as north Wales where most farms are small and struggling. The research in this chapter predated the foot-and-mouth crisis, which plunged rural communities into a deeper abyss.

31. B. Doherty, M. Paterson, A. Plows and D. Wall, 'The fuel protests of 2000: implications for the environmental movement in Britain', *Environmental Politics*, 11, 2 (2002), pp. 165–73. B. Doherty, M. Paterson, A. Plows and D. Wall, 'Explaining the fuel protests', *British Journal of Politics and International Relations*, 5, 1 (2003), pp. 1–23.

32. A. Melucci, *Challenging Codes: Collective Action in the Information Age* (Cambridge: Cambridge University Press, 1996).

33. An aid worker liaising with farmers on Anglesey, north Wales, in the aftermath of the foot-and-mouth outbreak of 2001, noted that whilst much small farm discourse mirrored green discourse in terms of critiques of the EU common agricultural policy and so on, many farmers were simultaneously highly sexist and racist.

34. It is tempting to speculate that this is a process bound to repeat itself, as it has in the past, with the radical lessons learned by groups of society who become involved with radical action taking time to diffuse themselves through society. It is even perhaps necessary that things should take this route – capacity building for a social movement society is bound to take time. This, however, is an idea relegated to a short note, as it threatens to become a paper in its own right!

35. The research work on social movements in India by the postmodern geographer Paul Routledge is a significant contribution to our understanding of the way movements globally have built capacity through decades of resistance. See http://www.geog.gla.ac.uk/~proutledge

36. Activist in interview, 1999.

37. http://www.risingtide.org.uk.

38. From http://www.n30.org.

39. See Kreisi, 'The political opportunity structure of new social movements: its impact on their structure'; Tarrow, *Power in Movement: Social Movements, Collective Action, and Politics.*

40. See I. Welsh and G. Chesters, 'Re-framing social movements: margins, meanings and governance', Cardiff School of Social Sciences, Working Paper Series, 19 (2001), p. 29.

41. My notes from this draft read: '24.3.03 – still frozen from four hours blockading the runway at RAF Valley!'

42. A slogan coined (I think) by London Reclaim the Streets.

43. D. Meyer and S. Tarrow, 'A movement society: contentious politics for a new century', in D. Mayer and S. Tarrow (eds), *The Social Movement Society: Contentious Politics for a New Century* (Oxford: Rowman and Littlefield, 1998).

# Chapter 7   Keyboard Protest: Hacktivist Spiders on the Web

My initial cooperation with Ricardo Dominguez was made possible by funding from the UK's Economic and Social Research Council (ESRC) and its seminar series, Living in the Matrix: Immateriality in Theory and Practice. Quotations cited in nn. 25, 26 and 43 below were taken from an interview entitled 'Performance art in a digital age: a conversation with Ricardo Dominguez' that took place on 25 November 1999, at the Institute of International Visual Arts. The interview was heavily edited by Coco Fusco and transcribed by InIVA staff. It was republished on Centrodearte.com and Latinarte.com.

1. K. Marx and F. Engels, *Selected Works in One Volume* (London: Lawrence and Wishart, 1968), p. 39.

2. See S. Levy, *Hackers, Heroes of the Computer Revolution* (New York: Dell, 1984) and P. A. Taylor, *Hackers: Crime in the Digital Sublime* (London: Routledge, 1999).

3. Levy, *Hackers*, pp. 84–5.

4. See Taylor, *Hackers*, for a fuller treatment.

5. Ibid.

6. The schema is inevitably 'rough' because real-world hacking activity often

involves elements from more than one particular generation – the schema has been used to give a simplified idea of hacking's evolution. Again, see Taylor, *Hackers*, for a full treatment.

7. D. Coupland, *Microserfs* (London: Flamingo, 1985).

8. See Taylor, *Hackers*, for a full discussion of hacking and instrumental reason.

9. T. Adorno, *The Cultural Industry* (London: Routledge, 1991), p. 54.

10. Coupland, *Microserfs*, p. 211.

11. P. Borsook, *Cyberselfish: A Critical Romp through the Terribly Libertarian World of Hi-tech* (London: Little Brown, 2000).

12. Critical Art Ensemble, *The Electronic Disturbance* (New York: Autonomedia, 1994), p. 24.

13. For a full account, see R. Grether, 'How the etoy campaign was won', *Teleopolis*, January 2000, available at http:www.heise.de/tp/English/inhalt/te/5843/1.html. Also, A. Wishart and A. Bochsler, *Leaving Reality Behind: The Battle for the Soul of the Internet* (London: Fourth Estate, 2002).

14. See ®™ark press release available at http://www.rtmark.com/etoyprtriumph.html.

15. See http://theyesmen.org.

16. J. Baudrillard, *For a Critique of the Political Economy of the Sign* (New York: Telos Press, 1981).

17. ®™ark, 'Sabotage and the New World Order', available at http://www.rtmark.com/etoyprtriumph.html.

18. The group's website (http://www.rtmark.com) provides numerous examples of past and present projects. These are deliberately modelled to imitate the financial mutual fund system.

19. ®™ark, 'A system for change', available at http://www.rtmark.com/etoyprtriumph.html.

20. M. McLuhan, *Understanding Media* (New York: New America Library, 1964).

21. G. Debord, *The Society of the Spectacle* (Detroit: Black and Red, 1983).

22. M Hardt and A. Negri, *Empire* (Cambridge, Mass.: Harvard University Press, 2000).

23. ®™ark, 'Curation', available at http://www.rtmark.com/etoyprtriumph.html.

24. S. Wray, 'The Electronic Dissonance Theater and electronic civil disobedience', available at http: www.thing.net/~rdom/ecd/EDTECD.html.

25. R. Dominguez, quoted in C. Fusco, 'Performance art in a digital age: a conversation with Ricardo Dominguez', unpublished paper, 1999.

26. Ibid.

27. S. Lash, *Critique of Information* (London: Sage, 2002), p. 25.

28. J. McKenzie, *Perform or Else: From Discipline to Performance* (London: Routledge, 2001).

29. See, for example, Ricardo Dominguez's paper 'Post-media impossibilities (part one) or Mayan technologies for the people', at http://www.thing.net/~rdom.

30. U. Eco, *Travels in Hyperreality* (London: Picador, 1987).

31. Ibid., p. 142.

32. Baudrillard, *Critique*, pp. 173–4.

33. Ibid., p. 182.

34. Ibid., p. 183.

35. K. Marx and F. Engels, 'The Manifesto of the Communist Party', in *Selected Works in One Volume* (London: Lawrence and Wishart, 1968), p. 38. The

historical and perennial significance of this analysis by Marx is explored in detail in M. Berman, *All That is Solid Melts into Air* (London: Verso, 1983).

36. T. Frank, *One Market Under God: Extreme Capitalism, Market Populism and the End of Economic Democracy* (London: Secker and Warburg, 2001), p. 200.

37. McKenzie, *Perform or Else*, pp. 18–19.

38. J. Vallee, *The Network Revolution: Confessions of a Computer Scientist* (London: Penguin, 1984).

39. Lash, *Critique of Information*, p. 127.

40. Ibid., p. 112.

41. N. Dyer-Witherford, *Cyber-Marx: Cycles and Circuits of Struggle in High Technology Capitalism* (Chicago: University of Illinois Press, 1999), p. 13.

42. Ibid., p. 143.

43. Dominguez, in Fusco, 'Performance art'.

44. M. Maffesoli, *The Time of the Tribes: The Decline of Individualism in Mass Society* (London: Sage, 1996), p. 7.

45. N. Klein, *No Logo* (London: Flamingo, 2001), p. xx.

## Chapter 8    Consuming Heresy: Theoretical and Practical Problems of Challenging Consumerism in Contemporary Protest Cultures

As ever I owe considerable gratitude to Chayley Collis for both personal support and, on this occasion, useful discussions of contemporary religious attitudes to consumption.

1. There are a number of methodological matters that a chapter on challenges to consumption within a book on anti-capitalism inevitably raises. Anti-capitalism is, of course, as old as capitalism, and especially the state-organized market system of the last 250 years. This chapter is concerned less with the history of anti-capitalist movements of the left and more with the genealogies of groups that have sprung out of the so-called new social movements, particularly their more anarchist elements. However, in identifying a pre-history of anticonsumerism there are inevitable overlaps with the radical communist and utopian socialist tradition.

2. G. Monbiot, 'We will pay the price for believing the world has infinite resources', *Guardian*, 31 December 2002, p. 16.

3. In some anticonsumerist literature, notably the Manchester-based Enough group (1993–2000), the hyphen is dropped, perhaps to change the negative associations of the prefix 'anti'.

4. There are a number of exceptions to this. One of the higher-profile ones was Friends of the Earth's support for the 1997 national No Shop Day actions organized by the anticonsumer group Enough. This temporary excursion into radical consumer politics only took place because one of the founding members of Enough – Anna Thomas – had recently got a job with Friends of the Earth and had been able to influence its rigid campaigning agenda.

5. This appropriation from the astronomical sciences appears in B. Doherty, A. Plows and D. Wall, 'Comparing radical environmental activism in Manchester, Oxford and North Wales', paper at the Workshop on Local Environmental Activism, European Consortium for Political Research, Grenoble, 6–11 April 2001. I am using this as a metaphor to explain the all-encompassing but underacknowledged role that material possessions have in determining our psychology.

6. I. Welsh, *Mobilising Modernity: The Nuclear Movement* (London: Routledge, 2000).

7. A. Dobson, *Green Political Thought* (London: Harper Collins, 1990).

8. U. Beck, *Risk Society: Towards a New Modernity* (London: Sage, 1992).

9. A. Giddens, *The Consequences of Modernity* (Cambridge: Polity Press, 1990).

10. U. Beck, A. Giddens and S. Lash, *Reflexive Modernization* (Cambridge: Polity Press, 1992).

11. Beck, *Risk Society*, p. 137.

12. Ibid., p. 4.

13. M. Rustin, 'Incomplete modernity: Ulrich Beck's risk society', *Radical Philosophy*, 67 (1994), pp. 3–12.

14. R. McKechnie and I. Welsh, 'Between the devil and the deep green sea', in J. Weeks (ed.), *The Lesser Evil and the Greater Good* (London: Rivers Oram, 1994).

15. D. Bell, *The Cultural Contradictions of Capitalism* (London: Heinemann, 1976).

16. K. Eder, 'The institutionalization of environmentalism: ecological discourse and the second transformation of the public sphere', in S. Lash, B. Szerszynski and B. Wynne (eds), *Risk, Environment and Modernity* (London: Sage/TCS, 1996).

17. G. Chesters and I. Welsh, 'Reflexive framing: an ecology of action', Research Committee 24: Globalization and the Environment, XV World Congress of Sociology, 6–13 July 2002, University of Brisbane, Queensland, Australia.

18. A. Durning, *How Much Is Enough?* (London: Earthscan, 1992).

19. Figures quoted in D. McLaren, S. Bullock and N. Yousuf, *Tomorrow's World: Britain's Share in a Sustainable Future* (London: Earthscan, 1998), pp. 316ff.

20. C. Lodziak, *The Myth of Consumerism* (London: Pluto Press, 2002).

21. The British sociologist Alan Warde has written at length on the selective theorizing of consumption in sociology and cultural studies. See, for instance, A. Warde, 'Consumers, identity and belonging', in R. Keat, N. Whitely and N. Abercrombie (eds), *The Authority of the Consumer* (London: Routledge, 1994). See also N. Abercrombie, 'Authority and consumer society', in Keat, Whiteley and Abercrombie (eds), *The Authority of the Consumer*.

22. R. Williams, *Keywords* (London: Flamingo, 1983).

23. J. Bowen, 'The curse of the drinking classes', in J. Purkis and J. Bowen (eds), *Twenty First Century Anarchism* (London: Cassell, 1997).

24. J. Purkis, 'Modern millenarians? Anticonsumersim, anarchism and the new urban environmentalism', in B. Seel, M. Paterson and B. Doherty (eds), *Direct Action in British Environmentalism* (London: Routledge, 2000).

25. This is not an exclusively new claim in terms of examining moments of literary subversion or heresy and tracing them through the centuries. In *The Movement of the Free Spirit* (New York: Zone Books, 1994), the Situationist writer Raoul Vaneigem popularized the Heresy of the Free Spirit, and Greil Marcus's book *Lipstick Traces: A Secret History of the Twentieth Century* (London: Secker and Warburg, 1990) took the millenarian sensibility right through to the Sex Pistols (1990). See also K. Goaman and M. Dodson, 'A subversive current? Contemporary anarchism considered', in J. Purkis and J. Bowen (eds), *Twenty-First Century Anarchism* (London: Cassell, 1997) for another anarchist analysis of this material.

26. N. Cohn, *The Pursuit of the Millennium: Revolutionary Millenarians and*

*Mystical Anarchists of the Middle Ages* (New York: Oxford University Press, 1970).

27. F. Perlman, *Against His-Story, Against Leviathan* (Detroit: Black and Red, 1983), p. 183.

28. N. Chomsky, *American Power and the New Mandarins* (Harmondsworth: Penguin, 1969).

29. M. Maffesoli, *The Time of the Tribes* (London: Sage, 1996).

30. M. Bookchin, *The Ecology of Freedom* (Palo Alto: Cheshire Books, 1982).

31. Bookchin has recently become something of a controversial figure in radical environmental and anarchist circles, not least because of his own frustrations at irrational, new age, postmodern or primitivist tendencies within the contemporary milieu. The pick of the serious engagements with his ideas is A. Light (ed.), *Social Ecology after Bookchin* (London: Guilford Press, 1998).

32. M. Barkun, *Disaster and the Millennium* (Syracuse: Syracuse University Press, 1986), p. 18.

33. C. Hill, *The World Turned Upside Down* (London: Penguin, 1982).

34. Not dissimilar arguments are offered in B. Szerszynski, 'The varieties of ecological piety', in *Worldviews: Environment, Culture, Religion*, 1, 1 (1997), pp. 37–55, with his comparison of contemporary groups such as Earth First! and Greenpeace with the differences between post-Reformation Protestant sects and the Catholic Church. He argues that the former organizations organize their own agenda, utilize the language of egalitarianism, develop their own iconography and rely on themselves to define their experience, while the latter are committed to hierarchy, mediation of experience and a predefined 'corporate' iconography.

35. D. Hardy, *Alternative Communities in Nineteenth Century England* (London: Longman, 1979).

36. Ibid., p. 2.

37. P. Bagguley, 'Beyond emancipation? The reflexivity of social movements', in M. O'Brien, S. Penna and C. Hay (eds), *Theorising Modernity* (London: Longman, 1999).

38. D. Pepper, *The Roots of Modern Environmentalism* (London: Routledge, 1993); P. Marshall, *Nature's Web* (London: Cassell, 1994).

39. L. Cox, 'Reflexivity, social transformation and counter culture', in C. Barker and M. Tyldesley (eds), *Alternative Futures and Popular Protest Conference Papers III* (Manchester Metropolitan University, 1997).

40. The work of a number of anti-technology writers such as the American primitivist John Zerzan. His *Elements of Refusal* (reprint; Columbia, Mo.: CAL Press, 1999) has been influential on certain sections of the current milieu, especially the more anarchist and green anarchist ends of the spectrum. The debate about spiritual matters and ecological thought is pivotal to the debate between social and deep ecologists from the mid-1980s – for example, B. Devall and G. Sessions, *Deep Ecology: Living as if Nature Mattered* (Salt Lake City: Peregrine Smith, 1985); M. Bookchin, D. Foreman et al., *Defending the Earth* (Boston: South End Press, 1991). A useful collection on psychological issues is T. Roszak, M. E. Gomes and A. D. Kanner (eds), *Ecopsychology* (San Francisco: Sierra Club Books, 1995).

41. S. McBurney, *Ecology into Economics Won't Go* (Bideford, Devon: Green Books, 1990), p. 154.

42. A. Melucci, *Nomads of the Present* (London: Hutchinson/Radius, 1989), p. 76.

43. This has been assisted by a number of established studies about the

difficulties of relating increased standards of living to levels of happiness: for example, M. Argyle, *The Psychology of Happiness* (London: Methuen, 1987).

44. D. Gribble, *Real Education: Varieties of Freedom* (Bristol: Libertarian Education, 1998).

45. C. Ward, *Anarchy in Action* (London: Freedom Press, 1982); C. Ward, *Housing: An Anarchist Approach* (London: Freedom Press, 1983).

46. C. Harper, *Anarchy: A Graphic Guide* (London: Camden Press, 1987).

47. It would be true to say that some of the aforementioned examples are perhaps less consistent on issues of anthropocentrism.

48. A number of texts cover this period and the emergence of more ecological communities: G. McKay, *Senseless Acts of Beauty: Cultures of Resistance since the Sixties* (London: Verso, 1996); W. Schwarz and D. Schwartz, *Living Lightly: Travels in Post-consumer Society* (Charlebury, Oxon: Jon Carpenter, 1998).

49. R. Lowe and W. Shaw, *Travellers: Voices of the New Age Nomads* (London: Fourth Estate, 1993).

50. B. Seel, 'Strategies of resistance at the Pollock Free State Road Protest Camp', *Environmental Politics*, 6, 4 (1998), pp. 108–31.

51. B. Lawley, 'The ecological libertarian approach: what role in UK social housing development?', *Anarchist Studies*, 9, 1 (2001), pp. 53–7.

52. Doherty, Plows and Wall, *Activist Networks*.

53. Local Exchange Trading Systems operate in many British cities and towns. Originating on Vancouver Island in Canada in 1982 as a local response to the impact of a recession on the community, it spread to the UK in the early 1990s, reaching a high point of perhaps 200 separate schemes by about 1995.

54. P. Kennedy, 'Business enterprises as agents of cultural and political change: the case of green/ethical marketing', in C. Barker and P. Kennedy (eds), *To Make Another World* (Aldershot: Avebury, 1996).

55. B. Seel and A. Plows, 'Coming live and direct: strategies of Earth First!', in B. Seel, M. Paterson and B. Doherty (eds), *Direct Action in British Environmentalism* (London: Routledge, 2000).

56. T. Fotopoulos, 'The limitations of lifestyle strategies', *Democracy and Nature*, 6, 2 (2000), pp. 287–308.

57. T. Trainer, 'Where are we, where do we want to be, how do we get there?', *Democracy and Nature*, 6, 2 (2000), pp. 267–86.

58. I am using common sense here as it appeared in the work of Antonio Gramsci, whereby it constitutes aspects of the dominant ideas within the society.

59. B. Szerszynski, 'Marked bodies: environmental activism and political semiotics', in J. Corner and D. Pels (eds), *Media and Political Style: Essays on Representation and Civic Culture* (London, Sage, 2002).

60. J. Habermas, *A Theory of Communicative Action*, vol. II (Boston: MIT Press, 1987).

61. Chomsky, *American Power*.

62. See the article 'Stop making sense: direct action and action theatre', *Do or Die*, 6 (1997).

63. J. Purkis, 'A sociology of environmental protest: Earth First! and the theory and practice of anarchism', PhD thesis, Manchester Metropolitan University, 2001.

64. J. Purkis, 'The city as a site of ethical consumption and resistance', in D. Wynne and J. O'Connor (eds), *From the Margins to the Centre* (Aldershot: Arena, 1996).

65. K. Goaman, 'Globalisation versus humanisation: contemporary

anti-capitalism and anarchism', *Anarchist Studies*, 11, 2 (2003), pp. 150–71;
D. Graeber, 'The new anarchists', *New Left Review*, 13 (2002), pp. 61–73.

66. Lodziak, *The Myth of Consumerism*.

67. Welsh, *Mobilising Modernity*.

68. D. Wall, 'Capacity building in the British direct action environmental movement' (unpublished manuscript, 2002).

69. T. Lang and C. Hines, *The New Protectionism* (London: Earthscan, 1993); C. Hines, *Localization: A Global Manifesto* (London: Earthscan, 2000).

70. N. Klein, *No Logo* (London: Flamingo, 2000).

71. The Christian Ecology Network is devising something on the same level as what is proposed here.

## Chapter 9    Anti-Capitalist Resistance in Genoa: A Personal Reflection

An earlier version of this chapter first appeared in *On-Fire: Genoa and the Anti-Capitalist Movement* (One-Off Press, 2002).

1. *Guardian*, 23 July 2001.

# Index